DATE DUE

Crime Reduction and
Problem-oriented Policing

Crime Reduction and Problem-oriented Policing

Edited by

Karen Bullock

Nick Tilley

WILLAN
PUBLISHING

Published by

Willan Publishing
Culmcott House
Mill Street, Uffculme
Cullompton, Devon
EX15 3AT, UK
Tel: +44(0)1884 840337
Fax: +44(0)1884 840251
e-mail: info@willanpublishing.co.uk
website: www.willanpublishing.co.uk

Published simultaneously in the USA and Canada by

Willan Publishing
c/o ISBS, 5824 N.E. Hassalo St,
Portland, Oregon 97213-3644, USA
Tel: +001(0)503 287 3093
Fax: +001(0)503 280 8832
e-mail: info@isbs.com
website: www.isbs.com

First published 2003

ISBN 1-84392-050-6 (hardback)

British Library Cataloguing-in-Publication Data
A catalogue record for this book is available from the British Library

Project management by Deer Park Productions
Typeset by GCS, Leighton Buzzard, Beds
Printed and bound by T.J. International, Padstow, Cornwall

Contents

Figures, tables and boxes

Figures

Tables

Boxes

Acknowledgements

This collection is a function of Home Office money, researcher quizzing and practitioner hard work. On behalf of all our contributors we would like to thank those long-suffering practitioners whose endeavours are scrutinised here and who suffered extra burdens in dealing with our queries.

The book was produced to a very tight deadline. We are grateful to our contributors and to those involved in the production process, including Brian Willan the publisher, for agreeing to take part in this venture and for sticking more or less to deadlines in the middle of busy lives. And we apologise for all the nagging. You were all very patient, at least to our faces. We would especially like to thank Chris Kershaw, Fiona Mclean, Verity Ridgman and Steve Wilkes of the Home Office for their support and help in putting this together.

We are delighted that this volume is appearing in the crime science series, and appreciate Gloria Laycock's inclusion of it.

Finally KB has decided, as with every previous editing assignment, never again to embark on this stress-filled lunacy!

Karen Bullock
Nick Tilley

London, July 2003

Notes on Contributors

Karen Bullock is a Senior Research Officer in the Research Directorate at the Home Office. Most of her research has focused on the evaluation of programmes and projects that aim to reduce crime and implement problem-oriented policing.

Chris Hale is Professor of Criminology and Dean of the Faculty of Social Sciences at the University of Kent. His main research interests include the socio-economic determinants of crime and punishment and fear of crime. His latest project has been advising the Home Office on issues around crime forecasting.

Jalna Hanmer is Professor of Women's Studies at the University of Sunderland, and UK and Associate Director of the International Centre for the Study of Violence and Abuse. She has researched and published on domestic violence since the early 1980s. Her publications include *Arresting Evidence: Domestic Violence and Repeat Victimisation* (co-author, Home Office 1999); and *Home Truths About Domestic Violence: Feminist Influences on Policy and Practice – A reader* (co-editor, Routledge 2000).

Charlotte Harris was formerly Research Fellow at the Kent Criminal Justice Centre at the University of Kent at Canterbury. She is now doing doctoral research at the London School of Economics looking at the processes of murder investigation in France and England.

Matt Hopkins is a research consultant with Morgan Harris Burrows. Formerly a Lecturer in Criminology at Nottingham Trent University, he has published widely, for example in the *British Journal of Criminology*, *International Review of Victimology*, the *Security Journal* and the *International Journal of Risk, Security and Crime Prevention*. He is currently working on the evaluation of the DNA Expansion programme for the Home Office and the evaluation of national New Arson Reduction Projects Initiative for the Office of the Deputy Prime Minister.

Tim John is Senior Lecturer in Criminology and Criminal Justice at the Centre for Criminology, University of Glamorgan. He has been engaged in research on intelligence-led policing since 1994 and (with Professor Mike Maguire) has published widely on the area. Other areas of research include the policing of environmental protest, and more general issues in criminal justice. He has also been involved in several evaluations of local crime prevention initiatives.

Bethan Jones is a Senior Research Officer in the Research Directorate at the Home Office. Most of her research has focused on the evaluation of projects and strategies that aim to reduce anti-social behaviour and tackle disorder.

Gloria Laycock is Professor of Crime Science and Director of the Jill Dando Institute of Crime Science at University College London. She previously worked in the Home Office as Head of the Police Research Group and later as Head of the Policing and Reducing Crime Unit. She has commissioned research on crime prevention and policing on behalf of the Home Office for many years and has published widely in this field.

Mike Maguire is Professor of Criminology and Criminal Justice at Cardiff University. He has researched and published widely in the crime and justice field, including recent studies of criminal investigation and intelligence-led policing. He is co-editor of *The Oxford Handbook of Criminology* (OUP, third edition, 2002).

Mario Matassa is currently Senior Research Fellow, Mannheim Centre for Criminology, London School of Economics. For the past four years he has been involved in three major studies of the policing of hate crimes and has written numerous reports for government on this subject. Recent publications include *Community Safety Structures: An International Literature Review* for the Criminal Justice Review Programme (HMSO: Belfast, with Adam Crawford), and 'Policing and Terrorism' (with Tim Newburn) in *Handbook of Policing* (ed. T. Newburn, Willan Publishing, 2003).

Tim Newburn is Professor of Criminology and Social Policy at the LSE. He is the author or editor of 20 books, many of which are on the subject of policing and security. His latest books include, *The Future of Policing* (with Rod Morgan, Oxford University Press, 1997); *Private Security and Public Policing* (with Trevor Jones, Clarendon Press, 1998); *Policing, Surveillance and Social Control* (with Stephanie Hayman, Willan Publishing, 2001); and, *Handbook of Policing* (Willan Publishing, 2003).

Ken Pease is currently Professor of Criminology at Huddersfield University and Visiting Professor of Crime Science at the Jill Dando Institute, University College London. He is a Chartered Forensic Psychologist.

Jan Stockdale is Senior Lecturer in Social Psychology at the London School of Economics and Political Science. Her research interests are focused on policing, crime reduction and community safety. Recent work includes evaluations of targeted action against gun crime in London and of an initiative to combat vehicle finance fraud, and analyses of the role and impact of neighbourhood and street wardens and of young people's involvement in street crime.

Nick Tilley is Professor of Sociology at Nottingham Trent University and Visiting Professor at the Jill Dando Institute of Crime Science, University College London. He was seconded as a consultant to the Home Office Research, Development and Statistics Directorate from 1992 to 2003.

Michael Townsley has worked on a range of operational policing projects focused on crime reduction in Australia and the UK. He is currently managing the crime and community safety theme for the North Huyton New Deal for Communities project, a ten-year regeneration programme to turn around deprived communities. He is affiliated with the Jill Dando Institute of Crime Science, University College London.

Steve Uglow is Professor of Criminal Justice at the Law School at the University of Kent where he is the Director of the Kent Criminal Justice Centre. He teaches and researches in the area of policing and has undertaken several evaluations of intelligence-led policing projects. His most recent book was *Criminal Justice* (2002).

Barry Webb is Deputy Director of the Jill Dando Institute of Crime Science, University College London. He has spent his career in crime reduction research, publishing on a range of crime topics including vehicle crime, burglary, violence, vandalism, and fraud. Prior to joining the Institute, he worked in the Home Office and before that at the Tavistock Institute of Human Relations researching the influence of environmental design on crime.

Christine Whitehead is Professor of Housing at the London School of Economics and Political Science and Director of the Property Research Unit, University of Cambridge. Her expertise includes the economics of social policy and urban economics, including cost effectiveness, value for money and cost benefit analysis in the context of public resource allocation.

Foreword

Evidence-based policy and practice are currently in vogue, and some may say about time too. The UK government took a major step in promoting this in the crime control field when in 1998 they launched the Crime Reduction Programme (CRP) which ran from 1999 to 2002. It involved the expenditure of some £400 million, though only £250 million was originally allocated. The programme represented a brave effort at implementing and building an evidence-based response to crime and disorder problems. It began with a review of the research base for crime prevention (Goldblatt and Lewis 1998). It attempted to fund work for which there was either already evidence of effectiveness or for which further evidence was deemed necessary.

To begin with 10% of the £250 million budget was earmarked for systematic evaluation in order to build up the evidence base. The announcement of such a significant investment, together with the promise of evaluation, generated a great deal of interest and support in the academic community. Although practitioners were faced with a plethora of bidding opportunities for various funding streams arising from the programme, they too supported its principles.

Many of the products of the CRP are now coming off the assembly line and it is time to take stock and ask what was learned, what could have been done better, where do we go from here? The chapters of this book, which is the second to be published in the Crime Science Series, contribute to that process. This volume reports the main findings from one stream – the Targeted Policing Initiative – which was concerned specifically with implementing problem-oriented policing. Several of the following chapters bring out how difficult it is in practice. Large-scale funding regimes where there is an understandable impatience for action and results are not necessarily best placed to yield carefully crafted, research-based project designs, that are then conscientiously and systematically implemented, monitored, adjusted and tracked to try to find out what is working for whom in what circumstances. Instead they can lead to opportunistic bidding, poor project design, hasty and inconsistent implementation, weak record keeping and disappointing results.

Crime science and problem-oriented policing are natural bedfellows. Problem-oriented policing calls for the routine application of the scientific method to policing. Crime science requires a problem-oriented police service to deliver on many of its findings. Problem-oriented policing begins with problems. It then tries to understand those problems well enough to work out what to do to deal with them – to eliminate them, reduce the harm caused by them or manage them more effectively. It draws on careful analysis of the presenting problem and systematic research that has worked out effective responses. It then checks whether the responses have been effective and adjusts them as necessary. Its focus is on police-relevant community problems. It will entertain any of a variety of ethical means for dealing with them. The problem and working out what to do about it takes precedence over all else in problem-oriented policing; in this it is akin to evidence-based medicine. Both are unremittingly concerned with drawing on the best evidence to deal with significant problems. Both call for professional, well-trained, thoughtful and open-minded practitioners. Both realise that strong research is essential to continuing improvements. In both, at their best, reflective practitioners work alongside applied researchers to forge improvements in understanding and treatment.

Crime science is an emerging discipline which, like problem-oriented policing, takes crime problems as its starting point. As with medical science its focus is on understanding conditions calling for attention in ways that will improve responses. Crime science potentially speaks to those in a host of organisations. Product designers, architects, planners, and managers of public and private sector organisations, for example, all also have much to learn from crime science. All are implicated in creating conditions that may either facilitate or disable crime. But crime science has a special relationship to those who have a specific responsibility to address crime and disorder problems: the police, Crime and Disorder Partnerships, and the various non-police agencies of the criminal justice system. These agencies and organisations have a duty to address crime issues, and in most cases the evidence base for what they do is far from strong. Much discretion is exerted in terms of issues focused on and in terms of the responses chosen. Tradition and agency culture play a large part in habitual ways of defining and dealing with issues. For the police this tends to favour detection, enforcement and deterrence as methods of dealing with problems. It also tends towards dealing with incidents one at a time rather than looking at potential forms of aggregation that can open the door to non-standard preventive responses. Problem-oriented policing and crime science are united in their pursuit of wide-ranging preventive responses to crime problems making use of analyses of aggregate data which isolate families of incidents that can be pre-empted.

There is a danger that moves towards the adoption of an analytic approach to dealing with crime problems, and to learning how better to deal with them, will be discredited through programme design and operation shortcomings. It is crucial for the successful implementation of problem-oriented policing and for complementary work in crime science that space and resources be provided for well-designed, strongly implemented and systematically evaluated action projects to address the perennial crime problems that confront us. In this way a robust body of knowledge can be developed to improve treatment of crime problems, along lines similar to those found in much modern medicine.

There is a global appetite for crime prevention and for problem-oriented policing. There are some excellent examples of well-documented research projects that have produced substantial achievements, for example Forrester *et al* (1988, 1990), Braga *et al* (2001), and Clarke and Goldstein (2002). There are a growing number of invaluable problem-specific guides produced by the United States Office of Community Oriented Policing Services. Finally, the Center for Problem-Oriented Policing has launched an excellent website at www.popcenter.org, where existing and newly emerging materials relating to problem-oriented policing can be found.

The coming years should provide rich opportunities for delivering problem-oriented policing and for engaging in the research entailed by it. Capitalising on the potential benefits from this work will require money and patience from government departments, consistency and commitment from police and other agencies with crime prevention responsibilities, and flexibility and engagement by the crime scientists who will need to participate in and report results from individual initiatives.

Gloria Laycock
Jill Dando Institute of Crime Science
University College London
July 2003

References

Braga, A., Kennedy, D., Piehl, A. and Waring, E. (2001) *Reducing Gun Violence: The Boston Gun Project's Operation Ceasefire*. Washington DC: US National Institute of Justice.

Clarke, R. and Goldstein, H. (2002) 'Reducing theft at construction sites: lessons from a problem-oriented project', in N. Tilley (ed.) *Analysis for Crime Prevention. Crime Prevention Studies* 13. Cullompton, Devon: Willan Publishing.

Forrester, D., Chatterton, M. and Pease, K. (1988) *The Kirkholt Burglary Prevention Project, Rochdale. Crime Prevention Unit Paper* 13. London: Home Office

Forrester, D., Frenz, S., O'Connell, M. and Pease, K. (1990) *The Kirkholt Burglary Prevention Project: Phase II. Crime Prevention Unit Paper* 23. London: Home Office.

Goldblatt, P. and Lewis, C. (1998) *Reducing Offending: An Assessment of the Research Evidence on Ways of Dealing with Offending Behaviour. Home Office Research Study* 187. London: Home Office.

Chapter 1

Introduction
Problem-oriented policing: the concept, implementation and impact in the UK and USA

Karen Bullock and Nick Tilley

The basic concept of problem-oriented policing

The term 'problem-oriented policing' was coined by Herman Goldstein, an American professor of law who had earlier worked as an adviser to the Chicago Police Department. Goldstein first outlined his ideas about problem-oriented policing in a journal article published in 1979 (Goldstein 1979). He later produced a fuller, book-length discussion (Goldstein 1990). In its very broadest sense problem-oriented policing describes a framework to improve the way that the police service operates. Its basic premise is that the core of policing should be to deal effectively with underlying police-relevant problems rather than simply to react to incidents calling for attention one by one as they occur. Goldstein saw problem-oriented policing as a way of delivering a scientific approach to finding solutions to core aspects of police business (Sampson and Scott 2000).

Goldstein discusses eleven 'basic elements' of 'problem-oriented policing':

1 Grouping incidents as problems.
2 Focusing on substantive problems as the heart of policing.
3 Effectiveness as the ultimate goal.
4 The need for systematic inquiry.
5 Disaggregating and accurately labelling problems.
6 Analysis of the multiple interests in problems.
7 Capturing and critiquing the current response.
8 An uninhibited search for a tailor-made response.

9   Adopting a proactive stance.
10 Strengthening the decision-making processes and increasing accountability.
11 Evaluating results of newly implemented responses.

These basic elements steer policing towards delivering and being held accountable for an outcome-focused and strongly analytic way of working. In it substantive police-relevant problems are aggregated and interrogated intelligently, the context for responses is looked at systematically, existing practice is examined critically, alternative responses rooted in the analysis are pursued and the effectiveness of new, proactive measures is evaluated rigorously. Goldstein does not, of course, rule out enforcement responses to problems though he vigorously advocates looking beyond conventional uses of enforcement and the criminal justice system. He stresses, too, the need for developing ethical responses to problems.

Why implement problem-oriented policing?

Goldstein highlighted shortcomings in the so-called 'professional model' of policing. The professional model had developed in the USA to deal with police inefficiency, corruption and abuse of discretion. Organisational streamlining, appointment of better staff and use of modern equipment had all been called for in the interest of making policing more professional and business-like. The policing delivered through this involved tight central control, standard operating procedures, fast responses and increasing use of cars, computers and modern communications technologies. Police officers were supposed to be neutral and to act within the law in enforcing the law.

Goldstein highlighted several weaknesses in this model. Research had shown that it was not in practice what was delivered and also that many standard police responses were in any case ineffective (see Eck and Spelman 1987 for a full discussion of this). Implementation of the model had led to a preoccupation with management issues and with the efficient processing of incidents rather than with substantive problems and with responding to them effectively. Resources for dealing effectively with problems in the form of community capacities and rank-and-file police officer talents were not being drawn on and used. And the reform efforts themselves had attended insufficiently to the complexities of policing.

Problem-oriented policing thus emerged out of a critical encounter with the 'professional model' of policing, which was itself a response to previous problems in the ways in which policing in the USA was conducted and organised. There is no wish in problem-oriented policing to return to some imagined 'good old days' before the professional model. Nor is there any wish to deprofessionalise policing. Rather, problem-oriented policing calls for the ethical and accountable policing stressed in the professional model. It also wants officers if anything more closely to resemble professional people by adopting an informed and analytic approach to defining problems and working out what to do about them.

Techniques and problem-oriented policing in practice

Two techniques have come to dominate the ways in which problem-oriented policing is conducted in practice. The first is known as 'SARA' and the second 'PAT'. SARA refers to scanning, analysis, response and assessment. The acronym was devised and used by Eck and Spelman in a demonstration project implemented in the USA in Newport News (Eck and Spelman 1987). SARA attempts to capture the main processes in doing problem-oriented policing. 'Scanning' describes work undertaken to identify problems that call for attention. 'Analysis' refers to efforts to find the underlying conditions giving rise to the problem. 'Response' describes the strategy and tactics put in place in the light of the analysis to deal with the problem. And 'assessment' relates to measurement of the impact on the problem. This way of rendering problem-oriented policing is almost universally used, and its headings are required in entries to the annual Goldstein Award competition for the best US problem-oriented policing initiative.

'PAT' refers to the problem analysis triangle. This highlights three defining features of all problems addressed in problem-oriented policing – their location(s), the offenders or those behaving in ways leading to calls to the police and the victims or complainants. The provenance of the problem analysis triangle is not clear. It connects most clearly, however, to 'routine activities theory' (RAT). According to RAT, predatory crimes require that three conditions converge in time and space. There must be a likely offender, a suitable target, and the absence of intermediary, be it a 'capable guardian' (to intercede on behalf of the target) or an 'intimate handler' (to demotivate the likely offender) (see Cohen and Felson 1979; Felson 2002). Since all three conditions are needed for a crime, manipulation of each element offers preventive opportunities. The three sides of PAT correspond to the three elements in

RAT. Likely offenders and suitable targets are obviously associated with offenders and victims/complainants, even though a target is rather different from a victim or complainant. Location equates roughly to capable guardian or intimate handler, as it is attributes of the location that are liable to offer higher or lower levels of guardianship, more or fewer handlers and a greater or lesser sense that the target or victim is likely to be protected. PAT has been found useful by many in thinking through problems and potential points of intervention.

The SARA process has been deemed by some to be rather mechanical. The application of the tidy four-stage process is something of rarity and indeed to be hamstrung by it would risk losing many opportunities to improve effectiveness and learning opportunities. Ideally programme elements and programme theories are tentatively developed, challenged and changed as interventions are developed and unfold. In practice, problems are often identified and responses picked from an established menu, thought up from scratch or borrowed from other known projects. The chief weaknesses found within the SARA structure rather con-sistently relate to analysis and assessment (see, for example, Read and Tilley 2000; Scott 2000). In practice a range of alternative models has been used to try to capture and describe the process of problem-oriented policing. Recently Paul Ekblom has developed a conceptual knowledge management framework based around what he term the '5 Is' of crime reduction (2002):

1. *Intelligence:* crime problems, patterns, trends, consequences, causes, and risk and protective factors.
2. *Intervention:* blocking causes and risk factors.
3. *Implementation*: targeting and delivery.
4. *Involvement*: mobilisation and partnership in the community.
5. *Impact*: impact, cost-effectiveness, process evaluation.

The implementation of problem-oriented policing

It would be difficult to exaggerate the influence on Goldstein's ideas about problem-oriented policing. Police services around the world have attempted to implement them. Goldstein's vision for policing has been widely taken up in Britain, even though in many respects the conditions in which policing is conducted are different from the USA.

Surrey Constabulary has been involved in attempts broadly to implement problem-oriented policing since the early 1980s. The Metropolitan Police Service undertook some demonstration projects in the 1980s. Police services in Northumbria, Thames Valley, West Yorkshire and Merseyside all put in place problem-oriented work during the early to mid-1990s. In the latter part of the 1990s, quite a large-scale demonstration project was undertaken in Leicestershire (Leigh *et al.* 1996, 1998). Cleveland and Merseyside police services also put in place ambitious schemes to spread a problem-oriented approach throughout the force areas (Leigh *et al.* 1998). Lancashire was close behind and has probably a more mature form of problem-oriented policing across the whole force area than any other at the time of writing. As one element of the HMIC Thematic Inspection on Crime and Disorder, a specific study was undertaken of problem-orientation in police services (Read and Tilley 2000). This found that problem oriented policing had become an orthodoxy. Nearly all police services purported to endorse it and few individual officers at any rank were critical of the concept. Crawford (1998) noted that now there is almost a consensus that problem-oriented policing is a suitable, pragmatic means of policing.

The appeal of problem-oriented policing on both sides of the Atlantic, indeed across the globe, is not difficult to understand. It appears to offer a way of dealing constructively with the gap created through the much faster growth in call demand on the police compared with the police resources. Identifying patterned problems, interrogating their under-lying sources and finding some points of intervention that will reduce the problems seem to make sense. It promises a way of better managing resources and of improving services to the community at the same time. Problem-oriented policing describes the application of the scientific method, which has apparently delivered successfully in other spheres, to the problems the police are expected to address. It also seems to take policing back to its roots in the sense that it is about dealing with problems effectively rather than about feeding prisons and the criminal justice system more generally.

Impact of problem-oriented policing on crime

There have been significant reductions in crime brought about through adopting problem-oriented policing. Examples include the Boston Gun Project, which successfully reduced gang-related shootings in Boston, mostly by providing leverage via publicised gang-focused crackdowns following shootings (Braga *et al.* 2001). The Kirkholt Burglary Reduction Project substantially reduced the overall domestic burglary rate; in particular by focusing on repeat victimisation (Pease 1992). In Charlotte

Mecklenburg thefts of white goods from construction sites were reduced by non-installation of appliances before new dwellings were occupied (Clarke and Goldstein 2002).

There is also a plethora of examples of good practice in problem-oriented policing in the police service generally. The winners of the annual Goldstein and Tilley Awards, in the USA and UK respectively, are notable examples. Typically, these cases begin with a sharply defined problem, they reveal careful analysis, responses are developed on the basis of the analysis, the responses put in place go beyond standard enforcement methods, non-police as well as police agencies are involved and there is systematic evaluation of achievements.

Implementation difficulties

The widespread implementation and mainstreaming of problem-oriented policing has, however, proven difficult. Though Lancashire Constabulary has probably most comprehensively put problem-oriented policing in place, few if any of those in the service would claim that it describes the way all in the force are operating.

Common obstacles experienced in forces where problem-oriented policing has been tried include the following:

1 *The imperative to respond to emergencies.* Habits of response to a wide range of incidents have been hard to shift. It is often not clear at the point of receipt of a call that nothing can be gained by an immediate response.

2 *Middle-ranking officers, especially sergeants and inspectors, caught between needs to respond and needs to steer and facilitate a problem-oriented way of working.* The here and now calls for a response tend to take precedence. Attention to them takes away resources needed if problem-oriented policing is to be conducted.

3 *Cynicism among many officers about headquarters-inspired reform movements.* These officers are apt to conform minimally and sit out what they construe as the latest fad (Leigh *et al.* 1998).

4 *Pitching responsibility for problem-solving at beat officers.* Early efforts to implement problem-oriented policing in this country allocated responsibility for problem-oriented policing to community beat officers at a time when being a community beat officer was not a popular or well regarded specialism. The result was a shortage of

officers with the energy and ability to deliver what is demanding work. Some commendable efforts were made but they tended to be very parochial and to make use of traditional police detection and enforcement methods. Clarke (1998) has suggested that this kind of work be construed as 'problem-solving' rather than 'problem-oriented policing' properly speaking, the latter term to be reserved for larger-scale work including systematic analysis.

5   *Hasty, inadequately thought-through implementation.* In some cases chief constables wanting to have problem-oriented policing in their forces underestimated what would be needed to make it happen. In one case a sergeant came to the Home Office to ask for advice on implementing problem-oriented policing force-wide in three weeks' time. His was an extreme version of quite a common underestimate of what is required.

The review of problem-solving conducted with the HMIC inspection of 2000 also identified the following specific inhibitors:

• Weaknesses in analysis and shortage of analysts.
• Limitations in data quality and data sharing.
• Inadequate use of crime reduction specialists.
• Inadequate time set aside for problem-solving.
• Exclusive focus on local low-level problems.
• Crudely operated performance management arrangements.
• Inattention to and weaknesses in evaluation.
• Inadequate involvement of partners in problem-solving.

Progress was being encouraged in some forces by:

• presence of a committed, enthusiastic, knowledgeable and involved leadership;
• provision of practical help and advice in planning and doing problem-solving;
• provision of data, analytic software for analysis and competent analysts;
• provision of information, training and experience to inform problem-solving;
• development of methods to disseminate good practice;
• development of structures to encourage problem-solving;
• development of units or taskforces dedicated to specific areas of problem-solving;

- allocation of staff on the basis of their aptitudes; and
- use of rewards to incentivise problem-solving.

Misconstructions of problem-oriented policing

There have been some significant misunderstandings of problem-oriented policing and what it entails in practice. First, there is the notion that problem-oriented policing relates only to very local problem-solving, say at individual or beat level. This is not the case. Problem-oriented policing can operate at all levels of problem definition up to and including the national and transnational. Secondly, problem-oriented policing is equated with community policing. They are quite different. Problem-oriented policing may sometimes begin with problems experienced in neighbourhoods and it may sometimes involve mobilising those in neighbourhoods, but not necessarily. Moreover, much done in the name of community policing has nothing to do with problem-oriented policing. Thirdly, problem-oriented policing has been confused with intelligence-led policing. The primary focus of problem-oriented policing is on dealing with police-relevant problems, where enforcement is but one means and generally not the preferred one. In intelligence-led policing the key focus is on smart (informed) enforcement in part in the belief that this will effectively contribute to crime control. Fourthly, problem solving has been taken to be synonymous with problem orientation. This is not so. Much problem-solving is unrelated to the substantive problems for which the police have responsibility and much that is related to substantive police issues does not require the systematic analytic approach that lies at the heart of problem-oriented policing.

The Crime Reduction Programme and the Targeted Policing Initiative

The Crime Reduction Programme

The British government established the Crime Reduction Programme following the 1997 Comprehensive Spending Review. It was based on a review of crime reduction literature that identified gaps in knowledge about what is effective in reducing crime (Goldblatt and Lewis 1998). The Crime Reduction Programme subsequently spent £400 million over three years on projects and research to increase the evidence base about:

- what works in reducing crime;
- rolling out (mainstreaming) good practice; and
- the cost-effectiveness of crime reduction initiatives and programmes.

The money was allocated via a series of funding streams. The streams and details of finances and projects are set out in Table 1.1.

The remainder of the £400 million was spent on research, partnership development, vehicle crime awareness raising, a series of web-based

Table 1.1: Crime Reduction Programme funding streams

Initiative	Projects	Total allocated	Use of funding
CCTV	683	£169,000,000	For funding schemes nationally
Targeted policing	59	£30,000,000	For helping the police to develop and implement a problem-oriented approach
Reducing domestic burglary	246	£24,000,000	For targeting neighbourhoods in England and Wales with high burglary rates
Drug arrest referrals	1	£20,000,000	For the development of face-to-face arrest referral schemes that aim to impact upon drug-related offending in England and Wales
Treatment of offenders	1	£14,362,000	For a range of initiatives to develop effective practice in working with offenders
Effective school management	38	£10,330,000	To integrate approaches to improving schools' management of pupils' behaviour and reducing truancy and exclusion
Violence against women	58	£9,655,000	To fund projects on domestic violence, rape and sexual assault
Youth inclusion	70	£8,620,000	For youth inclusion schemes

Table 1 continues overleaf

Table 1 continued

Initiative	Projects	Total allocated	Use of funding
Locks for pensioners	1	£8,000,000	For improvements to home security for pensioners living in low-income households in neighbourhoods suffering high domestic burglary rates
Neighbourhood wardens	85	£6,000,000	To develop a strategy for neighbourhood renewal
Vehicle crime	13	£5,218,000	For improvements to vehicle licensing and registration systems
On Track	26	£4,390,000	To identify and assist children and families at risk of getting involved in crime
Sentencing	3	£3,900,000	To develop the evidence base for sentencing and enforcement practices
Summer play schemes	147	£3,600,000	For diversion schemes during school holidays in low-income areas
Design against crime	4	£1,570,000	To encourage crime resistance in the planning and design of goods, services and buildings
Distraction burglary projects	3	£1,010,000	For projects aimed at reducing distraction burglary amongst the elderly
Distraction Burglary Taskforce	1	£1,000,000	For staffing of dedicated policy team to reduce distraction burglary
Tackling prostitution	11	£871,000	For local agencies working within a multi-agency context to implement local strategies for reducing prostitution-related crime and disorder

crime reduction tool kits and grants to the charitable organisations – for example, Rape Crisis and the Suzy Lamplugh Trust.

Much of the Crime Reduction Programme has followed the logic of problem-oriented policing in calling for evidence-based definitions of issues to be addressed, analysis of the problems, the use of evidence in proposing responses, involvement of partnerships and systematic evaluation. However, as described below, the Targeted Policing Initiative (TPI) comprises the stream specifically associated with problem-oriented policing.

The Targeted Policing Initiative

The TPI was one of the larger funding streams. About £30 million was spent over the three-year period on projects that sought to reduce crime through adopting problem-oriented approaches. It was hoped that the initiative, though providing specific funding, would deliver the necessary incentives for police forces and their partners to implement systematic problem-oriented principles and therefore show what can be achieved through following this approach to crime reduction. Fifty-nine projects were funded over all.

Police forces and their partners could apply for funding in a variety of ways. Two rounds of competitive bidding for funding were held. The first round was held in early 1999 and funded 11 projects.[1] The second round was held in 2000 and funded 27 projects. Most (65%) of the projects were funded this way. The two bidding rounds were managed slightly differently but in both police officers and their partner agencies had to complete a basic application form that focused on the size and nature of the problem that was to be addressed and the details of the proposed responses to tackle it. Box 1.1 shows the application requirements in the two rounds.

Applicants had about a month to complete the forms. A team of Home Office researchers, policy officials and an external assessor reviewed applications and made recommendations for funding. In both rounds short development visits from academics and Home Office staff were undertaken to short-listed projects in order to help them improve their proposals. Proposals were selected using a variety of criteria. The aims of the Crime Reduction Programme were multifaceted. There was an emphasis on both research and learning lessons but also on delivery and having an impact on crime. Criteria included value for money, sustainability and geographical spread to the projects.

A number of other projects received funding based on different criteria, which were considered on a case-by-case basis. One such

Box 1.1: Application requirements of round-one and round-two proposals

Round-one application requirements	Round-two application requirements
• To provide a description of the problem that they sought money to tackle	• An outline of the size and the nature of the problem
• To indicate how the problem related to the findings from local crime and disorder audits and strategies	• A description of why the problem was worth tackling
• To show how the problem related to the local policing plan	• An explanation of why the problem was amenable to a problem-oriented approach
• To spell out how the problem would be tackled, specifying in particular whether the project would make use of:	• Objectives/targets for dealing with the problem
– structured crime/incident data	• Possible interventions to tackle the problem
– new structures/ arrangements and	• An outline of funding required
– innovative tactics	• Details of planned or ongoing initiatives
• To show what crime reduction targets could be achieved	• A timetable
• To note related initiatives	
• To list other factors affecting the area	
• To indicate what resources would be required	

example was a project that sought to tackle fear of crime in rural communities. This was funded because it addressed the issue of rural crime, which had gained a high profile following the fatal shooting of an intruder by a householder in a remote part of the east of England. Another example was the evaluation of the roll-out of the National

Intelligence Model, which was funded because it was a matter of national interest.

Evaluation of the Targeted Policing Initiative

It had been anticipated that all the funded projects would be evaluated by either the Home Office or universities/contractors. All the projects funded from the round-one bidding process were evaluated independently through the Home Office but a change in policy halfway through the Crime Reduction Programme resulted in only nine of the 27 round-two projects being evaluated in this way. Overall, 20 of the projects funded through the bidding rounds were evaluated by Home Office research staff or by contracted staff from universities or consultancies. Other projects were evaluated though this depended on local circumstances.[2]

Overview of this collection

This collection draws together some of the key lessons learnt about the processes of problem-oriented policing as they were applied in the TPI. Nine of the following chapters cover altogether about a third of the projects funded under the TPI, as shown in Table 1.2. Nineteen of the 59 projects are included with a combined expenditure of about £8.5 million. Over a quarter of the 43 forces in England and Wales participated in the projects discussed here, including metropolitan forces, county forces with large cities and largely rural, sparsely populated forces. The projects considered are not a statistically representative sample. They are, however, wide ranging in the issues covered and the types of force participating.

Where possible these nine chapters have been ordered broadly into the stages associated with conducting problem-oriented policing – from analysis to implementation to evaluation to lesson learning and thence to replication – though in practice there is much overlap.

Chapter 2 (Townsley and Pease) discusses the role of crime analysis in a project that aimed to implement evidence-based, problem-oriented policing in Knowsley (Merseyside). Chapter 3 (John and Maguire) discusses the roll-out of the National Crime Intelligence Service's National Intelligence Model, a form of policing different from but with some affinities to problem-oriented policing (see Tilley 2003). Chapter 4 (Jones) describes the origins and implementation of a project aiming to implement problem-oriented policing to address issues in a rural area

Table 1.2: Targeted Policing Initiative projects discussed in this book

Project	Approx. allocated funding*	Chapter
Bringing evidence-based problem-oriented policing to Knowsley	£145,000	2
Implementation of the National Intelligence Model	£1,010,000	3
Using problem-oriented policing in a rural area – the Fens	£600,000	4
Cycle theft in Cambridge	£167,000	5
Gang-related shootings in Manchester	£500,000	5
Violent crime linked to alcohol abuse in Nottingham	£1,199,000	6
Alcohol-related violence in Cornwall	£950,000	6
Alcohol-related street violence in Cardiff	£499,990	6
The stolen goods market in a northern town	£431,000	7
The stolen goods market in a southern town	£462,000	7
Racially motivated crime in Hounslow, Greenwich, Merton and Tower Hamlets	£1,125,000	8
Hate crime in Southwark	£688,000	8
Hate crime in Brighton and Hove	£1,215,000	8
Anti-social and low-level criminal behaviour in a large housing estate in Hull	£393,000	9
Drug use and drug-related crime in Dalston	£760,000	9
Vehicle crime in Islington, Camden and Southwark	£597,000	9
Crime and disorder in remote rural locations in Northumbria	£40,000	9
Vehicle crime in Calderdale	£180,000	9
Repeat domestic violence and other repeat hate crimes in West Yorkshire	£488,000	10

Note: *In many cases this does not represent the total costs. Local contributions frequently supplemented the grant received. The costs exclude those incurred for the evaluations reported here. Some of the projects did not spend all their allocated money. Some projects received extra funding. Cost- effectiveness evaluation of projects included measurements of all costs associated with the project (for an example, see Chapter 9 of this volume).

covering parts of Norfolk, Cambridgeshire and Lincolnshire. In practice what was done was closer to intelligence-led than problem-oriented policing. Chapter 5 (Bullock and Tilley) takes two projects addressing very different problems – the one concerned with cycle theft in Cambridge (Cambridgeshire) and the other gang-related shootings in Manchester (Greater Manchester Police, GMP), and describes their origins, implementation and apparent effects. Chapter 6 (Maguire and Hopkins) takes three projects, but this time ones that addressed a similar problem – that of alcohol-related violence in Cardiff (South Wales), Nottingham (Nottinghamshire) and Cornwall. Chapter 7 (Harris, Hale and Uglow) examines two projects that attempted to implement a market reduction approach to address property crime in particular towns in forces in the north and south of England. Chapters 8 and 9 concentrate on issues of assessment. Chapter 8 (Matassa and Newburn) focuses on projects broadly concerned with hate crime: one in four London boroughs addressing the issue of racially motivated crime (Metropolitan Police Service, MPS), another in a fifth London borough addressing hate crimes generally (MPS), and a third in Brighton and Hove (Sussex) addressing racist and homophobic crime and domestic violence. Chapter 9 (Stockdale and Whitehead) is specifically concerned with economic evaluation. It discusses one project in three London boroughs (MPS), and another in Calderdale (West Yorkshire), both of which attempted to tackle vehicle crime. Stockdale and Whitehead also cover a project in Dalston (MPS) concerned with drug-related crime and two more in Tynedale (Northumbria) and Bransholme (Humberside). Chapter 10 (Hanmer) discusses the effort in West Yorkshire to take the Killingbeck project that had been found to have successfully addressed repeat domestic violence in part of Leeds and to implement it across the force, as well as to extend attention to homophobic violence. The final chapter, by Laycock and Webb, tries to gather together what has been learnt about ways of implementing and encouraging problem-oriented policing in the context of the Crime Reduction Programme. It is written from the perspective of two key players in the development of the programme and arrangements for its evaluation, who were members of the Home Office Research Development and Statistics directorate at the Home Office.

A number of general themes emerge from the chapters collected here:

1   Rolling out, replication and transference of findings from one project to another are highly problematic. In regard to efforts to address repeat victimisation, an approach widely advocated and widely found to have promise as a way of reducing crime, two projects

discussed here report implementation problems (Chapters 4 and 10). The implementation of the project described here to build on the work of a successful project in Boston to reduce shootings similarly experienced significant difficulties in translating strategy into action (Chapter 5).

2   The separation of the research, analysis and evaluation functions from implementation caused difficulties. The successful Killingbeck project, which was the foundation of the roll-out in West Yorkshire, had extensive researcher involvement, whereas this was not the case in the roll-out itself (Chapter 10). The Boston project likewise had continuing researcher involvement, while this was confined to the early stages of the Manchester project (Chapter 5). There are strong arguments here that researcher/evaluator involvement is important for effective implementation (Chapter 8). Establishing the role of the researcher as contributor to project development is tricky, but ultimately seems to pay off in enabling informed, monitored and adjusted interventions successfully to be put in place (Chapter 2). The continuing involvement of the analyst/researcher/evaluator in projects is uncommon and brings potential risks of bias in evaluation. The benefits, though, probably outweigh the costs (see also Bullock and Tilley 2003).

3   Consistent implementation comprises a consistently found problem (Chapters 2–5 and 7–10). The sources of the difficulties are quite numerous, but failures by project personnel fully to understand or embrace the rationale for the projects in which they are involved appear to be quite common. Problem-oriented policing becomes relevant where standard ways of dealing with issues rooted in standard understandings are not working. It is difficult to introduce non-standard ways of working to well established agencies, especially where teething troubles confirm the doubts of sceptics. These teething troubles are likely where new strategies are being implemented for the first time and where exactly what can be done is unclear.

4   In several cases, problems in data/problem analysis emerge (Chapters 2, 3, 5, 7, 8 and 10). There are issues of analyst capacity and training, data quality, data sharing and use of analysis.

5   Though anathema to problem-oriented policing as conceived by Goldstein, national performance indicators play a large part in shaping policing. They are unavoidable, but sometimes undermine

projects where targeted issues cease to be priorities (see, for example, Chapters 2 and 7).

The chapters collected here bring out something of the very wide range of issues the police are called on to deal with. They also bring out the intractability of many of the problems confronted. The efforts made by those involved in these projects are to be commended and the obstacles, hiccups and failures that independent scrutiny inevitably brings to the surface should not detract from the work undertaken. The problems addressed are, however, hard to deal with and standard forms of response are generally inadequate. It is to be hoped that there will be further experimentation, with a proper appreciation of the realities of working on the ground. Armchair critics have it easy. We would like in particular to see academics tempted to strike critical poses becoming more involved in the engaged business of working with the police and other agencies with crime reduction responsibilities. They could usefully help with the careful unpacking of problems seen in the best of problem-oriented work, along lines pioneered by the likes of Pease (1992), Braga *et al*. (2001) and Clarke and Goldstein (2002). Their help with evaluation would also improve understanding of the processes through which projects work and the measurement of outcomes.

One final point should be made. The findings reported here in no sense represent a test of problem-oriented policing per se. The notion of testing problem-oriented policing scarcely makes sense. It is akin to testing science per se. Testing hypotheses in science is crucial. Testing science as a hypothesis is another matter. Problem-oriented policing attempts to bring scientific method to policing. That many hypotheses in science, operating at the frontiers, are found to be flawed is to be expected. The same will be the case at the frontiers of problem-oriented policing. Equally many scientific experiments are flawed in their execution. Again the same should be expected of experiments in problem-oriented policing, especially as they are conducted well away from the controlled conditions of the laboratory where the scientist is in charge. Moreover, as Laycock and Webb argue in Chapter 11, the conditions set by the centre for local problem-oriented work were themselves in practice less than helpful.

In the chapters that follow it is sometimes not clear that problem-oriented policing, as described at the start of this chapter, was what was being done at all. Where it was implemented imperfectly or ineffectively, this is a cause, as Laycock and Webb stress, for learning not for sneering, jeering or castigating.

Notes

1 Though one of these was so late in submitting a fully developed proposal that it actually didn't start until the same time as the round-two projects. As such, it was evaluated using the money available for round two.
2 For example, sometimes there was pressure from the projects themselves and a number of projects funded outside the bidding rounds were evaluated as well.

References

Braga, A., Kennedy, D., Piehl, A. and Waring, E. (2001) *Reducing Gun Violence: The Boston Gun Project's Operation Ceasefire*. Washington, DC: US National Institute of Justice.

Bullock, K. and Tilley, N. (2003) 'The role of research and analysis: lessons from the crime reduction programme', in J. Knuttson (ed.) *Problem-oriented Policing: From Innovation to Mainstream*. Cullompton: Willan.

Clarke, R. (1998) 'Defining police strategies: problem-solving, problem-oriented policing and community-oriented policing', in T. O'Connor Shelley and A. Grant (eds) *Problem-oriented Policing: Crime-specific Problems, Critical Issues and Making POP Work*. Washington, DC: Police Executive Research Forum.

Clarke, R. and Goldstein, H. (2002) 'Reducing theft at construction sites: lessons from a problem-oriented project', in N. Tilley (ed.) *Analysis for Crime Prevention*. Crime Prevention Studies 13. Cullompton: Willan.

Cohen, L. and Felson, M. (1979) 'Social change and crime rate trends: a routine activities approach', *American Sociological Review*, 44(3): 588–608.

Crawford, A. (1998) *Crime Prevention and Community Safety*. Harlow: Longman.

Eck, J. and Spelman, W. (1987) *Problem Solving: Problem-oriented Policing in Newport News*. Washington, DC: Police Executive Research Forum.

Ekblom, P. (2002). Towards a European knowledge base. Paper on 5Is presented at EU Crime Prevention Network Conference on Exchange of Good Practices, Aalborg, Denmark, October 2002.

Felson, M. (2002) *Crime and Everyday Life*. Thousand Oaks, CA: Sage.

Goldblatt, P. and Lewis, C. (1998) *Reducing Offending: An Assessment of the Research Evidence on Ways of Dealing with Offending Behaviour*. Home Office Research Study 187. London: Home Office.

Goldstein, H. (1979) 'Improving policing: a problem-oriented approach', *Crime and Delinquency*, 25(2): 234–58.

Goldstein, H. (1990) *Problem-oriented Policing*. New York, NY: McGraw-Hill.

Leigh, A., Read, T. and Tilley, N. (1996) *Problem-oriented Policing: Brit Pop*. Crime Prevention and Detection Series 90. London: Home Office.

Leigh, A., Read, T. and Tilley, N. (1998) *Brit Pop II: Problem-oriented Policing in Practice*. Crime Prevention and Detection Series 75. London: Home Office.

Pease, K. (1992) 'The Kirkholt project: preventing burglary on a British public housing estate', *Security Journal*, 2(2): 73–7.

Read, T. and Tilley, N. (2000) *Not Rocket Science? Problem-solving and Crime Reduction*. Crime Reduction Research Series 6. London: Home Office.

Sampson, R. and Scott, M. (2000) *Tackling Crime and other Public Safety Problems: Case Studies in Problem-solving*. Washington, DC: Office of Community-oriented Policing, US Department of Justice.

Scott, M. (2000) *Problem-oriented Policing: Reflections on the First 20 Years*. Washington, DC: Office of Community-oriented Policing, US Department of Justice.

Tilley, N. (2003) 'Models of policing: community policing, POP, and intelligence led policing', in T. Newburn (ed.) *Handbook of Policing*. Cullompton: Willan.

Chapter 2

Two go wild in Knowsley: analysis for evidence-led crime reduction

Michael Townsley and Ken Pease

Introduction

This chapter describes the work carried out by academic advisers assisting Merseyside Police's efforts to conduct evidence-led policing routinely. The project had an ambitious objective: conduct an operational basic command unit (BCU) under the precepts of evidence-based practice. As will be made clear in the body of the chapter, the progress made in a two-year pilot towards such a goal, in an organisation such as the police, was only ever going to be embryonic.

The project became an attempt to introduce individual initiatives on the basis of analysis, either of Knowsley or imported data. Two of these which are believed to be promising will be described. However, in the interests of balance, one aspect of the work which we found particularly frustrating will be documented.

Background

This project was intended to operate a BCU consistent with the principles of evidence-led practice. Unlike other policing experiments involving the reduction of crime and disorder, the remit of the project was not restricted to discrete crime types. The entire gamut of operational policing problems was available for experimentation and study.

Evidence-led practice was taken to mean using best practice from both national and international applied criminological research as well as conducting aggressive data analysis to identify patterns in crime and disorder data. The theoretical framework used to underpin operational policing was problem-oriented policing. Two criminologists, located within the police station, sought to realise the envisioned enterprise.

In preliminary discussions, it was agreed that for the duration of the project the BCU would not be driven by Performance Indicators (PIs), and therefore subject to the fickle reprioritisation which plagues such regimes, but *would* be accountable for outcomes. This reprieve from the PI treadmill was envisaged as a mechanism to establish and facilitate a more proactive operational environment. Also agreed was that the area commander would remain unchanged for the period of the project to ensure a consistent management style of the area. In the event, it did not prove possible to make good on either of these undertakings. In retrospect, both were always unrealistic. In the fast-changing and often competitive world of the policing organisation, creating a time bubble, however rich the rewards of possible success might be, is not practicable. Even if it were, the external validity of such an approach would be very limited. Further, the project manager was changed nine months into the project. Both project managers were involved in other duties in addition to this project. It is against this backdrop that our description of what happened should be viewed.

Neighbourhood policing: a new model of service delivery

We came to Knowsley at a time when the Merseyside force was about to implement a tripartite division of police officers, consisting of neigh-bourhood, response and detectives. Neighbourhood policing was designed to build on the success of the existing community policing style. Detectives operated in a largely similar fashion as before, response officers would attend all urgent calls for service (categorised as 'incidents requiring immediate response' (IRIR calls) and neighbour-hood officers would attend non-urgent matters as well as consulting with the community and problem-solving. Neighbourhood officers were assigned to particular beats that they 'owned'. Neighbourhood inspectors had complete autonomy to determine tactics for their area and geographical accountability.

The new style of service delivery was so conceptually appealing the decision was made to implement the approach in every BCU in the force, not just the pilot BCU. The intention was that if the pilot BCU demonstrated and identified effective practices, they could be 'rolled out' to the other areas relatively seamlessly because there existed a consistent organisational infrastructure. This would not be the case if the BCU's structure was unique. If that had been the case, the external validity of the BCU work would be called into question. In practice, the transition to the new arrangements proved a time-consuming process for all concerned within the pilot BCU. Issues such as staffing levels (what is the optimal ratio of response to neighbourhood officers?), shift patterns (should neighbourhood officers do shift work?) and role responsibility (what constituted an IRIR incident? If response section could not attend, should this be given to the neighbourhood section or remain for evermore with response?) required an extensive development and implementation plan. The consequences, in brief, were as follows:

1   It was perhaps six months into the project before the new working arrangements were sufficiently settled for the command team to turn its attention to the project to the extent that it would have wished from the beginning.

2   By the time the project began in earnest, the writers had assumed roles within the BCU from which it was difficult to break out. They had attempted to be helpful people trying to bring the results of research and new analytic techniques to bear on local policing, but not as instigators of anything more profound.

For these reasons, the writers feel that accidents of history conspired against the project as originally conceived. The end of the project comes with some innovations having been made, and a wish that the project were starting, rather than ending, now. Having described the project glass as half empty, we must go on to record the fact that the BCU was very welcoming to us, we have made many friends and that in research terms the glass is half full – and we are still pouring. One of us is now working in Huyton as a manager in a New Deal for Communities initiative, and the other has chosen to work in Huyton beyond the end of the designated project period.

A conscious effort was made to make neighbourhood policing consistent with problem-oriented policing. Problems – groups of related incidents – were either defined internally, through crime pattern analysis or officer observation, or externally, through identification by citizens, business people or public servants or voluntary agencies. Problems were dealt with through the well-known SARA (scanning, analysis, response and assessment) process.

In general, we found understanding of the SARA process to be excellent in Merseyside. However, its application was not equally good. The SARA process tended to become a formula into which officers fitted what they intended to do anyway, rather than a process which sought to gain a deeper understanding of what was happening. At their worst, SARAs were a delaying tactic, buying time in which hard-pressed officers could address an issue for which immediate action might otherwise be demanded. There is every reason to suppose that these are hazards for any police organisation seeking to routinise the SARA process. The first output of the project external to Merseyside Police was a specification of 'what makes a good SARA' which appeared on the Home Office crime reduction website.

The signal failure

This section details a problem that was a constant irritant to our efforts and severely limited any perception of effective police work. We observed early in our time at Knowsley that the mechanism for calculating performance targets, performed at the force level, was irrational. Our advice to alter the way targets were calculated was not compelling enough during our tenure but between the end of the project and the drafting of this chapter Merseyside Police made a decision to calculate targets along the lines we suggested.

BCU performance in Merseyside is assessed by periodically flagging up BCU crime and detection levels relative to previously agreed targets. These are referred to as 'traffic lights' because they are coded green if they signal rates in line with targets, amber if on the margins and red if BCUs are failing to meet targets. The difficulty with such a system is that the targets fail to take account of seasonal cycles. The problems and their potential resolution are set out in more detail below.

Priorities within a police area are fluid. The importance placed on controlling certain crimes is related to, but not totally determined by, the magnitude and direction of the disparity between the recorded level of incidents and the targets set in place for the area. Where recorded incidents exceed the target level greatly, much activity is expended to reduce this difference. If the target is greater than the level of recorded incidents then attention can be shifted to other crime types. The same can be said of detections. Thus, targets are powerful entities; they can rapidly transform the delivery of police service in an area. It therefore follows that great care must be taken when selecting targets. If targets are unrealistic, they divert resources and undermine the efforts of officers.

The method of target-setting used during the BCU pilot had a number of deficiencies. It could be best described as *unweighted*. BCUs are informed that a certain percentage reduction (in the case of recorded crime) is required compared with the previous year. This amount gives the annual target. Monthly targets are then calculated by dividing by 12. The problem with this approach is that one assumes that the supply of crimes is uniform throughout the year. Many studies have shown this to be a false assumption (e.g. Farrell and Pease (1994) using Merseyside data). By way of illustration, consider the offence of theft from motor vehicle (TFMV), one of the largest single crime types in Knowsley. Taking median monthly totals for the years 1998 to 2000 yields the graph in Figure 2.1. Each year follows much the same pattern, so we shall treat the above as representative of the underlying frequency of TFMV offences in Knowsley. It is clearly apparent that the frequency of offences varies greatly over the course of a calendar year.

Suppose that targets were set so that the total for TFMVs in 2001 were to be 10% less than 2000's TFMV total. Taking the 2000 TFMV total (1,481 stolen cars), we can compute that the 2001 target is approximately 1,333 (0.9*1,481). How should this target be spread out over the year? The convention in Merseyside is to set targets uniformly so that each month has the same target, regardless of seasonal patterns for that crime type. Figure 2.2 demonstrates the difference between the historical pattern of TFMV in Knowsley and the target.

Figure 2.1   Annual predicted trend of TFMV in Knowsley

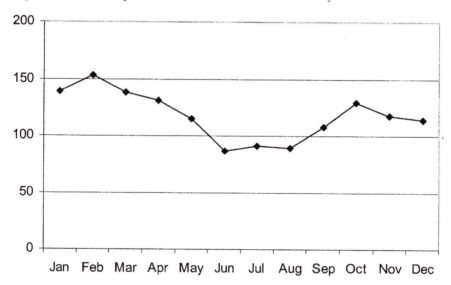

Figure 2.2   Seasonal crimes compared with uniform targets

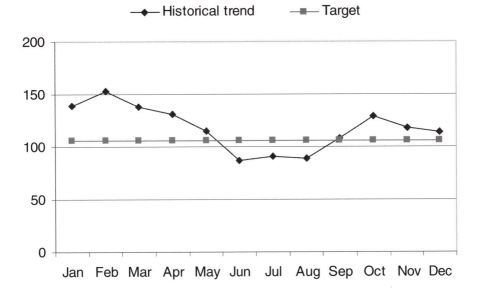

It is obvious that, based on past results, Knowsley's efforts to achieve the set targets will be very difficult for January to April as well as October and November (six months of the year!). On the other hand, May to September should be relatively easy. The overall result will be that management will be depressed during the high months and elated at other times – despite the fact that their (in)ability to reach the monthly target is in large part a function of seasonal trends. While the patterns ensure that senior officers will be cheerful when they go on their summer holidays, this seems insufficient justification for a process which separates them from an accurate knowledge of the results of their efforts.

Given the seasonal variation of TFMV, a *weighted* method of target-setting is recommended. This would be performed by attributing the reduction throughout the year not evenly but according to each month's historical share of the annual total. For example, the annual target is 1,333 TFMVs (using the imaginary 90% of last year's total). To achieve this total, or less, BCUs should be able to attribute reduction across months according to seasonal proportions. In the case of TFMV incidents, monthly targets should be weighted by that month's historical share of the total.

Three years of data, 1998–2000, were used to construct a historical TFMV trend (median monthly values were chosen). This was subjected to an arbitrary 10% reduction per month to determine the weighted targets. Unweighted targets were determined by reducing 2000's TFMV total by 10% and then dividing this amount by 12. The observed number of TFMVs in the year 2001 were obtained to compare how the different targeting styles provide contrasting messages to management. The different interpretations possible were considered if contrasting targeting schemes were used (see Figure 2.3). Under the unweighted targets Knowsley met its target on three occasions (August, November and December), and even then by the barest of margins. Weighted targets give a different picture. Here, about five months conform to the standard. The picture is much less bleak than when unweighted targets are used.

The point of weighting targets is not merely to make an area look good; it should not be used just because to do so is to have more 'green light' months. The point is that it is unrealistic to expect anyone to suppress crime uniformly when the underlying distribution of crime is not uniform. Nor should months when crime is traditionally high be seen as the time to relax or take a holiday because 'there is nothing that we can do'. The point of demonstrating that crimes have a seasonal component is that it is pointless beating yourself up during the high crime season. It is just as pointless to do the opposite, to accept the status

Figure 2.3 Contrast between weighted and unweighted target setting

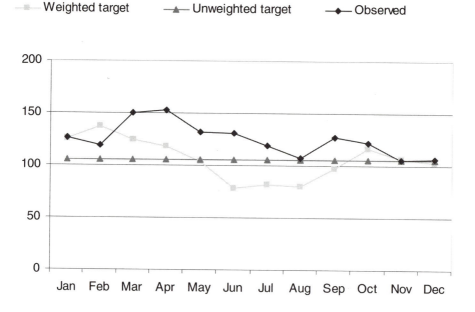

quo. Rather than being apathetic during the high season, the seasonal approach should be seen as similar to running a long-distance race over hilly terrain. More effort is applied when going up a slope and less on the decline. Applying equal effort throughout the race would result in an ineffectual performance.

An effective way of utilising the weighted targets would be to apportion resources to what crime is high for the season. If burglary and car crime have an inverse relationship, then during burglary's low season resources can be diverted towards the impending car crime high season. If seasonal trends are not known, one will be caught out every year. Once a prediction about impending increases is cast, work can be carried out to try to falsify it.

Unweighted targets are illogical devices for assessing police performance and greatly harm any objective decision-making about resource allocation. There are two main problems with unweighted targets: police do not have an accurate picture of how they have performed and, in our opinion worse, they have no idea how to plan for the impending wax or wane of crime levels as their targets never change. PIs are very influential in determining police action. The magnitude of this influence, however, should be commensurate with the underlying rationality of the mechanism.

Casual readers may feel we have spent an inordinate amount of time on this topic. However, it is one where a relatively minor change of practice would place the force in which we have invested so much of our time in a better position to know when its efforts make a difference.

Preventing repeat residential burglary

A significant proportion of the project's activities was devoted to developing a burglary initiative. Prior work by existing staff yielded a number of initiatives but these were imperfectly implemented. For example, Merseyside police developed a repeat victimisation policy that required officers to comply with a series of steps to reduce the chance of repeat burglaries. When audited, this process was being carried out in very few instances (about one in 60 cases). Fortuitously, the then area commander for Knowsley had been responsible for developing the force repeat victimisation policy, so was well versed in the merits of preventing repeat incidents and was keen to see the policy applied routinely.

The burglary initiative was designed to take advantage of the empirical research on burglary prevention. Along with the well-known repeat victimisation literature, the results of emerging research were incorporated into the prevention strategy. Recent studies show there is evidence that a form of elevated victimisation risk occurs in the properties surrounding burgled houses. What is intriguing is that this elevated risk is time limited, in much the same way as the time course of repeat victimisation diminishes as time elapses. This phenomenon has been described as a penumbra of risk (Shaw and Pease 2000), near repeat victimisation (Townsley *et al.* 2003) or isomorphic victimisation (Johnson and Bowers 2003) by various researchers.

Thus, the aim of the burglary initiative was to reduce the incidence of domestic burglary via the prevention of repeat victimisation and near repeat victimisation. This was attempted through a series of actions. First, there existed a repeat victimisation (RV) strategy which was underpinned by the well-known Olympic model of tiered response (Chenery *et al.* 1999). This is where crime prevention action is directed to victims and the extent of this action is directly proportional to the extent of victimisation history. This system, however, is at the mercy of the mechanism that identifies repeat victims. In Knowsley's case, the identification of repeats relied on a system of a manual twelve-monthly search for every reported burglary.

Therefore, a RV database was developed. Burglary incidents were entered daily. The database was designed such that every new entry was automatically scanned for incidents with similar location information during the preceding 12 months. The matching procedure is sensitive enough to discern definite matches and possible matches. Possible matches can be further investigated to determine if the same household is involved. Using the RV database, the crime reduction officer was in a far better position to respond to repeat victims swiftly. Prior to the database development the process of identifying repeat victims was exceedingly time-consuming and tedious.

The second measure developed to prevent repeat burglaries was a security assessment for victims of burglary. The security assessment was based on a version first developed in Queensland, Australia (for full details, see National Crime Prevention (2001)). The assessment is contained within a booklet providing advice and assistance on securing premises. The Knowsley booklet consists of general crime prevention advice, a security audit, information about alarms, a property inventory and useful telephone numbers for the police, Victim Support and the local authority. The security assessment was designed to be easy to fill out in a short amount of time and provide customised recommendations for each victimised household.

The first officer attending a burgled household completes the security audit of the premises. This includes the condition of the front and rear doors, windows, lighting, alarms, property marking, vehicle security and general housekeeping. For each of the 24 security points in the assessment, officers needed to determine the condition of the feature in the immediate wake of a burglary and whether a security upgrade was appropriate. In most cases where a feature was non-existent or in-adequate the recommendation to upgrade would logically follow. The questionnaire was on pressure-sensitive paper enabling the response officer to take a copy, leaving the other with the householder as a reminder of the suggested recommendations.

Householders were asked to sign the assessment to facilitate house-holder ownership of the security upgrading. They were also informed that a police officer would make a follow-up visit after approximately one month to confirm that the recommendations have been carried out and to encourage further security upgrading that had been recom-mended but not carried out. Fears of police intimidation were expressed in the drafting stage, but a key element in the training given to police officers was that they were providing a service to the householder – not coercing victims into modifying their residence, but telling motivated people what to do. There were no sanctions for individuals who opt not to carry out recommendations.

The third mechanism to prevent repeat burglaries was used to prevent near repeats and conventional repeat burglaries. The crime reduction officer developed and designed 'burglary alert' cards. Originally intended to be used by officers at the scene of burglaries when the neighbours were not at home, their purpose has evolved to incorporate cocoon Neighbourhood Watch, known locally as Chrysalis Watch – where neighbours of a burglary victim are informed of the incident and agree to look out for nearby dwellings and suspicious individuals – as well as provide crime prevention advice for those properties most at risk of near repeat victimisation. After the first officer attending completed inquiries with the burgled household, burglary alert cards were distributed to neighbouring houses to three homes either side of the burgled premises. Officers had discretion to distribute cards to other nearby homes which circumstances suggested might be at elevated risk.

Figure 2.4 shows the total number of residential burglaries per month for Knowsley and the remainder of the force, indexed to 100 six months prior to the introduction of the booklet. The commencement of the booklet's use is indicated by the solid vertical line. It is clear that there was a difference between the level of burglary in Knowsley and the rest of the force. While fluctuating, the amount of burglary in Knowsley was

Figure 2.4 Total monthly residential burglaries

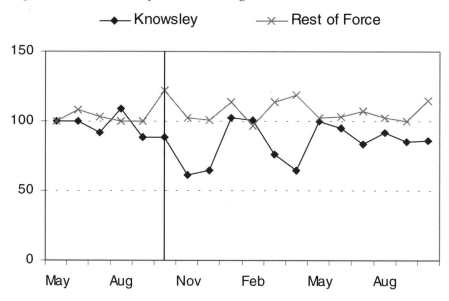

less than the force aggregate, in relative terms, for all but one month since the introduction of the booklet.

An obvious next step would be to examine the temporal patterns of repeat burglaries. However, the monthly volume of repeats in most areas was too small to compare reliably. Small fluctuations in the number of repeat victims would produce erratic patterns. Table 2.1 shows for the first six months of the initiative the percentage change in the volume of repeat incidents compared with the same period last year. The table shows that Knowsley experienced a reduction in the amount of repeat burglaries over the first six months of the initiative. This runs counter to St Helens (which shared the initiative but did not implement it to the same degree), the contiguous areas and the rest of the force.

We surveyed police officers to elicit opinions about the security assessment three months after implementation. We asked three questions: (1) do you think it helps you do your job?; (2) do you think the victim found it useful?; and (3) is it easy to fill in? Overall the replies were negative for the first two but positive for the third. The only benefit the officers could perceive was the ease of use, despite an over-whelmingly positive response by victims (see below).

Further analysis was then undertaken of common features/weak-nesses that afforded the offender a greater opportunity to burgle – for

Table 2.1: Percentage change in repeats for first six months compared with same period twelve months previously

	Percentage change
Knowsley	–9.1
St Helens	+13.6
Contiguous	+37.4
Rest of force	+10.0
Total excluding Knowsley	+27.2
Total including Knowsley	+23.3

example, condition of windows and doors, whether the front door had a view panel, etc. This information was then fed back in two ways. First, response officers were given personal feedback with regards to their personal style. For example, some officers would tick lots of weak points but then vary in which ones they would highlight to be repaired or upgraded. Alternatively, some officers noted many security short-comings but never made a recommendation for improvement – this was fed back to the officers concerned on an individual basis. Secondly, a 'common weak points' list was prepared for the Knowsley Housing Trust in order that they can update their security as required by s. 17 of the Crime and Disorder Act 1998.[1] Also, the information will be utilised as a guide in the planning office for other forthcoming building developments.

Response officer visits to burglaries increased in their quality as the series of questions gave them a structured and practical approach to dealing with burglary dwellings. Utilising the booklet and the red cards sensitised response officers to the issues surrounding repeat victimisation. The system of neighbourhood policing provides owner-ship at constable level and the second visit encourages staff to engage with the community. Similarly, the scheme encourages social cohesion in the community as neighbours support one another following a neighbour being victimised. In the follow-up visits, the reaction of burglary victims was overwhelmingly positive and they stressed their feelings that they had been given a professional service and a reduced fear of repeat victimisation. Also, 67% of victims are found to have upgraded their security as per the recommendations.

The police and local authority Crime and Disorder Reduction Group have now made the updates with regards to weak points an agenda item in their meetings. This feedback loop will provide information and focus for the local authority, housing association and planning committee when sanctioning new buildings. They can determine set criteria under s. 17 of the Crime and Disorder Act as, previously, the weak points were not known. This continues to be a developmental area.

A note on the value of pilot testing to encourage compliance

In order to gauge officer reaction to the security assessment booklets, a number of draft copies were distributed to a particular section of officers with a request to pilot them and provide feedback. The majority of the feedback was negative. This provided the opportunity to rethink elements of the initiative to accommodate the genuine concerns of the officers. One comment ('how are we going to carry them?') prompted the purchase of leather-look folders emblazoned with the Merseyside Police shield. They were distributed to every response officer at the launch of the booklet. Prior to the launch, officers viewed the booklets as just another task that was not really their job (it fell under the responsibilities of the crime reduction officer). Incorporating the folders alongside the burglary book enabled the task to be viewed as less onerous as well as implicitly demonstrating how important the organisation viewed the proper completion of the burglary books.

Operation Safeground – self-selection

Prior research has shown that offender self-selection (letting individuals *volunteer* for police attention by their commission of minor offences) provides a greater hit rate than picking individuals at random (Chenery *et al.* 1999; Maple, 1999). The principle is that career criminals commit offences of a broad spectrum, ranging in frequency. In order to prevent rare, but serious, events, one focuses attention to those people who commit minor, but common, infractions of the law. In this way, attention is diverted to that group of people who are most likely be involved in serious crime. The advantage of this approach is that because individuals volunteer for police attention, officers do not waste time on innocent people, there is no basis for allegations of harassment and more people come in contact with the police who are already subject to police powers.

There are a number of published examples of offender self-selection. The Transit Police of New York found that by preventing those individuals who jump turnstiles there was a corresponding drop in crime in the subway and trains. The explanation for this drop was that fare evaders also commit other offences in the transit system (Maple, 1999). Drivers who illegally park in disabled parking bays were found to be subject to police attention at far higher levels than drivers who parked legally. One fifth of the individuals who used the disabled bays illegitimately were subject to immediate police interest compared with 2% for legally parked cars (Chenery *et al.* 1999).

There were three distinct attempts to implement a self-selection style experiment. In the first a replication of the disabled parking bay trigger was executed. There was only one trial and the results, on the surface, did not merit further experimentation. In one morning 17 vehicles were found to be illegally parked. Of these, 9 were checked and they were of no police interest – i.e. the drivers were not wanted, there were no traffic violations, etc. The officer responsible deemed the experiment to have produced no positive results and implied that the underlying premise was flawed.

The analysis, as presented to us, had one major omission. Not every illegally parked vehicle was checked. Eight vehicles were able to depart the scene before they could be stopped by the police officer. In light of this, a hit rate of zero out of 9 becomes a hit rate of zero to 8 out of 17. The point here is not that the 8 vehicles got away without being scrutinised, but that the results were viewed in a particular context which served to dissuade further experimentation of the technique.

The second self-selection experiment involved cars driving through a bus interchange. The police had received from the transport department a number of complaints of cars driving through a bus-only zone – the restricted area was clearly marked – and it was thought an ideal opportunity to retest the self-selection hypothesis. The results were dire. An officer recorded no cars driving in the restricted area for the duration of the trial. It was not clear whether the time period used to test the premise was selected based on the peak times of illegal bus-lane driving. The test was abandoned after the first attempt. Again, self-selection was seen to have failed.

The third attempt to execute self-selection was dubbed Operation Safeground. The police, DVLA and Knowsley Taxi Licensing col-laborated in a vehicle inspection programme where they would pull over any vehicle in which the driver was not wearing a seatbelt. In the four-hour time period the hit rate of offences was significantly greater than would be expected by chance. A summary of the hits in various categories is displayed in Table 2.2. Apart from the disturbing statistic concerning taxis and private hire vehicles – about half of them were deemed not safe to drive – the rate of hits for private vehicles is quite

Table 2.2: Percent of drivers/vehicles displaying characteristics where the 'non-use of seatbelt' self-selection trigger was used

	Total (%)
Private vehicles (n = 62)	
Arrest	2 (3.2)
VEL offences	9 (14.5)
Prohibitions (dangerous vehicles)	7 (11.3)
Taxis and private-hire cars (n = 40)	
Defect notices	14 (35.0)
Stop notices (removal of plate)	6 (15.0)

high. By way of comparison, a similar operation was conducted without the self- selection triggers where officers would stop all vehicles of a particular age at a specific time of day (these were both selected for likelihood of theft). The number of vehicles or drivers that the police had further powers over amounted to about 5% of the vehicles stopped. While too much cannot be read into single observation trials, in this case the seatbelt trigger had an greater hit rate than random stop checks by a factor of five.

The message from this is that by using a minor infraction of the law (not wearing a seatbelt) as a trigger for scrutiny, a greater chance of hits is possible. For the police, this means their actions are more likely to be cost-effective and most importantly do not run the risk of accusations of harassment because the behaviour or action selects individuals for police attention in an objective and non-contentious way.

Conclusions

Our conclusions will be impressionistic. We believe that the perspective we espoused is only now permeating police colleagues in Knowsley. An operation targeting Huyton offenders with outstanding warrants came after we quantified the problem. The burglary security assessment booklet is to be rolled out across Merseyside, suitably amended. The principle of self-selection has recently been taken up and developed with a variety of vehicle-related triggers for action, and in conjunction with the adoption and use of automatic number-plate recognition equipment. Any change we have achieved comes through the availability of local analyses and national perspectives which would, with the best will in the world, have been beyond the fevered working schedule of analysts. Indeed one of the lessons we have learnt and had repeatedly reinforced is just how time intensive some of the more interesting analyses turn out to be. Our belief now is that, rather than imposing some pre-packaged approach (based on routine activities theory, situational crime prevention or problem-oriented policing), change will come on the back of painstaking accretions of analytic skill and their incorporation of perspectives, to generate analyses which speak to ever more sophisticated conceptions of the policing task.

Finally, the overarching aim of the Targeted Policing Initiative was to conduct evidence-based practices routinely. One of the results of incorporating an evidence-based approach is a heavy reliance on intelligence and data analysis. While the promise of evidence based approaches is to lower the incidences of crime and harm in our community and to use resources more effectively, crime analysts are among the few in any police force that are guaranteed to experience increased workload as a result of a move towards evidence-based approaches.

A theme that recurs in several reports (HMIC 1998; Read and Tilley, 2000; Scott, 2000) concerns the quality of training provided for analysts. Most training consists of techniques to interrogate information systems. Analysts become very good at obtaining data, but not how to analyse it. Without adequate training, the unpacking of problem components will be beyond the skill of most crime analysts, individual predilections aside.

Analysts will contribute to the policing endeavour when they provide officers with an understanding of the plethora of crime situations. Most analysts know how to *describe* data, but less common is the ability to make *inferences* from the data (Lamm Weisel, 2003). The difference between description and inference is similar to the difference between (human) intelligence and wisdom. An intelligent person can tell if it is raining outside, but a wise person knows to take an umbrella.

A descriptive analysis of vehicle crime would include hot-spots and times of the car crime, what types of car are subject to crime and what different methods were used to commit the offence. Inferences develop explanations about the observed patterns. If the descriptive phase identifies a concentration of offences at particular locations, explanations are developed for why this is so (e.g. improper place management, links to public transport, neglible risk of apprehension, supply of vulnerable targets).

Inferences made about crime data provide the clues that should be used to reduce crime. If only descriptive statements are used to diagnose crime problems, solutions generated will either be superficial or not explicit enough to be relevant. Descriptive analyses will help reduce crime by virtue of chance or good fortune.

The single most beneficial activity that analysts could do to increase their effectiveness would be to stop thinking about crime problems in terms of their legislative labels and instead describe them by the activities of the participants. Scott (2000) encourages problem-solving to be recalibrated away from crime types to offending behaviours. He points out that shorthand labels for problems tend to aggregate a host of actual and implied behaviours that ultimately serve to muddy the analytic water. For example, the police term violence, while descriptive, can encompass a wide array of behaviours. It can include violence between immediate family members, both intergenerational and intimates (domestic violence); violence between individuals known to each other (acquaintance violence); and violence between people unknown to each other (stranger violence). One may also wish to categorise another type of violence as those incidents involving alcohol, although this would probably confound matters. For the purposes of illustration we will not do that here, mainly as alcohol is likely to be involved in both domestic and stranger violence (Chapter 6 in this volume considers the relationship between alcohol and violence).

A descriptive analysis of violence, in the legislative sense of the word, is therefore an amalgam of the three major types of violence. The picture that emerges will be the result of the relative proportions of each different type of violence. There is a risk, therefore, that the patterns of acquaintance violence will cancel out the patterns of stranger violence, say. The problem of violence needs to be partitioned into discrete elements so that individual incidents within an element are very similar. Even if every incident of violence was partitioned into the three categories suggested, there may be merit in partitioning categories further. Domestic violence between intimates could be further split into two groups – where the individuals are cohabiting or not.

The point of grouping incidents by behaviour and not legislative category is that legal definitions are crude typologies when it comes to describing the full gamut of human emotion and actions. One cannot hope to gain an understanding of a crime problem if it is not described properly. In quite a few cases partitioning incidents within a crime classi-fication will be an arduous and time-consuming task. Some of the greatest gains in analytical insight are to be made in these circumstances, however. If data problems have prevented a process of penetrating analysis, it is likely that not much is understood of the problem beyond the superficial.

In conclusion, recorded crime information is useful, but inadequate recording practices combined with cumbersome and rigid recording mechanisms bedevil efforts to understand patterns of crime. 'Crime will be high where it is easy to commit' is one of the theoretical underpinnings of applied criminology. We could also make the case that 'where crime analysis is difficult, meaningful results will be rare'.

Note

1 This section obliges local authorities to consider the implications on community safety of any decision-making.

References

Chenery, S., Henshaw, C. and Pease, K. (1999) *Illegal Parking in Disabled Bays: A Means of Offending Targeting.* Home Office Briefing Note 1/99. London: Home Office.

Farrell, G. and Pease, K. (1994) 'Crime seasonality: domestic disputes and residential burglary in Merseyside 1988-90', *British Journal of Criminology*, 34: 487–497.

HMIC (1998) *Beating Crime. Thematic Inspection Report.* London: HM Inspectorate of Constabulary.

Johnson, S.D. and Bowers, K. (2003) 'The burglary as clue to the future: the beginnings of prospective hot-spotting', *European Journal of Criminology*, in press.

Lamm Weisel, D. (2003) *Form and Function of Analysis in Solving Problems.* Crime Prevention Series 14. London: Home Office.

Maple, J. (1999) *Crime Fighter.* New York, NY: Broadway Books.

National Crime Prevention (2001) *Lightning Strikes Twice: Preventing Repeat Home Burglary.* Canberra: Attorney-General's Department.

Read, T. and Tilley, N. (2000) *Not Rocket Science? Problem-solving and Crime Reduction.* Crime Reduction Research Series 6. London: Home Office.

Scott, M. (2000) *Problem-oriented Policing: Reflections on the First 20 years.* Washington, DC: Office of Community-oriented Policing, US Department of Justice.

Shaw, M. and Pease, K. (2000) *Research on Repeat Victimisation in Scotland.* Crime and Criminal Justice Research Findings 44. Edinburgh: Scottish Executive.

Tilley, N. and Laycock, G. (2002) *Working out What to Do: Evidence-based Crime Reduction.* Crime Reduction Research Series 11. London: Home Office.

Townsley, M., Homel, R. and Chaseling, J. (2003) 'Infectious burglaries: a test of the near repeat hypothesis', *British Journal of Criminology*, 43(3): in press.

Chapter 3

Rolling out the National Intelligence Model: key challenges

Tim John and Mike Maguire

Introduction

As many other contributors to this volume illustrate, there is an accelerating shift away from 'reactive' or 'fire brigade' policing towards a variety of more strategic, targeted and future-oriented approaches, based on the identification and analysis of recurrent (and emerging) problems, assessments of risk, planned responses and clearer prioritisation in the use of resources (for broader discussions of these trends, see Ericson and Haggerty 1997; Gill 2000; Maguire 1999, 2000, 2003; Tilley 2003). However, until now, the development of such approaches has been piecemeal and patchy across the country, as well as handicapped by a confusing range of labels and terms: 'community' policing, 'problem-oriented' policing, 'intelligence-led' policing and so on. This chapter focuses on the core model which has recently been adopted by the Association of Chief Police Officers (ACPO) as a means of bringing these diverse strands together into one universal system with standard procedures and terminology, and which, its designers and 'champions' intend, will ultimately provide the vehicle through which all major police business is channelled and delivered: the National Intelligence Model (NIM).

Despite its name, despite its origins in the National Criminal Intelligence Service and despite many misapprehensions both inside and outside the police, the NIM is not simply about the use of criminal intelligence. It is in essence a *business model* – a means of organising knowledge and information in such a way that the best possible decisions can be made about how to deploy resources, that actions can be co-ordinated within and between different levels of policing, and that lessons are continually learnt and fed back into the system. While at present strongly associated (both in perception and practice) with the world of serious crime, the CID and law enforcement activities, it is in fact designed to be applied much more widely – for example, to facilitate multi-agency crime prevention and responses to non-crime problems such as disorder and anti-social behaviour. It is thus right at the heart of the current movement towards 'problem-solving' in police work, which provides the framework for this book.

The chapter is based largely on a research study of the early stages of the 'roll-out' of the NIM (John and Maguire forthcoming), which entailed both an overview of developments at a national level and fieldwork in three police force areas, selected as 'pilot sites' for its implementation. We first provide a simplified description of the NIM and the thinking behind it. This is followed by an account of progress with the 'roll-out', focusing on a number of key issues which were identified in the course of the research as posing serious challenges to the successful implementation of the model in practice. Finally, we use one of the forces as a case study through which to explore the extent to which the NIM 'fits with' another important policing model, problem-oriented policing (POP). As POP is already well established in several forces, the compatibility of the two models may have an impact upon the implementation of the NIM and how easily it is accepted and understood by officers on the ground.

Origins of the National Intelligence Model

One of the key strands of thinking that led directly to the emergence of the NIM was the conviction that criminal intelligence should play a more central role in crime control, and in the policing agenda more generally. This was by no means a new argument, having been reiterated in a series of high-level reports since the 1970s (ACPO 1975, 1978, 1986, 1996; HMIC 1997). However, while the systematic collection, pooling and analysis of intelligence were generally agreed to be vital to the work of specialist squads (especially those dealing with serious and organised crime in a cross-border context), even here it did not 'drive the business' to the extent that was sometimes claimed, many detectives preferring to run their own informants and keep information to themselves, as well as responding *ad hoc* to specific pieces of intelligence rather than being guided by deeper analysis and planning (see, for example, Maguire and Norris 1992). Where more mainstream policing was concerned, intelligence systems remained grossly underdeveloped in most forces, and it was not until the Audit Commission report of 1993, which contrasted a 'vicious circle' of failure to control crime through reactive policing with the 'virtuous circle' of effectiveness that was possible through proactive and targeted policing, that serious and determined attempts began to be made to use intelligence systematically in local responses to crime. One of the first forces to grasp the nettle was Kent where, largely due to a powerful lead from the Chief Constable, local police stations began to engage in a genuine form of 'intelligence-led' policing. This involved significant reallocations of resources from 'reactive' CID teams to intelligence units and the setting up of core management groups (tasking and co-ordination groups), which met regularly to consider the latest intelligence reports and analysis, to set priorities and to 'task' teams or individuals to collect further intelligence or to carry out tactical operations (Maguire and John 1995; Amey *et al.* 1996). The 'Kent model', indeed, has been very influential in the development of the NIM, which echoes many of its aims and processes.

Despite the pioneering lead of Kent and a number of other forces, and despite increasing promotion of intelligence-led policing by the Home Office, ACPO, HMIC and other central bodies, it became clear in the late 1990s that intelligence structures and processes remained under-developed and ineffective in a large number of forces. Common problems included lack of co-ordination and integration of key elements; failure to create a 'culture of intelligence' (Friedman *et al.* 1997) in which information is 'owned' by the whole organisation; and lack of strategic thinking and prioritisation (for further comment and descriptions of a variety of successful and unsuccessful initiatives, see Maguire and John 1995, 1996; Howe 1997; Hook 1998; Barton and Evans 1999; Fogg 2000a, 2000b; Martindale 2000; Innes and Fielding 2002; Sheptycki 2003).

Moreover, huge variations in practice reflected the fact that intelligence systems had developed in a piecemeal, individualistic fashion, with little centrally co-ordinated direction. This divergence of practice not only hindered the spread of good practice, but created barriers to the effective flow of information between forces, as well as between the local, national and international levels. As the National Criminal Intelligence Service (NCIS 1999) emphasised, such barriers undermined the potential impact of intelligence-led policing in achieving both its business goals (value for money, best value) and its criminal justice goals (accurate targeting and best evidence).

It was largely in response to these concerns that NCIS developed the NIM (Flood 1999; NCIS 1999, 2000).[1] However, while one of the key aims was to improve and standardise practices around the collection, analysis and dissemination of intelligence, it was designed with a considerably wider vision than this.

Key concepts and components of the NIM

The NIM is essentially the design for a comprehensive 'business process' to rationalise and systematise the ways in which the police service handles information and makes key decisions about the deployment of resources. Its overall structure is actually quite simple, although this tends to become obscured by jargon and by the detail of its individual components (John and Maguire forthcoming). A frequent criticism of the NIM from within and outside the police is that its terminology and presentation are unapproachable, too technical and not geared to use by police officers (see, for example, Gill 2000; Sheptycki 2003). As one of our respondents put it:

> NIM is a simple concept made very difficult. It is academic. If you carve it up you can get the hang of it. In fact, it can be insulting, it's so simple. But also police officers can be very basic in their approach. My own impression is that it was meant to be a management tool, that it was never meant for police officers. And with this apparently not being the case, I don't see why the structure has to be so formal for police officers, for them to do their job. It contains a level of sophistication that turns people off.
>
> (intelligence sergeant)

To help readers unfamiliar with the model to understand it, we seek in this section to avoid the trap of excessive detail by summarising its essential characteristics in as simple a manner as possible. The outline will be divided into four sections, discussing (1) how the NIM defines levels of policing; (2) how it defines policing 'business' and its outcomes; (3) the main mechanism through which the business is done and the outcomes are achieved, the 'tasking and co-ordinating process'; and (4) the main 'products' that are created and used in this process.

Defining and linking levels of police activity

A number of studies and commentators have highlighted a perennial difficulty with raising the status and impact of intelligence. This is to maintain a regular flow of reliable information and intelligence between different units and areas of the police service – a process which should

contribute to an effective overall 'intelligence cycle'. It is well documented that such flows experience frequent interruptions and blockages
due to a variety of cultural, bureaucratic, geographic and technical
factors (see, for example, Maguire and John 1995; Barton and Evans 1999;
Innes and Fielding 2002, Sheptycki 2003). This can be a problem even
between neighbouring units of the same force, but is particularly
apparent between different 'levels' of the police organisation. One of the
most serious problems identified in this context is the so-called 'regional
void' – the lack of systematic co-operation between forces to share
information about, and to develop joint operations against, 'travelling
offenders' such as professional burglars, whose activities fall below the
threshold of 'serious and organised' crime dealt with by the National
Crime Squad, but are difficult for individual forces to tackle alone.

The NIM defines three 'levels' of policing activity, as follows:

Level 1: basic command unit (BCU) and local.
Level 2: force and cross-border.
Level 3: national and international.

It includes a set of processes designed to create and maintain an effective
flow of intelligence both within and between these three levels. As Flood
(1999: 9) points out, if this can be achieved in practice, it will be a major
advance for the police service:

> The model is, therefore, very ambitious, for in describing the links
> between the levels it offers for the first time the realisable goal of
> integrated intelligence in which all forces might play a part in a
> system bigger than themselves. How can we have a sound crime
> strategy if we cannot paint the picture of crime and criminality
> from top to bottom?

A point emphasised to the researchers during the evaluation of the roll-
out was that complex crime problems are experienced – albeit in
different ways – at more than one level and may be most effectively dealt
with by simultaneous strategies and actions undertaken at different
levels. In other words, the levels are not mutually exclusive and it should
not be assumed that they exist in order for ownership of a problem
simply to be passed upwards or downwards to the 'right' level and then
forgotten. Illicit drug supply forms an appropriate example, and one
which forms the basis of a more detailed case study in John and Maguire
(forthcoming). Importation is primarily a level 3 (national/inter-
national) concern; dealing has an impact at levels 1 and 2; and the

community consequences of drug use will primarily affect level 1. Each level can play a part in the overall response by dealing with its own aspect of the problem, and they can contribute to one another's effectiveness by sharing information and co-ordinating strategies.

Developing Flood's analogy, therefore, the various pictures painted at level 1 will, when combined, paint much of the picture for level 2. The pictures painted by each of the 43 police forces (and other agencies) will, when put together, contribute to the national/international picture needed at level 3. This will in turn influence subsequent activities at levels 1 and 2 through the setting of national policing priorities and objectives.

Defining policing business and outcomes

The NIM seeks to reinforce the key areas of policing activity – or policing 'business', as it is usually referred to in the model – at each of the three levels defined above. It identifies the core business areas of policing as 'managing crime', 'managing criminals', 'managing localised disorder', 'managing enforcement and community issues' and 'reducing opportunities for crime'. The outcomes sought through the NIM process are defined in similarly wide-ranging terms: 'community safety', 'reduced crime', 'arrested/disrupted criminals', 'managed hot-spots' and the control of 'potentially dangerous offenders'. It is further specified that they may be achieved through a variety of policing methods and resources: 'intelligence, reactive investigation, proactive operations, and patrol resources' (NCIS 2000).

The above definitions make it clear that it is a misconception to regard the model solely as a more sophisticated form of the kind of 'proactive policing' advocated by, for example, the Audit Commission (1993) in its exhortation to 'target the criminal, not the crime', or simply as an advance from the use of individual 'proactive' tactics (intelligence, surveillance and informants) to a more integrated 'intelligence-led' system for targeting prolific offenders, like that adopted in the early days of the 'Kent model' (Maguire and John 1995). Certainly, many elements of the latter are present in the NIM, but this is only part of the story. The model specifies its 'business', its 'outcomes' and available resources as encompassing a considerably broader remit than that previously understood as being the preserve of intelligence-led policing (ILP). It specifically includes tasks such as managing 'disorder' and 'community issues' within its 'business', and places 'community safety' among its desired outcomes. It also recognises ownership of reactive and patrol resources, and not just of resources like surveillance teams and informant handling.

The mechanics of the NIM: the tasking and co-ordinating process

At the heart of each of the three levels is an identically constituted 'tasking and co-ordinating process'. At the core of this process lies the Tasking and Co-ordinating Group (TCG), one of which is set up in each of the geographical areas through which policing is managed at the level in question (for example, in each BCU at level 1, and each force at level 2).[2] The TCG, whose key members include heads of intelligence units and senior managers with control over police resources, becomes the owner of all policing 'business' for that level, and is responsible for achieving the relevant 'outcomes'. The TCG is the prime recipient of analytical and intelligence products (see below), and decides on which priorities to address (or not to address) and which resources to allocate to these priorities.

The TCG operates in two distinct modes. In its strategic form (Strategic Tasking and Co-ordinating Group, or STCG) it is primarily concerned with setting the *control strategy* for a relatively long period (typically ranging from 3 to 12 months). The control strategy sets the main intelligence requirements for this period (normally aimed at filling gaps in the picture of crime and disorder problems as currently known), and the main direction for the prevention and enforcement activities that will be carried out. The setting of these requirements (or priorities) will be informed by intelligence products and by a range of other con- siderations, such as priorities set at other levels, by government or by partner agencies.

The Tactical Tasking and Co-ordinating Group (TTCG) is convened on a more frequent basis (typically every week, fortnight or month). Its prime responsibility is to monitor performance, and where necessary adjust responses, against the priorities set in the control strategy. It will also respond to new problems that have arisen in the intervening period and adjust priorities and the deployment of resources accordingly. Again, its membership will be the relevant managers who have the authority to allocate (or reallocate) resources.

The NIM 'products'

The tasking and co-ordinating process at each level is informed by four key *intelligence products* and nine *analytical products*. It is important to understand the functions of these products and the differences between them, so a very brief outline will be given of each.[3]

Feeding the tasking and co-ordinating process: the intelligence products
The four intelligence products are generally (but not exclusively)

produced by analysts. Their main purpose is to inform the work of TCGs in setting priorities and planning strategies and interventions.

The *strategic assessment* is the principal document used by the STCG to determine the priorities that will form the basis of the control strategy. As such, it will be a substantial document summarising policing issues for the relevant level (crime trends, changes in patterns of criminal activity or disorder, etc.). It will also include a broad range of information about, for example, priorities set by other levels, relevant legislative changes and partnership objectives. As would be expected, there will be differences in emphasis of focus and content across the three levels.

The *tactical assessment* is a similarly central document that forms the basis for decision-making by the TTCG. It will recommend appropriate actions to implement the control strategy, drawing upon what is referred to as the *tactical menu* – that is, a list of available options such as targeting, surveillance, crime series investigation, hot-spot management or preventive measures. It will combine a review of previously set priorities and activities with an assessment of newly arising problems needing decisions on prioritisation.

Target profiles are strongly geared towards operations managers, providing specific intelligence on criminals and their activities. This intelligence product is most frequently used by TTCGs as the basis for deciding which individuals or groups will be targeted, and by what methods.

Problem profiles are similar in nature, although focused upon crime and disorder issues rather than specific offenders – usually identifiable crime series occurring in particular 'hot-spots'. Again, the product will inform the TTCG's decision-making process and selection of responses from the tactical menu.

Feeding the intelligence products: the analytical products

The intelligence products are, in turn, based on nine *analytical products*, which are simply analytical techniques specified by the model. Table 3.1 diagrammatically illustrates the NIM's recommendations for which analytical products (techniques) will contribute to each of the four intelligence products described above. Most represent the first stage in developing raw information into actionable intelligence. As such, there can be close inter-relationships between these techniques. For example, network analysis will often form the basis for the selection of offenders who will form the basis of subsequent target profiles.

Below is a very brief summary of the nine analytical products, based on both NCIS and force-produced guidance, and on a review of the content of a range of such products collected throughout the course of

Table 3.1: Inter-relationships between analytical and intelligence products

	Intelligence products			
Analytical products	Strategic assessment	Tactical assessment	Target profile	Problem profile
Results analysis	√	√	√	√
Crime pattern analysis	√	√	X	√
Market profile	√	√	X	X
Demographic/social trend analysis	√	X	X	√
Criminal business profile	√	√	X	X
Network analysis	√	√	√	√
Risk analysis	√	√	√	√
Target profile analysis	X	√	√	√
Operational intelligence assessment	X	X	√	X

the research (for a more detailed discussion of these products, see Cope 2003):

1 *Results analysis*: assesses the impact of the tactical menu options selected. Forms a means of identifying 'what works' and disseminating good practice.

2 *Crime pattern analysis*: identifies crime series, crime trends, hot-spots and general profiles of those responsible. Provides detailed information on the basis of which prioritisation and tactical response decisions can be made.

3 *Market profile*: an ongoing assessment of the details of criminal markets – key actors, networks, criminal assets and associated criminal trends. Owing to its breadth, it will frequently encompass other analytical products (such as network or crime pattern analysis), dependent on the nature of the market. Allows prioritisation of which elements of the market can be addressed and resourced, by applying the tactical menu.

4 *Demographic/social trend analysis*: allows longer-term predictions of future demands on police activities, partly by more in-depth analysis of social factors underlying aspects of crime or disorder. Will also be used to identify (predict and therefore resource) seasonal trends in crime and other relevant activity.

5   *Criminal business profiles*: builds up a detailed modus operandi of criminal enterprises. Used to inform decisions on tactical responses and to identify legislative or policy needs.

6   *Network analysis*: a detailed breakdown of the individuals and activities that constitute an identifiable criminal network. Used to inform strategic planning and tactical operational decisions.

7   *Risk analysis*: identifies the risks posed by criminal individuals or organisations to the public, individual victims or categories of victims and law enforcement agencies. Will form the basis for decisions on prioritisation at both strategic and tactical levels.

8   *Target profile analysis*: provides a detailed picture of the activities, associations and lifestyles of individuals identified as meriting special attention in relation to a particular crime or disorder problem (e.g. as serious or prolific offenders). Will include a breakdown of techniques that have worked, or failed, against the target in the past. Will be an important determinant of target selection (prioritisation) and appropriate tactical responses.

9   *Operational intelligence assessment*: based around specific operations, this is an ongoing assessment of, for example, new intelligence about associates or activities. One stated purpose is to maintain the focus of the operation (prevent 'mission creep').

Summary of the model

In summary, then, the model splits policing into the two overarching fields of core policing 'business' and its required 'outcomes'. The link between them is the tasking and co-ordinating process. Tasking and co-ordinating operates in two mutually dependent modes, strategic and tactical, and is informed by four key 'intelligence products'. These, in turn, are based upon nine 'analytical products' (or techniques). The key resulting driver is the control strategy, which is addressed through the tactical menu (or set of operational responses).

This general structure is replicated at three distinct levels of policing: level 1 (local), level 2 (cross-border) and level 3 (national/international). Mutual dependence is again apparent, with priorities set at each level ultimately influencing those at the others.

The breadth of the model is, therefore, considerable. The introduction to this volume discusses some common misconceptions about problem-oriented policing. We would argue that the NIM is similarly vulnerable to a major misconception: that it is *only* about ILP. Admittedly, police-generated information and intelligence, analysed and presented through standard techniques and products, make up a large proportion of the inputs to the model and form the main basis for the decision-making processes within it. However, as inter-agency partnerships develop, more information is coming from sources outside the police; the use of demographic and social trend data is also growing, opening a bigger window on social factors underlying changes in crime rates and patterns. Importantly, too, in terms of *outputs* and *outcomes*, the NIM departs substantially from the narrower understanding of proactive/ILP responses. Depending on the problem and its dynamics, the TCG, applying the NIM principles, controls the full range of policing responses and will apply them through the tactical menu. Hence, a community policing response might be most appropriate to address difficulties in a particular area. Or a local partner with the relevant resources might be identified to address particular social factors believed to underlie a policing problem. In these respects, the NIM exhibits many similarities to POP. Indeed, we would argue that, if properly implemented, it encourages, supports and facilitates problem-oriented approaches. We shall return to this topic near the end of the chapter through a brief discussion of the interaction between POP and the NIM in a force in which the former was already well established. First, however, we present some of the general findings from our evaluation of the early days of the national 'roll-out' of the NIM and its implementation in three 'pilot' forces.

From theory to practice: implementing the model

As has been described by Leigh *et al.* (1996, 1998) in relation to force-wide adoptions of POP, and by Maguire and John (1995), Amey *et al.* (1996) and Barton and Evans (1999) in relation to ILP, major difficulties are often experienced in attempting to introduce a new 'model' of practice into the busy and somewhat conservative world of operational policing. Similar difficulties are being encountered in implementing the NIM. This section focuses upon the major challenges to successful implementation which were identified by the researchers, both in the national 'roll-out' and in the three forces studied. Two general themes are singled out as critical prerequisites of progress: strength of leadership, and broad ownership and understanding of the model. Key areas of difficulty are then discussed in relation to each of the four main elements of the model outlined above (links between levels, definitions of business and outcomes, the work of TCGs, and the intelligence and analytical products). We begin, however, with a brief description of the aims and methods of the evaluation, which – in common with several other evaluations of projects funded under the Targeted Policing Initiative – was hindered to a considerable degree by 'implementation drift' away from the original policing project plan.

The NCIS project, the evaluation and 'implementation drift'

The research was originally commissioned, in April 2001, to evaluate an NCIS project funded under the Home Office's Targeted Policing Initiative (part of the wider Crime Reduction Programme). As noted earlier, the project in question was a 'roll-out' of the NIM in three selected 'pilot forces'. The plan was for NCIS to set up a 16-strong expert team. The core members of this team would be based in its headquarters in London, their main tasks including the provision of national advice and the development of training materials. The remaining staff were to be based in appropriate NCIS regional offices to provide close guidance and assistance to the three selected forces (Lancashire, Surrey and West Midlands) to implement the NIM in a systematic manner. The researchers would observe this process and evaluate its effectiveness, drawing out lessons from which a future 'national roll-out' would benefit.

However, the NCIS project never materialised as planned. Owing to major problems in persuading forces to release suitably qualified officers, NCIS managed to recruit only four staff to the new team (known as the National Intelligence Model Implementation Project, or 'NIMIP' team). Consequently, the NIMIP team largely abandoned the plan of assisting the roll-out in the three selected areas and concentrated instead upon other tasks, in particular developing national training packages for the NIM, acting as a reference point for queries about the model from any force (including making advisory visits when requested) and setting up a system for monitoring progress with the NIM in all forces across the country. In the mean time, the three development forces were left largely to their own devices in terms of introducing the NIM. However, in spite of the relatively insular and unguided nature of the force roll-outs, common themes were apparent within their experiences of implementing the NIM.

Research methodology

In each development site, a variety of research methods was adopted, depending to some extent on the force's approach to implementing the model. These included, *inter alia*, collection of documents relating to the implementation scheme and process; interviews with those responsible for force roll-out; interviews (in 25 different BCUs) with those responsible for implementation at BCU level; analysis of NIM-related documentation, particularly intelligence products and a variety of analytical products; and observation of TCGs and other NIM-related meetings and processes. Three sets of interview and survey data were obtained which are large enough to allow a degree of quantitative analysis. These are as follows:

1 Semi-structured interviews with 31 intelligence analysts in the three 'pilot' forces.

2 Some 75 returns from a self-completion questionnaire distributed to delegates at a national analysts conference in November 2002.

3 Some 358 returns from a self-completion questionnaire distributed to police and civilian staff in Surrey and the West Midlands towards the end of 2002.

The research team also visited the NIMIP team offices at intervals to interview its members and to collect relevant data, including information from a 'gap analysis' (spring 2001) and a subsequent 'baseline assessment' (spring 2002) covering all forces. These are based on a combination of self-assessment returns from each force and follow-up visits by NIMIP staff. The result is, essentially, a 'traffic lights' system, in which each force is categorised as red, amber or green in terms of its progress with each of a defined set of developments which are required to introduce and run the model as designed.

General themes

We begin with a discussion of two general, or pervasive, themes which emerged consistently from the research as critical to the successful implementation of the NIM: leadership; and ownership and under-standing.

Leadership

It was apparent from the experiences of the three development sites, and from interviews with the NIMIP team, that commitment of leadership at ACPO level was an important precursor to making substantive progress with the implementations. At the time of the national gap analysis in early 2001, it was apparent that only a minority of forces had clear and committed ACPO leadership. Only 15 (37%) of the 40 forces surveyed were rated as 'green' in the traffic lights system, and a further two (5%) as 'amber' at that time (see Table 3.2). The leadership of directors of intelligence in relation to the NIM was rated somewhat higher, but even here, 32% were assessed to be in the 'red' zone. However, by the spring of 2002, the situation in both cases had changed dramatically: in the first baseline analysis, all but one forces were rated as 'green' on both criteria, meaning that each force now had lead officers in place with specific responsibilities and commitment to introducing the NIM.

Table 3.2: 'Traffic lights' assessments of forces' leadership in implementation of NIM via gap analysis (spring 2001) and first baseline assessment (spring 2002)

Criterion	Assessment			
	Green %	Yellow %	Red %	(n)
2001 ACPO leadership	37.5	5.0	57.5	(40)
2002 ACPO leadership	98.0	2.0	0.0	(44)
2001 Director of Intelligence	60.0	7.5	32.5	(40)
2002 Director of Intelligence	98.0	2.0	0.0	(44)

Strength of leadership is also important in other areas. Perhaps foremost among these is the chair of the TCG. Knowledge of, and commitment to, the model and the benefits that it can bring to policing in a BCU is an important determinant of the viability of the model in that area. Survey respondents from the national analysts' conference were asked to state whether the chairs of their TCGs 'fully understand' the NIM. Sixty- two per cent thought that they did, but 24% thought that they did not and 14% did not know. This factor also came through strongly in the interviews in all three development sites and through observation of a number of TTCGs. Without effective chairing, TCGs, in particular, tended to revert to simply a 'bidding-for-resources platform', where personality rather than evidence from products was most likely to prevail. The more effective chairs, however, were able to maintain a focus on the issues within the tactical assessment and prioritise resources on that basis. Additionally, they were more likely to review the effectiveness of previous activities and seek to improve on results rather than to dismiss them and move on to the next short-term 'blip' or apparent crisis. Further comment on TCGs is given below.

Outside the TCG itself, the commitment of the chair (or divisional superintendent if different) was also an important determinant of the centrality of the NIM within a BCU, particularly in terms of the status, and therefore the influence, of the intelligence unit. A number of Detective Inspectors running such units expressed frustration with senior managers who did not understand the NIM, were not committed to it and, hence, were not equipped to drive the business effectively.

Ownership and understanding of the model
Throughout the research it was clear that ownership and understanding of the model was still very much concentrated within the intelligence unit, and (sometimes) the TCG. For example, in one of the development sites only 36% of the general officer respondents were familiar with the operation of the NIM, and 45% with the operation of the TCG. As the intention is for the NIM, through the TCG process, to own and allocate all problems and resources, this is a discouraging finding. In terms of the ILP aspects of the model, the need to encourage all officers to engage with intelligence and submit accurate and timely reports has been established elsewhere (e.g. Maguire and John 1995; Sheptycki 2003). Failures to spread the sense of ownership and involvement undermine the potential effectiveness of the strategy. As one superintendent put it:

> If officers doing the job generally have no idea why they are doing it, they will have less commitment to intelligence-led policing and will only be interested in response methods. Inspectors in general have identified that sectors and individual officers need to understand the link between what they contribute in intelligence, and the feedback and tasking that comes from the [TCG]. They need to see that they are not feeding into a 'black hole' and that it is not a one-way process.

In terms of the NIM itself, one of the most significant obstacles raised to spreading the sense of ownership is the difficulty of achieving widespread understanding of the model and its processes. Forming a full understanding is clearly a problem for many of those directly involved in the TCG process, let alone those at a greater distance from it. For example, the analysts in the development sites were asked whether they were 'confident that members of the TCG fully understand the NIM'. Twenty-eight per cent replied 'yes', 55% 'no' and 14% 'don't know'. The conference respondents were asked a similar question, but aimed at teasing out the *proportion* of TTCG members with a good understanding. Only 10% felt that all members fully understood the model, and a further 21% that the majority did. Sixty per cent of the respondents considered that only a minority fully understood the model (see Table 3.3).

Table 3.3: Understanding of the NIM among TCG members, as perceived by analysts

	%
All understand	10
Majority understand	21
Minority understand	60
Don't know	10
Total	100 ($n = 63$)

Respondents and interviewees frequently criticised the language of the model as a significant obstacle to understanding, and as a factor perpetuating the view that it is 'owned' only by specialists. For example:

The labels, jargon, and posh names will lose people. Cliques have evolved using jargon and buzzwords that confuse and frustrate many staff.

(intelligence unit inspector)

One major obstacle is the language of the model. People switch off, or they leave it all together. To rewrite it in simple language would be a big step forward.

(intelligence sergeant)

Defining and linking the levels: issues around standardisation

As noted above, one of the key aims of the NIM is to introduce standardisation of procedures and products. This is explicit in the structure of the model, as demonstrated in the replicated processes at levels 1, 2 and 3. Major variations in the content and structure of the product documentation make their effective collation and analysis throughout the level structure difficult to achieve. For example, 21 very different strategic assessments at level 1 will make the opportunities for level 2 prioritisation based upon them far more difficult to achieve. Similarly, if all 43 forces produce radically different strategic assessments, building a national picture will be difficult at level 3. Ultimately, indeed, such blockages in the transference of intelligence and analytical products may potentially undermine one of the main strengths of the model as a whole.

Given the fundamental nature of this issue, the early attempts made at standardisation by the NIMIP team may be viewed as an opportunity missed. The first tranche of guidance documentation provided very open exemplars of what should be done within each element of the process, and of what should be included within specific products. The more specific version 2 guidelines focused upon intelligence products, providing an overview of the aims and purpose of each product and recommendations as to the frequency of their production, appropriateness of their dissemination, etc. They also provided recommended formats for the four products, with fictional examples of each.

'Too little and too late' is probably the most accurate reflection of the views of intelligence personnel in the development sites about the usefulness of the latter guidelines. On the other hand, another frequently expressed view was that the guidelines represented an attempt to impose a national standard upon the process with little appreciation for policing at force, and particularly BCU, level. For example, one head of intelligence noted that the NCIS target profiles were suitable at BCU level, but 'insufficient' for level 2. In this regard, one of the development sites was particularly concerned at the lack of consultation between NCIS and the development sites in the creation of the guidance documents. It may well be that such difficulties are less pronounced in other forces which began their implementation in earnest at a later date.

In the absence of early clear national guidance, therefore, the three forces studied had adopted various mechanisms to develop their own in-house requirements and guidance for what the various processes should involve, and the content and format of their various products. The degrees of corporacy of these approaches varied. A constant feature, however, was that any such force-wide guidance and/or templates came into play a considerable time after initial implementation of the NIM, typically in the second half of 2002. In the intervening period, each BCU developed, and became comfortable with, using its own versions of the products. Consequently, later attempts to impose a template from an 'external' source tended to be met with resistance. This problem was particularly acute where leadership of the NIM at force level was relatively diffuse.

Defining business and outcomes

Although the broad areas of business and outcomes are identified within the model, the specific areas that will (or will not) be addressed and the desired outcomes that will be sought lie to a great extent within the decision- making processes of the STCGs. The research identified three main factors which hindered effective decision-making in these respects: insufficient input from partners; overdominance of performance indicators; and conflict with priorities set elsewhere. These will be outlined in turn.

Despite the intention behind the NIM that STCGs should involve not just police officers but partners from other agencies, and that control strategies should draw upon information from a wide range of sources, only a few STCGs were set up in this way. Some examples of good practice were identifiable in each of the development sites, with individual BCUs involving a variety of partners including local authorities and the National Probation Service. Outside these individual BCUs, however, such involvement was regarded as an area for future development. Without a more inclusive approach to partnership involvement being widely adopted, the broader business goals and outcomes of the model will be difficult to achieve – as will the diffusion of ownership of problems across relevant agencies. This also has negative implications for the potential of the NIM to deliver POP solutions.

Not only were most STCGs dominated by a 'police view' of local problems, but the concern was raised by some intelligence operatives that managers tended to take insufficient note of those aspects of the strategic assessment that fell outside police performance indicators. For example, the conference respondents were asked whether performance indicator considerations ever dominated their TCG too much (hence interfering with the strategic aims). A clear majority felt that this happened 'routinely/always' (35%) or 'often' (29%) in their TCGs, and only 36% that it happened 'rarely'. This narrow interpretation of goals, coupled with a general lack of partnership representation at the strategic level (only rarely did STCGs include non-police members), can lead to the priorities in the control strategy remaining too narrowly focused and based on only a superficial understanding of local problems. It was also found that this in turn could influence the way in which intelligence staff approached their tasks, and that in some BCUs the content, presentation and diversity of sources used were being steadily amended to meet the narrower information demands of the managers. The comments below are typical of many on this topic by local intelligence officers:

> The TCG is a concentration upon performance indicators and little else. This needs changing. When priorities are set at TCG, if the performance indicators were taken out, then the real problems of the BCU would show up accurately. There is a distinct conflict between ground-level police officers and the upper management (and their focus on performance indicators).

[I] don't always think that the performance indicators reflect the concerns of the community. Non-performance indicators can cause neglect and lose touch with the worries and concerns of the public.

Finally, and more generally, the NIM should allow policing organisations at each level to determine their policing priorities strategically over a set period of time. The setting of those priorities will be informed by a number of factors, including governmental and partnership priorities, issues of concern to the community and the resources available at any particular time. Once the NIM has matured (i.e. when the processes at the different levels, and the flow of information between them, are operating effectively) this should become a symbiotic, circular process: hence the priorities being set at BCU level will influence force priorities; in turn priorities set by the forces will influence governmental priorities; and so forth. At this early stage of implementation, however, the priorities set at the different levels often failed to keep these considerations in balance, and in some instances were in conflict. One frequently cited example of this kind of conflict was the impact of the government's Street Crime Initiative (SCI) (see Home Office 2002), which identified a 'top ten' of forces in which street robbery would be targeted as a major priority. However, the general view in one of these forces was that this type of crime was not a serious problem in most BCUs and the SCI had resulted in policing resources being diverted away from locally identified priorities. As one local intelligence officer put it: 'Here we need a vehicle squad, not a robbery squad.'

While some managers saw such conflicts as a major problem, other were hopeful that they represented simply 'teething troubles' and would be satisfactorily resolved over time. For example, one BCU-based intelligence unit sergeant observed:

What the government want contradicts what the BCU wants. But [we] must be patient. The strategic assessment will be up and running shortly and it is hoped that this document will assist the drive for the next 12 months with less reliance on government objectives and more on the real need of the BCU. Everyone will be a lot happier to argue when the strategic assessment is the basis of fact. Then if performance indicators match real need – fine. If not, we can address it with knowledge and evidence.

Mechanics of the tasking and co-ordinating process

Given its centrality to the running of the model as a whole, the successful operation of the tasking and co-ordinating process is a crucial to its overall success. This is a major issue which is discussed in some detail in our research report (John and Maguire forthcoming), but for the purposes of this chapter, two practical difficulties identified in the development sites will be presented as symptomatic of broader problems being experienced. These concern the frequency with which TTCG meetings are held and the ways in which they are conducted.

There was considerable variation between the development sites in the frequency with which TTCG meetings were held. In one force alone, for example, different BCUs convened the meetings at weekly, fortnightly or monthly intervals (although this is under review). Another force held its TTCG meetings fortnightly, with varying interim arrangements to review the priorities in the light of intervening events or results. Some BCUs, for example, held a weekly tactical update meeting, others daily briefings and others a combination of the two. Delegates to the national analysts' conference were asked to provide details of such arrangements in their own forces. Fifty-eight per cent of 71 respondents stated that TTCG meetings were held fortnightly, 21% weekly and 21% monthly. The great majority of those whose forces held monthly or fortnightly meetings were content that the interval they named was appropriate, but almost half those who mentioned weekly TCGs felt that they were too frequent.

There is some debate on what the most appropriate interval between TTCGs might be. The advantage of a monthly meeting is that it allows trends to become apparent and the proportion of analysts' time spent preparing tactical assessment documents is minimised. It also assists in preventing the process becoming dominated by 'knee-jerk', reactive activities based on responding to isolated crimes or short-term 'blips', and allows time for the agreed responses to have an impact. The major disadvantages, however, are that effective ongoing review of prioritised activities becomes more difficult, and the length of time can lead to the focus on those priorities being lost.

The comparative strengths and weaknesses of weekly meetings are essentially the converse of the above. They tend to encourage a short-term, non-predictive approach. Another recurrent problem is that the proportion of analysts' time spent preparing the tactical assessment documents becomes too great – typically a day to two days prior to the meeting is spent preparing these. This impacts considerably upon the analytical resources available to create other meaningful intelligence and analytical products. A two-weekly interval, possibly supplemented by an intervening update meeting, would appear to be a useful compromise between the two extremes.

Turning to the conduct of the meetings themselves, observation of TTCG meetings revealed some examples of good practice in each of the three forces. However, a number of common weaknesses were identified that detracted from the potential of TTCGs to perform their main functions. For example, frequently the members did not read the tactical assessment prior to the meeting, which necessitated the report being read out verbatim (usually by the analyst), reducing the time available for constructive discussion.

Also evident was a tendency for the discussion to become sidetracked into the details of individual crimes, even where there was no clear link to previously established priorities. In one BCU, indeed, the lack of attention being paid to the intelligence and analytical products had resulted in the analysts no longer attending the TTCG or producing tactical assessments. The civilian LIO now performed both functions.

In some instances, too, the TTCG more closely resembled a 'resource bidding' meeting rather than an intelligence-driven one. Again, arguments for resources tended to be built around the desire to rectify dips in performance-measured areas of policing, rather than the 'messages' emerging from intelligence products.

Despite these weaknesses, in those BCUs that had established the NIM early on and had clear leadership, there were indications that these difficulties were being resolved and this aspect of the process maturing.

Feeding the process: analysts and products

As has already been emphasised, the intelligence and analytical products are the basic currency on which the NIM is based. The quality of such products is therefore of major importance to the effectiveness of the system as a whole. Clearly, this depends to a large extent on the skills of individual analysts, but these can only develop with appropriate organisational support in the form of, for example, resources, training, guidance, and adequate pay and career structures. This section will briefly present the main findings of our research in relation to (1) the analyst role and (2) the quality of products. The latter discussion will focus on the two most important intelligence products: strategic and tactical assessments, but most of the issues raised were common to the full range of analytical and intelligence products.

The role of the analyst

The analyst role has been evolutionary in nature. Consequently, analysts have broad and divergent career backgrounds with differing levels of experience and qualifications. We found a fairly even divide between those who had reached their position by moving through a number of administrative roles (mainly with the police service), and those (typically younger and more recently appointed) who held degrees, often with social science research training, but relatively little practical experience. The different routes have their own advantages and disadvantages and none is necessarily 'the best', but the diversity in itself creates significant challenges for police forces in terms of developing and exploiting their analysts' skills.

In addition to the diversity in backgrounds, there is no single recognised training requirement for analysts to undergo in order to achieve recognised levels of skills and competencies. The effect of this is apparent in Table 3.4, which shows responses from delegates at the analysts conference when asked whether they had received specific training in relation to the four intelligence products and/or the nine analytical products. Only a small proportion had been trained on all of either category, and most had been trained on fewer than half the analytical products.

Table 3.4: Extent of analysts' training on NIM products

Trained in	*n*	%
Intelligence products		
All	6	10
Some	41	71
None	9	16
NA/don't know	2	3
Total	58	100
Analytical products		
All	5	9
Majority	18	31
Minority	26	45
None	6	10
NA/don't know	3	5
Total	58	100

Interviewees in the three 'pilot' forces and respondents to the above survey were also asked to what extent they had been involved in the creation of specific products. Where intelligence products were concerned, the great majority had created problem profiles (97% cent in the development sites and 80% of the conference analysts) and tactical assessments (93 and 75%, respectively), although there was somewhat less experience of strategic assessments (74 and 70%) and target profiles (52 and 70%). However, as one might expect from the statistics on training above, it was in analytical products that the main gaps in practical experience were to be found. As Figure 3.1 shows, with the important exceptions of crime pattern analysis and network analysis (and to some extent target profile analysis) large proportions of analysts had no practical experience of creating these products. The absence of experience was most striking in results analysis and risk analysis.

Figure 3.1   Percentages of development site and conference analysts who had created various categories of analytical products

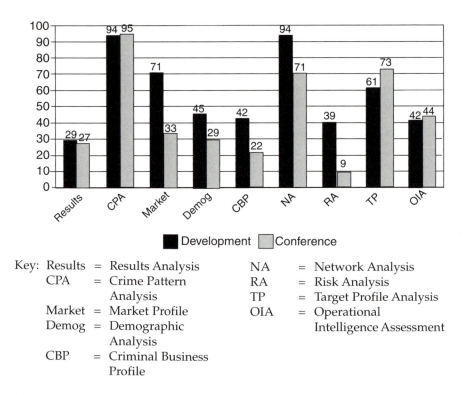

Key: Results = Results Analysis
     CPA   = Crime Pattern
               Analysis
   Market = Market Profile
   Demog = Demographic
              Analysis
     CBP   = Criminal Business
               Profile

NA   = Network Analysis
RA   = Risk Analysis
TP   = Target Profile Analysis
OIA = Operational
        Intelligence Assessment

The retention of existing analysts was a major issue for many of the police managers interviewed. At the present time there is no nationally agreed pay structure or clear (hierarchical) career path for analysts. This produces two significant problems. First, the lower-paying forces quite frequently lose analysts to more generous neighbours or to other, non-police, employers. For example, one of the development sites experienced a 48% turnover of analytical staff in the two-year period ending October 2001; in contrast, their higher-paying neighbouring force retained all its analysts over the same period. Given the expense of training analysts (estimated by one principal analyst at £5,500 for basic skills and £10,000–15,000 for comprehensive training), and the time taken for them to become accustomed to the way a BCU operates, this is a clear financial as well as human resources issue. Secondly, for those analysts who do remain within one force, there is little career incentive for them to seek to excel. Senior and principal analyst posts are very low in number. One principal analyst summed up the position thus:

> Staff retention depends upon job satisfaction, which includes professional development, career progression, salary and training. There is no professional structure within the analytical function to ensure analysts' development and to guarantee quality assured work. There is no career structure for analysts to enhance their development and to ensure their accountability for performance.

In the absence of a national career structure, a number of forces have taken an initiative in developing their own internal equivalents. Although this increases the prospects and job satisfaction for those analysts who remain, it does not solve the broader retention issues.

The combined effect of all the above factors is that few analysts are currently equipped to produce the full range of intelligence and analytical products, standards are inconsistent and products vary in form and content. It is suggested that a considerable national effort is needed to deal with these problems.

Strategic assessments

The strategic assessment is potentially the most significant document in the NIM process, due to its influence in determining the control strategy for a set period of time, and its distillation of priorities from a broad range of sources. Different police forces and their BCUs have approached the preparation and content of their strategic assessments very differently. In those BCUs which had produced several strategic assessments, it was clear that there had been a considerable learning curve between earlier and later documents, with evidence of increasingly sophisticated analysis. Interviews with their authors suggest that this process of development is assisted both by having the original document as a foundation on which to build, and the acquisition of a clearer understanding from the members of the STCG of what types of information are of most use to their decision-making.

This having been said, considerable extremes were evident in the quality of assessments. One BCU's strategic assessment, for example, was little more than a loose and unstructured collection of data on a range of crimes. Comment on the statistics was descriptive rather than analytical and no reference was made to sources for determining priorities other than the meeting of existing performance indicators.

On the other hand, other BCUs with similar analytical resources had managed to produce much more comprehensive and sophisticated strategic assessments. Examples of these were evident in all three forces. The knowledge, training and enthusiasm of analysts, and their protected abstraction of time from other duties by their managers, appear to be key factors in facilitating the production of high-quality documents. Those interviewed stated that up to two months of work was required to produce these comprehensive annual strategic assessments. It was common practice for intervening quarterly updates to be distributed to provide a summary of progress and to present updated information.

Tactical assessments

Due to the numbers and variety of tactical assessment documents produced, it is more difficult to make generalised comments about them. Examples were found ranging from the simple presentation of descriptive statistics to the employment of a range of analytical products to identify, quantify and assess the appropriate responses to a problem. It is apparent in reviewing these documents, however, that *standardisation* is a major issue which needs to be confronted. With one partial exception, uniformity of structure and approach was strikingly lacking within the three forces studied, let alone between them. This was clearly a factor in the further finding that the exchange of information between different TCGs was not common: for example, only one force's level 2 analysts routinely collected the tactical assessments from their BCUs and were able to supply them centrally to the evaluation team.

As with strategic assessments, concerns about performance indicators often dominated tactical assessments, at the expense of other priorities. Minutes and action plans arising from the TTCGs suggest that this was often perpetuated in the meeting itself. There was also a tendency for the tactical assessment to be retrospective rather than predictive in nature, focusing on trends that had arisen in the intervening period since the previous document was produced. This was further reflected in the tactical options decided upon, which tended to concentrate on short-term resolutions rather than looking at longer-term interventions. Examples of explicit and ongoing responses co-ordinated with relevant crime and disorder partners were found, but were in a small minority.

General issues

The effectiveness of the TCG process depends heavily on the quality of the intelligence and analytical products that it receives, but the research found that this was an area in which considerable improvement is still needed. Our main findings on this issue may be summarised as follows:

1   Different forces, BCUs, analysts and other individuals in intelligence roles are at different stages of what is a steep learning curve for coming to terms with the NIM and its associated products. Many of those who implemented the model in a structured way early on were able to demonstrate improvements in the level of analysis and sophistication of presentation over time.

2   Substantial investment in intelligence and analytical resources, and protection from abstraction, are necessary if products of a requisite standard are to be produced.

3   Something of a 'vicious circle' was also apparent. Without the above issues being addressed, it is likely that the products will remain comparatively weak, and their usefulness or 'added value' questionable to the members of the TCG. Without quality products it is less likely that senior managers (particularly the less knowledgeable or committed among them) will see the potential value of investing further in analytical resources. Further development of the model could therefore become 'stuck' and its potential unrealised.

4   Formal training and networking opportunities are necessary for analysts to be able to acquire and disseminate good practice.

5   The current situation regarding standardisation undermines a key purported benefit to policing that the NIM might provide.

6   In order to assist TCGs to learn from experience, including mistakes, it is important that results analysis becomes fully integrated into the process and is not sidelined (see also Sheptycki 2003).

Lancashire Constabulary, POP and the NIM

Bullock and Tilley, in the introduction to this volume, have identified Lancashire Constabulary as operating a comparatively mature form of problem-oriented policing. Through its status as a NIM development site, the force is also relatively advanced in comparison with many others in its implementation of the NIM. Moreover, Lancashire has played a key role in developing the i2 analysts workstation, which provides technical support for creating many of the intelligence and analytical products and approaches.

In implementing the NIM, senior police managers in Lancashire were keen not to abandon the force's commitment to POP, and decided therefore to base their implementation of the NIM explicitly on the POP principles which had already been widely instilled among operational staff. They describe this as 'a united approach' (Billsborough and Keay 2002: 7; see also Tilley 2003), in which a clear equivalence is drawn between the main elements of the NIM and the SARA (see Chapter 1) approach to POP. This is demonstrated in Table 3.5.

For Lancashire, therefore, the business objectives define the remit, and provide the focus, for the scanning element. These are established by addressing the priorities set by each level, and through the Community Safety Partnerships. The TCG process provides the vehicle by which analysis is given a suitable forum for effective prioritisation and response decisions to be taken. Finally, the NIM outcomes provide the benchmark against which to assess if (or when) the responses have been successful. Billsborough and Keay (2002: 8) describe the interchange thus:

> Tasking and Coordinating Groups now build on the foundations of Problem Oriented Policing processes ensuring that intelligence led and problem solving activity is prioritised (against the control strategy), actioned and resourced according to these priorities. Tasking and Coordinating Groups also co-ordinate and ensure the accountability of intelligence and operational staff.

Table 3.5: Lancashire: equivalence between NIM and POP components

NIM	Business	Tasking and co-ordinating process		Outcomes
POP	Scanning	Analysis	Response	Assessment

Source: Adapted from a diagram in *Context* (2002: 6).

Crucially, therefore, the NIM potentially provides a remedy for several of the structural difficulties faced by policing organisations moving towards a problem-oriented (or problem-solving) approach. One of the established ideals of POP is that it should, at the very least, shift the *emphasis* of policing decision-making away from managers towards front-line officers – those in a better position to understand the causes and possible solutions for a perceived problem. Those officers, however, will frequently not have the resources to be able to solve the problem, or a suitable mechanism for voicing them. The NIM, through the TCG, provides a forum to allow problems to be identified, prioritised and resourced with ownership and responsibility existing at various points within the policing strata.

Equally important, the model provides far stronger, and more readily identifiable, mechanisms for professionalising the scanning, analysis and assessment phases of the SARA model. Much of this aspect will revolve around the contribution that analysts can make in using the analytical products (techniques) to build more accurate pictures of specific aspects of policing business. In turn, explicit use of the POP approaches (PAT and SARA – see Chapter 1) alongside the NIM might produce the advantage of a more ready understanding among general officers of what the NIM seeks to achieve, and hence of the importance of their roles within it. Whereas the NIM has been criticised for being technical, one of the lauded advantages of POP – and one of the reasons for its wide take-up – is its sheer simplicity. The compatibilities between the two models demonstrated in this chapter (and see Tilley 2003) suggest that a tandem approach has considerable merit.

Concluding comments

This chapter has sought to contextualise the development of the NIM, to provide an overview of its key features and to outline the early challenges experienced by forces as they implement the model. Where appropriate, comparisons and links have been made to POP in order to emphasise the relevance of the NIM to the concept of problem-solving in policing, which forms the central theme of this book.

Although we have drawn attention to some major implementation hurdles, it is important not to lose sight of the considerable enthusiasm for the model which was expressed by many of those police officers (at all levels) who had reached a full understanding of the NIM and of its potential contribution to policing within and across the various levels. Even so, the hurdles that have been identified undeniably pose serious challenges to the long-term viability of the model as the nationally favoured means of conducting policing business. As with many previous efforts to reform police practice, the size of the gap between the theoretical 'sense' that the model makes and how successfully it translates to the real world of policing will play a major part in determining its lifespan and its level of success.

At the time of writing, the most obvious requirements to close this gap are committed leadership (at both ACPO and TCG level), thorough training for participants at all levels, better support structures for analysts, better communication and understanding of roles between analytical and operational staff, and efforts to increase the standardi-sation of products and systems. Until the main implementation hurdles have been successfully negotiated and the NIM is operating much more as its designers envisaged, not only will those involved be handicapped and frustrated by continual 'malfunctions', but it will remain very difficult to give a conclusive answer to the most important question of all: whether the model 'works' in the sense of helping the police to reduce or control crime more effectively.

Notes

1 Its main designer was Brian Flood, a senior officer who had been influential in establishing intelligence-led policing in Kent.
2 Some forces have created the concept of a 'level half', and have set up further TCGs at subdivisional (sub-BCU) level.
3 For brevity and to avoid complication, two other sets of products used by TCGs, knowledge products and system products, will not be discussed in detail here. Knowledge products seek to inform the TCG process about operational standards, legislation and guidelines, and training needs. System products seek to improve areas such as technical support and access to data held by other agencies.

References

ACPO (1975) *Report of the Subcommittee on Criminal Intelligence* (the Baumber Report). London: Association of Chief Police Officers.

ACPO (1978) *Third Report of the Working Party on a Structure of Criminal Intelligence above Force Level* (the Pearce Report). London: Association of Chief Police Officers.

ACPO (1986) *Report of the Working Party on Operational Intelligence* (the Ratcliffe Report). London: Association of Chief Police Officers.

ACPO (1996) *Report on International, National and Inter-force Crime.* London: Association of Chief Police Officers.

Amey, P., Hale, C. and Uglow, S. (1996) *Development and Evaluation of a Crime Management Model.* Police Research Series 18. London: Home Office.

Audit Commission (1993) *Helping with Enquiries: Tackling Crime Effectively.* London: HMSO.

Barton, A. and Evans, R. (1999) *Proactive Policing on Merseyside.* Police Research Series 105. London: Home Office.

Billsborough, I. and Keay, S. (2002) 'A united approach', *The Standard (i2 User Group)*, 24 (May–Sept.): 8–9.

Context: The Newspaper of the Lancashire Constabulary (2002) Volume 4, issue 5, April.

Cope, N. (2003) 'Crime analysis: principles and practice', in T. Newburn (ed.) *Handbook of Policing.* Cullompton: Willan.

Ericson, R. and Haggerty, K. (1997) *Policing the Risk Society.* Oxford: Clarendon Press.

Flood, B. (1999) 'Know your business: NCIS has brought together best practice in intelligence led policing', *Nexus*, 7 (Winter): 8–9.

Fogg, E. (2000a) 'Deadly concoctions: the dangers facing officers who may discover evidence of the illicit production of synthetic drugs and how the National Criminal Intelligence Service has responded to them', *Police Review*, 4 August: 25–30.

Fogg, E. (2000b) 'Out of Africa: how the National Criminal Intelligence Service is tackling "419" letter fraud', *Police Review*, 28 July: 26–27.

Friedman, G., Friedman, M., Chapman, C. and Baker, J.S. (1997) *The Intelligence Edge.* London: Random House.

Gill, P. (2000) *Rounding up the Usual Suspects? Developments in Contemporary Law Enforcement Intelligence.* Aldershot: Ashgate.

HMIC (1997) *Policing with Intelligence: Criminal Intelligence.* London: Home Office.

Home Office (2002) *Street Crime Initiative: Figures to the End of September.* London: Home Office.

Hook, P. (1998) 'Gang wars: the new National Crime Squad response to organised transnational crime gangs', *Police Review*, 106(5460): 14–15.

Howe, S. (1997) 'Failing intelligence research in the UK is uncoordinated and unstructured', *Policing Today*, 3(2): 23–5.

Innes, M. and Fielding, N. (2002) 'Intelligence work: police practice in the information age.' Paper presented to the British Society of Criminology conference, Keele University, July.

John, T. and Maguire, M. (forthcoming) *Second Round Targeted Policing Initiative: Rollout of the National Intelligence Model. Final Report to Home Office.*

Leigh, A., Read, T. and Tilley, N. (1996) *Problem-oriented Policing: Brit Pop.* Crime Detection and Prevention Series 75. London: Home Office.

Leigh, A., Read, T. and Tilley, N. (1998) *Brit Pop II: Problem-oriented Policing in Practice.* Police Research Series 93. London: Home Office.

Maguire, M. (1999) 'Strategies of crime control: the shift to "proactivity" and its implications', in G. Bruinsma and C. van der Vijver (eds) *Public Safety in Europe*. Enschede, the Netherlands: University of Twente.

Maguire, M. (2000) 'Policing by risks and targets: some dimensions and implications of intelligence-led crime control', *Policing and Society*, 9: 315–36.

Maguire, M. (2003) 'Crime investigation', in T. Newburn (ed.) *Handbook of Policing*. Cullompton: Willan.

Maguire, M. and John, T. (1995) *Intelligence, Surveillance, and Informants: Integrated Approaches*. Police Research Group Crime and Prevention Series 64. London: Home Office.

Maguire, M. and John, T. (1996) 'Covert and deceptive policing in England and Wales: issues in regulation and practice', *European Journal of Crime, Criminal Law and Criminal Justice*, 4: 316–34.

Maguire, M. and Norris, C. (1992) *The Conduct and Supervision of Criminal Investigations*. Research Study 5, Royal Commission on Criminal Justice. London: HMSO.

Martindale, C. (2000) 'The Al Capone factor', *Nexus*, 9 (Autumn): 27–29.

NCIS (1999) *NCIS and the National Intelligence Model*. London: National Criminal Intelligence Service.

NCIS (2000) *The National Intelligence Model*. London: National Criminal Intelligence Service.

Sheptycki, J. (2003) *Review of the Influence of Strategic Intelligence on Organised Crime Policy and Practice*. London: Home Office.

Tilley, N. (2003) 'Models of policing: community policing, POP and intelligence led policing', in T. Newburn (ed.) *Handbook of Policing*. Cullompton: Willan.

Chapter 4

Doing problem-solving across borders in low-crime areas: the Fens experience

Bethan Jones

Introduction

Background

The Crime Reduction Programme (CRP) in general and the Targeted Policing Initiative (TPI) in particular have focused mainly on crime problems in urban areas. This is not surprising. Crime problems are disproportionately concentrated in towns and cities. This chapter, however, discusses the emergence, development and implementation of a project that was specifically concerned with rural crime problems in an area which crosses three force boundaries. The genesis of the project discussed here is unusual in a number of respects.

First, it emerged in the wake of a specific high-profile case. In August 1999 Tony Martin shot two men involved in the burglary of his house in the Fenland village of Enmeth, Norfolk. One of the men, Fred Barras, died from his injuries and Martin was convicted for the offence. Tony Martin was jailed for murder in April 2000, and in October 2001 the sentence was reduced from murder to manslaughter. The case prompted a great deal of concern in rural areas that their crime problems were not being addressed. It fuelled a sense of vulnerability experienced by many. There was pressure to act locally to address the problem and nationally to try to deal with rural crime and fear of crime issues. So, £600,000 was set aside for an initiative, as part of the TPI, and formally announced on 19 July 2000.

Secondly, the project involved three separate police forces in collaboration with one another. Enmeth, where the Martin incident took place, is close to the Lincolnshire and Cambridgeshire borders.

However, it is only one of 72 parishes that were ultimately included in the Fenlands project area. The Fens comprises quite a large rural area of roughly 700 square miles, 96,000 households and has a total population of 228,000. It covers specific beats in Western division Norfolk, South division Lincolnshire and Central division Cambridgeshire. On the ground the Fens makes sense as an entity but county and police force boundaries do not correspond to any natural social or geographical break. The Fens does, however, have its own geographical identity, and the area has a strong agricultural base and offers employment opportunities in farming, vegetable packing and food processing. The capital of the Fens is Wisbech, a large market town which sits on the border of two police force boundaries with a third police force boundary five miles away. This demonstrates one of the main problems of policing the Fens because two police forces have responsibility for the town of Wisbech.

Aims of chapter

The aims of this chapter are to describe:

- the background to the Fenlands TPI and some of the methods that were used to define and identify problems in the area; and

- the outputs and outcomes of this project.

Methodology

A very quick analysis of crime in the Fenlands area was undertaken by two Home Office researchers who attempted to identify local problems and some potential strategies to tackle them (Tilley and Smith 2000). Their analysis involved examination of crime, incident and intelligence data across the three forces and analysis of British Crime Survey (BCS) data. The results informed some modifications to the original project bid produced by the three forces and contributed to the agreed strategy. The project was then evaluated by Home Office staff. A wide variety of data were used in the evaluation including the following:

- Interviews with project staff.

- Interviews with grass-roots level staff including crime scene attenders, forensic scenes of crime officers (SOCO), community beat officers and intelligence staff from all three forces.

- Attendance at project board meetings and analysis of project board minutes.

- Analysis of detection rates, recorded crime and performance management data.

- Analysis of two fear of crime surveys to assess the impact of the initiative.

Defining the problem

What problem to tackle

The difficulty for those preparing the project proposals was that though there was a good deal of pressure to 'do something' about crime in rural areas, and the issue had been brought to a head by the Martin case, crime rates are comparatively low in rural areas. A project that merely played to a frenzy created by a tragic and high-profile case would go against the grain of the CRP, which had been funded to support evidence-based projects. What evidence was there of a problem in the Fens, and was there an evidence-warranted focus that could be found for a project there?

Recorded crime and the British Crime Survey

BCS data had shown that the prevalence rates of crime (the proportion of potential victims suffering one or more crime events) in rural areas are consistently lower than those in urban or inner-city areas (Mirrlees-Black 1997; Mirrlees-Black *et al.* 1998). For domestic burglary, the household rate in 1996 was 3.9% for rural areas, 6.3% for urban areas and 10.3% for inner-city areas. For violence, the individual rate was 3.6% for rural areas, 5.4% for urban areas and 7.1% for inner-city areas. For vehicle-related theft the rate for car owners was 15.7% for rural areas, 20.1% for urban areas and 26% for inner-city areas. This has been the case consistently across sweeps of the BCS. While rates have changed the relative positions of rural, urban and inner city areas have not.

All three forces code beats 'urban' and 'rural', though there are some acknowledged problems in clear assignment in all cases. In all forces the rural recorded incidence rates for crime (crime as a proportion of potential victims) are consistently lower than their urban counterparts. This goes for all crime categories, bar burglary other than a dwelling. Table 4.1 gives examples for the Fens area within one of the forces. Across the whole of this force the urban/rural contrasts are even more stark. For example, in relation to domestic burglary the rates per 1,000 households were 7.2 for rural and 27.5 for urban areas in the year ending June 2000.

Table 4.1: Urban and rural recorded crime rates in one force area Fen sector

Crime types	Recorded rates per 1,000 residents (year ending 30/6/00)	
	Urban beats	Rural beats
Violent crime	4.55	2.89
Burglary dwelling	9.35	6.34
Burglary other	6.53	7.00
Theft and handling	32.29	16.55
Vehicle crime	9.06	7.08
Criminal damage	13.20	7.55
Drugs	1.93	0.57
All	64.76	38.74

Prevalence and incidence rates from the BCS and the recorded crime data thus showed relatively low rates in rural areas, providing no evidence for targeting special resources at their reduction.

Fear of crime and disorder

Fear of crime and travelling criminals had been mooted as potential distinctive issues that could be addressed in a Fens project. This was in part due to the anxieties expressed in the wake of the Tony Martin case and because his victims – those burgling his house – were not locals.

Again, with regard to fear of crime the BCS showed nationally lower levels of worry in rural than urban areas, as shown in Tables 4.2 to 4.4.[1]

Table 4.2: Urban/rural differences in fear of crime

Offence type	Percent very worried about falling victim to crime			
	Inner city	Urban	Rural	All adults
Burglary	30	20	13	19
Mugging	27	19	10	18
Car theft	36	23	14	21
Theft from car	27	16	11	17
Rape	27	22	14	21
Attack by strangers	27	19	12	18
Racial attack	13	8	3	7

Source: From Mirrlees Black *et al*. 1998.

Table 4.3: Age and urban/rural fear of crime patterns

Age range	Percent feeling very or fairly unsafe walking alone in area after dark			
	Inner city	Urban	Rural	All adults
Age 16–29	14	9	7	10
Age 30–59	12	9	5	8
Age 60+	18	11	6	10
All ages	14	9	6	5

Source: From Mirrlees-Black *et al.* 1998.

Table 4.4: Patterns of perceived incivilities in urban and rural areas

Type of incivility	Percent seeing very or fairly big problems			
	Inner city	Urban	Rural	All adults
Noisy neighbours	16	9	4	8
Teenagers	39	29	15	27
Drunks/tramps	14	8	3	8
Litter	47	29	15	27
Vandalism	44	27	14	26
Drugs	40	25	14	24

Source: From Mirrlees-Black *et al.* 1998.

Across every measurement rural areas suffered lower levels of concern over crime. On the basis of these data the case for a rural initiative focusing on fear looked weak, though it was clearly likely that the Tony Martin case had provoked a substantial increase, at least in the short term. This was especially so in the Fens, though systematic data were not available for that particular area.[2]

Travelling criminals

There was a widespread view apparently held by police and public alike that 'travelling criminals' constituted a serious problem in rural areas, including the Fens. Four possible types of travelling offender were spoken of during force visits (types 3 and 4 are sometimes referred to as 'travellers'):

1   Criminals who happen to be away from home (for example, when on holiday) who commit crimes at some distance from their normal addresses.

2   Skilled criminals coming into an area intentionally to commit a high-value offence such as robbery or burglary.

3   Nomadic groups living in caravans, among some of whom crime is committed as part of their way of life.

4   Sometime members of nomadic groups who are more or less settled, some of whom belonged to criminal nomadic groups and persist in criminal activity.

The first type was not believed locally to be significant in the Fens. The remaining three were deemed by some in the police and evidently by many residents in the community to constitute a problem for the Fens though it was accepted that there was limited direct evidence as to their significance. With regard to 'travellers' in particular, one of the police services had attempted to cast around the information systems of four forces, and concluded in an unpublished report in 2000 that 'Nothing tangible can be found in the theory that "travellers are a problem" ... Norfolk, Cambridgeshire, Lincolnshire and Nottinghamshire have insufficient management information to establish what broad problems are caused by travelling criminals. There is no data set showing any links between rural crime and the travelling fraternity.'

Repeat victimisation

Research on repeat victimisation had shown that across a wide range of offences those who have been victims of crime are at increased risk of further incidents, and that this provides a strong basis for targeting preventive efforts on victims (Farrell and Pease 1993; Farrell 1995; Pease 1998). Could repeat victimisation provide an evidence-based focus for an initiative in the Fens? This would, after all, chime well with the Tony Martin case, since he had apparently been a repeat victim whose criminal response, that of shooting perpetrators, had led to his imprisonment.

Data from the 1995 BCS presented in Mirrlees-Black *et al.* (1998) showed that while only 3.9% of rural respondents had experienced one or more domestic burglary, fully 17% of those that had experienced one incident went on to experience another. For contact crime the figures are more dramatic: though only 3.6% experienced one or more incident, among those who had experienced one incident 33% went on to experience another. For vehicle-related theft, though 15.7% experienced one or more crimes 23% went on to experience another. It should be noted that these figures cover respondents' experience over 12 months. For those experiencing their first incident towards the end of the year there would have been very little time to experience another.

In one force, using a 'rolling year', for domestic burglary the prevalence rate was 17 per thousand households, and the incidence rate among victims was 60 per thousand, about three and a half times the prevalence rate. For offences against the person the prevalence rate was 8 per thousand residents, and the incidence rate among victims was 81 per thousand, about ten times the prevalence rate. In a second force, rural and urban beats were compared for domestic burglary. Urban victims had a victimisation rate that was 6.6 times that of all households (167.2 per thousand vs. 25.6 per thousand), rural victims with 4.9 times that for all households (56.6 per thousand vs. 11.5 per thousand), again using rolling years.

Among actual victims in rural areas, including those living in the Fens, crime rates appear to be high relative to the rates of crime among all potential victims, and to provide a plausible target for preventive attention.

Calls for service data from two of the Fens forces indicated that calls originating from rural areas were more likely to be screened out, although emergency response rates in rural and urban areas remained largely the same. Scene attendance was generally not high in rural areas, falling to just 40% in one force. Increased rates of scene attendance might provide opportunities to pre-empt repeat incidents and provide reassurance among those whose anxieties about crime had been raised.

The proposal

The modified proposal ultimately submitted by the three forces aimed to deliver 'marked reductions in crime, improve detection rates and bolster public confidence'. The project's resources would be used to achieve these by:

- concentrating on repeat victimisation – with a preventive orientation and stepped interventions where there are repeat incidents;

- increasing the rate and speed of crime scene attendance, with greater attention to the potential for collecting forensic evidence;

- providing a greater focus on cross-border crime – notably through increasing the collection, exchange and analysis of intelligence about travelling criminals, through enhancing the collection and analysis of DNA profiles and fingerprints of arrestees; and

- providing high-profile policing to reassure the public and restore public confidence.

The proposal also referred to public relations issues, in the interests of providing improved reassurance to the public by informing them of the measures being taken.

Interventions

Several specific measures were planned:

1 A target to attend 85% of specific crime scenes in 24 hours, except where force call grading policies demand an earlier response. The crimes targeted were:

  - burglary dwelling;
  - burglary other than a dwelling (BOTD);
  - vehicle crime;
  - violent crime (including domestic violence);
  - criminal damage; and
  - theft from agricultural premises.

2 Assessment for potential sources of forensic evidence (e.g. DNA, fingerprints and shoe marks) by officers first on the crime scene, with deployment of SOCOs if necessary. Scenes attended included burglary other than a dwelling and vehicle crime, in addition to domestic burglary which was already prioritised. The revised policy covers additional high-volume crime scenes that would have previously been screened out.

3 Introduction of a standardised stepped model to tackle repeat victimisation, to be adapted from the successful model developed in Huddersfield which reduced domestic burglary by 30% (Chenery *et al.* 1997).

4 Development of an IT system to link the intelligence systems of the three forces and enable the comparison of all crime and disorder data.

5   Establishment of a dedicated project team to analyse all three forces' crime, intelligence and command and deploy systems and generate intelligence on travelling criminals.

6   Introduction of formal policies for cross-border operations with regular cross-border tasking and intelligence meetings.

7   Increase in levels of police visibility via a mobile police station to reassure the public.

8   Funding for local community safety projects that tackle fear of crime.

In the original project plan funds were allocated as shown in Table 4.5.

Table 4.5: Project funds

Area	£
Staffing costs	320,000
Mobile police station	50,000
IT systems	150,000
Public attitude surveys	20,000
Community safety grants	60,000
Total	**600,000**

Implementation of the project

Implementation structures

The project aimed to implement the main interventions primarily through a dedicated project office and a bespoke IT system capable of focusing specifically on crime in the Fens project area. The remainder of the interventions, including the crime scene attendance, repeat victim and mobile police station work, were to be implemented using existing sector resources.

The project team staffing the office included the project manager (an inspector), an analyst and researcher (civilian support staff), three rural intelligence officers (police constables) and a community safety officer (police constable). However the analyst left the project in May 2002 and was replaced by one of the rural intelligence officers.

The terms of reference for the project office and objectives of the project team were as follows.

- To identify and arrest offenders committing crime in the Fens project area. This included all crime with particular reference to burglary, distraction burglary, burglary other than a dwelling including commercial burglary and vehicle crime.

- To collate intelligence and information on offenders, producing packages and bulletins for circulation or tasking in the three forces.

- To identify crime series and trends in the project area.

- To disseminate intelligence and information to all interested parties.

- To identify linked crimes across the project area and to provide officers arresting offenders with information to deal with all crimes committed throughout the three forces.

The staff in the project office would consequently be responsible for analysing intelligence from the three forces to produce intelligence packages and bulletins to be considered by the three forces and the cross-border tasking meetings.

The other proposed interventions such as increased scene attendance and use of SOCOs, introduction of a stepped repeat victimisation model and increased visibility would be carried out within the project area by the particular force responsible for policing the area from existing resources. No additional staff or resources were provided.

Project timetable

Table 4.6 shows the timetable in which the project was implemented.

Project outputs and outcomes

The project intended by way of the interventions listed previously both to reduce the occurrence of and to increase the detection of targeted crimes within the Fenlands area, particularly burglary dwelling, burglary other than a dwelling (BOTD) and vehicle crime and to reduce fear of crime.

Intelligence sharing and proactive operations

As of December 2002 the project office team had produced the following:

Table 4.6: Project timetable

Action	Date
Funding from Home Office agreed and project manager appointed	October 2000
Project board agreed*	December 2000
Advertise project staff posts, devise role profiles, interview and recruit	January to April 2001
Project office ready	April 2001
Policies agreed	May 2001
Appoint staff (excluding community safety officer)	May 2001
Project launch	June 2001
Individual IT systems provided. Separate Crime Pattern Analyst (CPA) system required	July 2001
Mobile police station launched	July 2001
Project is operational	August 2001
i2 analytical work is possible on separate CPA system	October 2001
Community safety officer and third rural intelligence officer appointed	December 2001
All staff IT trained	January 2002
Cross-border tasking policy agreed	May 2002
Analyst leaves project	May 2002
Proactive wing launched	July 2002
New analyst trained	December 2002
Project funding and proactive wing end	December 2002

Note *Three area commanders, project manager and two representatives from the Home Office.

- 160 information and intelligence bulletins.
- 337 intelligence forms (primarily the result of work by the rural intelligence officers).
- 13 packages (three main packages which resulted in operations running from November 2001 to December 2002).
- 87 arrests.
- 262 detections:
  - 76 Cambridgeshire;
  - 64 Norfolk;
  - 76 Lincolnshire;
  - 38 (Cambs., Lincs. or Norfolk); and
  - 8 other police forces.

Of the 190 information and intelligence bulletins and packages that were produced by the project team between July 2001 and January 2003, just over half (97) focused on suspicious vehicles and a third (67) concerned suspicious persons or known offenders.

Information and intelligence bulletins were a summary of collated information from the three forces' information systems, focusing on suspicious vehicles and known offenders. Future targets for packages were chosen based on the project's analysis of this information. These bulletins were distributed to the three forces, highlighting specific information for police observation. The intelligence bulletins were based on forms created by the Fens project team, intelligence generated by the three rural intelligence officers through their contact with known informants and force crime-recording systems. Intelligence submitted by the project typically differed from that kept by the three police forces' divisional and local intelligence units.

The original aim was to devise and install a single IT server capable of merging crime, incident and intelligence data from all three forces in the project office. This would allow the project analyst to compare all the crime, intelligence and command and deploy (CAD) data for the area on one system. But it became apparent in early 2001 that system in-compatibility made this unfeasible. This reduced the capacity of the project team to produce intelligence packages for forces' tasking and co-ordination meetings. Instead, the project team tended to produce bulletins and flyers resulting in the feeling among grass-roots level staff that the analytical capability of the project office had been under-utilised.

During the course of the initiative, the project team produced 13 packages that resulted in three main proactive operations that led directly to the arrest of ten suspects. Despite the proactive work, the project had found it extremely difficult to link the offenders targeted to specific crimes to a level that would satisfy the criminal courts. They consequently used the tactic of collaborating with insurance companies and other government agencies (including the DSS) to investigate the possibility of fraud. The case study below highlights three of the main proactive operations that the project co-ordinated.

Examples of proactive operations
One of the main analytical packages produced by the project office between November 2001 and April 2002 originally focused on three repeat offenders operating across force borders. The majority of the crimes were committed in Lincolnshire and involved taking vehicles without consent and commercial burglary/burglary other than a

dwelling. Details of all three offenders had previously been circulated in an intelligence bulletin produced by the project office. The project team collated further information on the three main individuals and four of their known associates. From August to October 2001, a total of £337,000 worth of crime was linked to the offenders. All lived on a permanent traveller site. Two of the three targets were arrested in December 2002.

A three-man proactive team headed by a detective inspector was affiliated to the project to undertake further investigation of prolific offenders between July 2002 and December 2002. They investigated past crime committed by 8–12 suspects to find evidence to substantiate charges. New crimes committed by the individuals would also be investigated, making use of intelligence and witnesses. The team engaged in surveillance of the prolific offenders and disruptive activities during this period. From this, over 200 items and £47,000 worth of property were ultimately recovered. In an attempt to link individuals to the scenes of crime, 16 vehicles were seized for forensic examination. Through this offenders were linked to four vehicles, with results out-standing for three other vehicles.

In total, the main suspects were linked to a total of 26 separate crimes in the Fens area and the proactive wing investigated these crimes with the aim of securing a criminal conviction. Ultimately nine of the suspects were arrested on 3 December 2002, with a further arrest made the following day. The ten targets are currently on bail pending further action for DSS and insurance fraud and several substantive burglary charges.

Repeat victims
Overall, 262 repeat victims (domestic burglary, burglary other than a dwelling and domestic violence) were identified between August 2001 and December 2002. Of these, 73% (190) received a stepped level intervention, the majority of whom were given a silver response (see Table 4.7 for details of interventions). In total, there were 19 bronze-level responses, 123 silver responses and 48 gold responses. This differed from the original model used in Huddersfield where all repeat victims were allocated a silver response. If the Huddersfield model had been im-plemented as it was originally intended, all victims of BOTD, burglary dwelling and domestic violence would have received a bronze-level response, and all repeat victims would have received a silver-level response. However, in the Fens, repeat victims had to be victimised two/ three times to receive a bronze/silver-level response, and three/four times to receive a gold response, depending on the force.

Table 4.7: Fenlands repeat victimisation model

Bronze	Silver	Gold
Scene visit	Level one plus	Level two plus
Victim visit for domestic violence victims	Community beat officer visit	Review by crime manager
Crime prevention advice given	Alarm installation	Covert operations
Victim support informed	Risk assessment to identify further action	
Scenes of crime attend	Crime pattern analyst to identify 'at-risk' periods for patrol	
Four week post-incident follow-up to assess implementation of crime prevention advice		
Alert Neighbourhood Watch		

If the Fens project had implemented the original model used in Huddersfield officers would have completed in excess of 1,625 bronze-level responses for burglary dwelling and BOTD victims (domestic violence figures are not available), and 262 silver responses. It is clear that the repeat victimisation element of the project received only token implementation, perhaps the result of limited resources and large geographical area covered by the project.

Mobile police station
Between July 2001 and December 2002 the mobile police station (MPS) was deployed a total of 199 times, was available to the public for 980 hours and dealt with 5,759 visitors (2,685 adults and 3,074 children). It usually visited either one or two locations for an average of 4.9 hours, and received an average of 2.7 visitors per hour of deployment. Use of the MPS did, however, vary between the forces, as did attendance by the public.

The most common reasons for visiting the MPS were to complain about speeding in the local area (70% of visitors), to raise the issue of youths causing annoyance (46%) and to ask for crime prevention advice (37%). Only 15% of visitors mentioned the lack of police or issues concerning police visibility in the local area. It would appear that fear of crime was not very high on the agenda and did not prompt many people to visit the MPS.

Other activities by MPS staff included:

- 33 school visits;
- 11 operations;
- 4 patrols; and
- 10 meetings attended.

Scenes of crime attendance
The aim was to attend 85% scenes of crime for burglary dwellings, burglary other than a dwelling (BOTD), vehicle crimes, violent crimes (including domestic violence), criminal damage and theft from agricultural premises. Two forces recruited dedicated scene attenders and consistently achieved this target. One force failed to meet this target for several months.

Outcomes

Repeat victims
It was anticipated that repeat victimisation would be reduced by 20%. Similar models to tackle domestic burglary in other areas have reduced domestic burglary by between 30% and 75% (Pease 1992; Chenery *et al*. 1997). But levels of repeat victimisation in the Fens actually increased year on year.[3] Domestic burglary increased by 55% (an extra 11 repeat victims) and burglary other than a dwelling increased by 38% (an extra 28 repeat victims). Lincolnshire did, however, achieve a small year- on-year reduction in repeat victims of burglary dwelling.

This increase in repeat victimisation and failure to replicate the success of previous projects is not surprising. The Fens project did not in practice attempt to follow the Huddersfield model, and the revised model was itself not implemented consistently across the three forces. The project also suggested that this increase was partly the result of their improved focus on repeat victimisation and implementation of a manual identification process.

Satisfaction and fear of crime
The results from two fear of crime surveys[4] show that both fear of crime and satisfaction with the local police have remained virtually un-changed (see Table 4.8). The number of respondents who reported feeling unsafe after dark increased slightly in the second survey, and the number of respondents who said they were fearful remained virtually the same. The inability of the project to impact on feelings of safety and reassurance may be partly the result of partial implementation failure,

Table 4.8: Satisfaction with the police and fear of crime (weighted at individual level)

Question	Year-1 survey respondents	Year-2 survey respondents
Satisfaction Percentage satisfied with police in local area	74 ($n = 726$)	73 ($n = 751$)
Fear of crime Percentage of respondents who are fearful	37 ($n = 381$)	37 ($n = 378$)
Safety Percentage of respondents who feel unsafe walking alone after dark	30 ($n = 304$)	33 ($n = 330$)

especially in relation to attending to repeat victims. Previous research has shown that tackling repeat victimisation is an important way of addressing high fear of crime (Borooah and Carcach 1997).

Respondents in the second survey were also asked to compare how the police were performing now compared with a year ago:[5]

- 14% said better (146);
- 72% said the same (736);
- 7% said worse (71); and
- 7% said don't know (74).

Despite increased police presence through the MPS and scene attendance no effect on satisfaction with policing or fear of crime was evident.

Crime

Data for two separate periods were examined to determine the impact of the project on recorded crime. The first period covered the year before and after the project's operational launch (August to July 2000/1 and 2001/2). The second period of analysis covered the first and second year of project funding. However, due to implementation delays, the point at which the work had actually begun was January 2001 and hence the second period analysed was January to December 2002 compared with 2001.

For the first period analysed crime increased in the project area by 26%, an additional 910 crimes. Burglary dwelling, burglary other than a dwelling and vehicle crime increased by 20%,[6] an extra 403 crimes. The increase in recorded crime was also seen in the second analytical period when crime rose 24% (an extra 889 crimes) and burglary other than a dwelling, burglary dwelling and vehicle crime increased by 14%,[7] an additional 284 crimes. Most of the project resources were directed towards enhancing analytical capability, identifying repeat travelling/ traveller offenders and improving detection rates, none of which reduced crime levels in the Fens project area.

Detections

The number of detections increased by 28% for the period August to July 2001/2 compared with 2000/1. This equates to an extra 183 detections. Specifically, notable increases were seen for BOTD, burglary dwelling and vehicle crime (see Table 4.9). This improvement continued into the second period of analysis with a 29% increase in detections seen between January to December 2002 compared with 2001. This amounts to an additional 200 detections. Again there were increases in each of the target categories of burglary dwelling, BOTD and vehicle crime (see Table 4.9).

Although improvement was seen in the numbers of detections achieved, the increase in recorded crime meant that for the two periods of analysis, detection rates in the project area only increased by 0.2% to 19.1% and 0.8% to 19.3%, respectively. However, within the particular target crimes of BOTD, burglary dwelling and vehicle crime, the improvement seen was more marked: +2.0% for the first period analysed and +1.6% for the second period equating to an extra 71 and 55 detections, respectively.

The project aimed to reduce recorded crime and increase the detection of targeted crimes within the Fenlands area, particularly burglary dwelling, burglary other than a dwelling (BOTD) and vehicle crime. However, although detection rates did increase during the evaluation

Table 4.9: Impact on detections

Outcome	August to July 2001/2 compared with 2000/1	January to December 2002 compared with 2001
All detections	+28% ($n = 183$)	+29% ($n = 200$)
Burglary dwelling detections	+86% ($n = 31$)	+26% ($n = 14$)
BOTD detections	+53% ($n = 17$)	+49% ($n = 17$)
Vehicle crime detections	+47% ($n = 23$)	+41% ($n = 24$)

period, these substantial increases in detection rates did not impact on recorded crime in the project area.

Displacement

In the surrounding area which received no additional resources crime increased by 30% (1,518) between August and July 2000/1 and 2001/2. The number of detections increased 23% for the same period (314) but detection rates decreased by 1.4% from 26.9 to 25.5%. It may have been that focusing resources at the Fenlands project area caused this decrease.

Summary

The project aimed to reduce crime and repeat victimisation, to increase public confidence in the local police and to reduce fear of crime. The research-based repeat victimisation element of the project was only very partially implemented. The main focus of the TPI-funded activity was on intelligence gathering and deployment of the MPS. Analysis shows that recorded crime and repeat victimisation increased and fear of crime and public satisfaction remained virtually unchanged. Increases may be partly due to improvements in recording and identifying repeat victims and changes to the crime recording system introduced in April 2002. However, detection rates did increase inside the project area, with burglary dwelling showing one of the largest improvements. They were not, though, associated with any fall in crime overall.

Notes

1 The differences between urban and rural patterns of crime and crime concern have been looked at in more detail recently in Aust and Simmons (2002). They report broadly similar patterns to those shown here. They provide a useful account of change over time, which generally shows consistency in urban areas having greater actual and perceived crime problems than rural areas.
2 A local newspaper poll had found that nine out of ten people in the Fens felt unsafe in their own homes. Findings of this kind, however, face well-known problems of self-selection and hence unrepresentativeness.
3 Comparison of repeat victimisation between August/July 2000/1 and August/July 2001/2.
4 The baseline survey was conducted in June 2001 prior to the operational launch of the project and the second survey was conducted in November 2002. Both surveys were conducted by telephone and lasted roughly 20

minutes. A response rate of 54% was achieved using Epsem random digit dialling (RDD) computer-assisted telephone interviewing (CATI). The sample was chosen using the last birthday rule for adults aged 16+. Fieldwork lasted for 7 weeks and interviews were mainly conducted in the evenings and at weekends.

5 Unweighted data.
6 There were an additional 205 BOTD, 72 burglary dwelling and 126 vehicle crimes.
7 There were an additional 99 BOTD, 47 burglary dwelling and 138 vehicle crimes.

References

Aust, R. and Simmons, J. (2002) *Rural Crime: England and Wales.* Home Office Statistical Bulletin 01/02. London: Home Office.

Borooah, V. and Carcach, C. (1997) 'Crime and fear: evidence from Australia', *British Journal of Criminology*, 38: 635–57.

Bullock, K., Farrell, G. and Tilley, N. (2002) *Funding and Implementing Crime Reduction Initiatives.* RDS OLR 10/02. London: Home Office.

Chee, E. (1999) 'Family violence: Findings from the 1998 Crime and Safety Survey' (unpublished report). Melbourne: National Centre for Crime and Justice Statistics, Australian Bureau of Statistics.

Chenery, S., Holt, J. and Pease, K. (1997) *Biting Back II: Reducing Repeat Victimisation in Huddersfield.* Crime Prevention and Detection Series 82. London: Home Office.

Farrell, G. (1995) 'Preventing repeat victimisation', in M. Tonry and D. Farrington (eds) *Building a Safer Society.* Crime and Justice. Vol. 19. Chicago, IL: University of Chicago Press.

Farrell, G. and Pease, K. (1993) *Once Bitten, Twice Bitten: Repeat Victimisation and its Implications for Crime Prevention.* Crime Prevention Unit Paper 46. London: Home Office.

Kershaw, C., Chivite-Matthews, N., Thomas, N. and Aust, R. (2001) *The 2001 British Crime Survey. First Results England and Wales.* Home Office Statistical Bulletin 18/01. London: Home Office.

Mirrlees-Black, C. (1997) *Rural Areas and Crime: Findings from the British Crime Survey.* Research Findings 77. London: Home Office.

Mirrlees-Black, C., Budd, T., Partridge, S. and Mayhew, P. (1998) *The 1998 British Crime Survey: England and Wales.* Home Office Statistical Bulletin 21/98. London: Home Office.

Pease, K. (1992) 'The Kirkholt project: preventing burglary on a public housing estate', in R.V. Clarke (ed.) *Situational Crime Prevention: Successful Case Studies.* New York, NY: Harrow & Heston.

Pease, K. (1998) *Repeat Victimisation: Taking Stock.* Crime Detection and Prevention Series 90. London: Home Office.

Shaw, M. and Pease, K. (2000) *Research on Repeat Victimisation in Scotland*. Crime and Criminal Justice Findings 44. Edinburgh: Scottish Executive Central Research Unit.

Tilley, N. and Smith, J. (2000) 'A Fenland targeted policing initiative?' (unpublished report, Policing and Reducing Crime Unit). London: Home Office.

Chapter 5

From strategy to action: the development and implementation of problem-oriented projects

Karen Bullock and Nick Tilley

Introduction

Background

This chapter looks at strategy development and implementation in two projects. The first, based in Cambridge, aimed to reduce a high- volume, relatively low-impact crime problem – that of cycle theft. Cycle theft had been found to account for 20% of all crimes in Cambridge city centre. There were some 2,793 recorded thefts in the financial year 1998–99. Cycling is a major mode of transport in Cambridge and the number of secure stands was not meeting demand. Some stands were too old and proving inadequate in their design. Some were damaged, some were poorly installed. The population of Cambridge was thought to be tolerant of cycle crime, thinking of it as a normal part of life and as such was apathetic towards bike security. Offenders were generally believed to fall into three groups: joy-riders, who dump bikes after 'borrowing' them to get from A to B; acquisitive thieves, who take opportunities to steal in order to fund other habits; and volume offenders, who use vans to steal large numbers of bikes, possibly to order.

The second project aimed to reduce a low-volume, high-impact crime problem – that of gang-related shootings. Between January 1997 and November 2000 there were 270 shootings in Manchester (Bullock and Tilley, 2002). Shootings were concentrated in small areas of south Manchester. Victims and offenders shared similar backgrounds and offending histories. The majority of these shootings were believed to be gang related. The original idea in Manchester was to replicate the seemingly successful Boston Gun Project (Braga *et al.* 1999), which had been associated with rapid falls in gang-related shootings. This project applied a 'pulling levers' approach to the identification and application of measures to those involved in undesirable behaviour (Kennedy 1997). In Boston this meant applying pressure on those liable to engage in serious violence and informing them that, if they engaged in certain violent acts, this would trigger a co-ordinated crackdown on all gang members. Pulling levers was the principal means of inhibiting gang-related violence identified in the published project reports, though a range of other conditions was also present that may also have played a part in the apparent success of the Boston project. These included the use of black outreach workers, the attachment of social workers to police stations, and joint probation and police patrolling around the clock.

Greater Manchester Police and their partners were granted about £500,000 to spend on their project over 18 months. Cambridgeshire Constabulary received just under £167,000 from the Targeted Policing Initiative (TPI) to which they pledged a further £120,000 to fund police officer involvement in their project. The Cambridge project began in autumn 2000 and the Manchester project commenced in autumn 2001.

Aims of chapter

The aims of this chapter are to:

- describe the processes through which the strategies were developed and turned into action on the ground;

- examine why some elements of the strategies were implemented, some were not, some were added and some were altered; and

- identify the significant obstacles and enablers of strategy implementation.

It will become clear that the two projects were very different in terms of problem type, scope and type of interventions. Cambridge became essentially a situational crime prevention project, while Manchester applied a range of social interventions. The intention is not to compare the two projects. Together, however, they provide an overview of the implementation issues faced by different forms of intervention in very different contexts.

Methodology

A range of methods was used to collect data on the implementation of the initiatives. Project staff and their managers were interviewed, in some cases several times. Minutes of meetings and other project records were analysed. In the Manchester gun project, the project staff also filled in quite detailed update forms for us. In addition, in Manchester the authors also attended a range of steering meetings and practitioner meetings. The details of the interviews are described in Box 5.1.

Role of evaluators

The authors had rather different relationships with the two projects. In the Manchester project, we were heavily involved in the early days of the project, collecting and analysing data about the nature of the shootings problem (Bullock and Tilley 2002). We also drew up in very broad outline the agreed strategy. As the strategy has been implemented we have become mainly observers, our active role being limited to giving occasional feedback to the project board. This was different from the part played by David Kennedy and his research team in the Boston Gun Project which inspired the Manchester work. Kennedy functioned as an action researcher. We did not do so. In regard to the Cambridge project, one of the authors had visited the force for a half a day as part of the development process. Apart from that we were observers throughout. The analysis of the problem and the formulation of the strategy were completed before we became involved.

Box 5.1: Details of interviews conducted in the Cambridge and Manchester projects

---

Cambridge bike project
Nine interviews:
- One with project manager.
- Three with Cambridgeshire Constabulary civilian staff.
- Two with police officers who had managerial responsibility for the project.
- Two with planners working for Cambridgeshire County Council.
- One with a member of the advisory group.

Manchester gun project
Thirty-two interviews with 38 people (32 interviews, repeat interviews of the same person, some joint interviews):
- Steering group – autumn 2001 (× 10).
- Practitioners – autumn/winter 2001 (× 12).
- Practitioners – spring/summer 2002 (× 10).

Strategy development and implementation

The strategies emerged in different ways in the two projects. In Cambridge the community safety manager developed the aims, specific objectives and detailed implementation timetable before the project manager was appointed.

The aims of the project were to:

- reduce the number of cycle thefts in Cambridge city centre by 5–10%;

- reduce the number of cycle thefts from students by 20%; and

- increase the number of detections by 10%.

The specific objectives were to:

- trial different types of secure cycle-parking racks to determine which were the most user-friendly, secure and appropriate for different locations in Cambridge;

- provide a secure cycle park in the basement of Park Street car park;

- identify additional locations throughout the city for installing secure cycle racking;

- install extra racks and replace inadequate existing racking and include publicity about racks;

- develop and set up a comprehensive and consistent university-wide cycle registration scheme;

- use a black and fluorescent 'police warning' campaign to warn cyclists of theft problems;

- set up a cycle squad of two police constables proactively to target prolific offenders;

- measure the change in numbers of securely parked cycles in a predefined city-centre location;

- determine current figures of under-reporting of cycle theft in Cambridge City; and

- work out what measures effectively reduce cycle crime.

In Manchester the situation was somewhat different and much more complicated. In the light of findings from the research phase of the project we proposed the broad focus of a strategy, which was endorsed by the local Crime and Disorder Partnership (see Bullock and Tilley 2002). The first three elements were inspired by the Boston project. These were:

- to apply co-ordinated leverage to gangs through highly publicised multi-agency targeted crackdowns, aimed at gangs using firearms, possessing firearms or taking part in serious assaults;

- to enhance community relations, to ensure that the community supported the strategy and to avoid the crackdown backfiring (in part on the basis of Scarman 1981); and

- to engage with gang members to elicit information, to transmit consistent messages about targeted crackdowns and to provide diversionary services.

A further three elements were considered necessary in view of the distinctive conditions in Manchester. These were:

- to develop inter-gang mediation services, to head off and defuse tensions that risk leading to serious incidents of violence, including shootings;

- to increase protection for victims and repeat victims; and

- to sensitise agencies to the implications of their actions for gangs and the risks to their members, especially in the light of the provisions of s. 17 of the Crime and Disorder Act 1998.

The logic of the proposed strategy is shown in Figure 5.1. As with the Boston project it was suggested that the main focus should be on reducing shootings and serious violence rates rather than on gangs and gang membership more generally. This broad strategy was presented to the Manchester City Crime and Disorder Partnership in March 2001 and was accepted. Detailed tactical planning was left to the project manager (a police inspector who was newly in post) and two other members of staff who had been employed to work on the project. This resulted in a number of sizeable documents, which presented large numbers of recommendations about how to proceed. For example, the final implementation strategy ran to some 41 pages and contained well over

Figure 5.1 The logic of the proposed strategy for Manchester

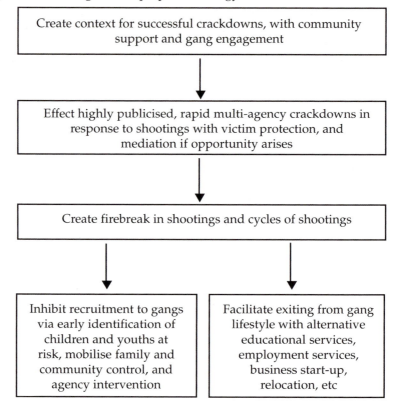

100 recommendations. Recommendations were divided under two headings: 'enforcement' and 'prevention'. These were further divided into a range of proposed activities. Boxes 5.2 and 5.3 give some examples.

The partnership decided it was not realistic to try to implement all the measures proposed. Each agency was asked to select a smaller number of interventions, using an abridged template of options based on the document described in Box 5.3, which were appropriate to their agency and which they would implement. Interventions were considered on the basis of desirability, viability, priority, and means of implementation. Agencies were also asked to consider naming individuals, who would be responsible for implementing the interventions, and also to provide estimates of how much each would cost. By May 2001, 31 interventions were agreed, as detailed in Table 5.1.

Box 5.2: Indicative examples of 'law enforcement' recommendations for Manchester

---

- Brief the head of the Crown Prosecution Service (CPS) and key prosecutors based on the findings of the research.

- Conduct regular sessions with clerks to keep the courts updated on developments within the gang landscape, the wider context of gangs and impact on the community.

- Ensure a detailed multi-agency assessment is carried out on all gang-involved youth and adults before the courts.

- Develop a procedure whereby marginal youth can be released under licence or bailed to intensive supervision by the Youth Offending Team (YOT) and probation also involving individuals from other agencies.

- In order to make deterrence work, adopt the pulling levers strategy in police crackdowns.

- Initiate practices in probation that allow for increased frequency of home visits during non-traditional hours.

- Rigorously enforce tenancy compliance, injunctions, evictions and (re)possession.

- Partner agencies considering pursuing an anti-social behaviour order inform other partners regarding who the target is for discussion.

- Establish a combined law enforcement/criminal justice agency gang unit with the aim of setting a precedent for a multi-agency taskforce on gangs and gang violence.

By June 2001 a name for the project and a mission statement had been agreed. The name was the Manchester Multi-Agency Gang Initiative (MMAGS). The mission was to:

- enforce the law through multi-agency targeted crackdowns;

- deter young people from entering into a gang/gun culture and divert them towards alternatives;

- provide support to young people and families who are most vulnerable;

- secure the conviction and/or rehabilitation of gang-involved offenders;

Box 5.3: Indicative examples of 'prevention' recommendations for Manchester

- Interventions must address the multiple factors which condition youth towards serious youth offending behaviour.

- Establish a multi-agency database containing basic information on gang-involved youth.

- Chronically affected areas be subject to the full range of interventions. Those with emerging gang problems be subject to a more limited set of interventions (e.g. a primary emphasis on work in the schools, outreach on the streets and increased police patrols at potential hot-spots).

- Greater Manchester Police (GMP) exchange information about known gang members with neighbouring police forces.

- Monitor the impact of gangs on non-gang offenders.

- Monitor problems or obstacles that youth and family members may encounter as each tailored intervention plan unfolds. Agencies must be flexible in this respect.

- Encourage partners and community-based grass-roots groups to collaborate in supervising youth while in school and immediately after school day ends.

- Establish information routes so that data on gang involved children and children vulnerable to gang influences get to appropriate school staff.

- Provide a mix of day/evening/weekend classes, crash courses and tutoring in the home and at youth centres, colleges and other centres: an 'alternative high school'.

- Provide simultaneous education/skills development and training to youth and youth's parent(s) and other family members.

- Identify signs of impending disputes and carry out timely mediation in schools.

- Ensure that Sure Start is aware of any history of gang involvement of young parents they work with.

- Identify non-statutory community-based groups to act as first point of contact/intervention in support of families with gang-involved youth.

- Prior to release of an incarcerated gang-involved youth, identify and work with other community members who may have latent antagonisms or disputes with the youth.

Box 5.3 continued

- Directly approach youth in the streets, parks and other public places 24 hours a day.

- Intervene at early stages of a dispute.

- Develop closer links with non-statutory groups.

- Develop models for risk assessment related to different categories of youth.

- Help to build relations between gang-involved youth and the wider civil society.

- Develop a jobs bank to provide work as an alternative to gang involvement.

- Practitioners to conduct regular briefings for senior managers of partner agencies to ensure they are familiar with the changing dynamics of the gang landscape.

- Develop regular workshop for practitioners from different agencies who deal with, or have dealt with, gang-involved youth and/or their families.

- Police officers to get out of cars and on to the streets more often to become visible as 'same cop, same neighbourhood' officers.

- Gang Involved Youth Service Providers Network to act as outreach organisation and as an interface between gang-involved youth and existing statutory agencies.

- Raise health professionals' awareness of gangs and impact of gang culture on youth.

- Visits of partner practitioners to project units/offices to elicit feedback from project staff and those in receipt of services from the project.

- reduce the incidence of death and injury to young people and the wider impact of gangs on the community; and

- create an environment for commercial investment.

In terms of strategy development, it is clear that the original objectives set out in March 2001 were greatly expanded upon by the project implementation team. The consequences of this will be described later.

Table 5.1: Interventions and lead agencies in Manchester

Strategy element	Lead and secondary agency
Conduct regular home visits and identify the changing needs of youth and family	Chief Executive's Department
Develop a jobs bank	Chief Executive's Department
Direct conflict mediation in all environments affected by gangs	Chief Executive's Department
Directly intervene with youth gang members if there is a likelihood of tit-for-tat reprisal	Chief Executive's Department
Encourage local businesses to support specific projects	Chief Executive's Department
Ensure employment for youth and family members in regeneration projects	Chief Executive's Department
Establish 'Streetworker' pilot project to conduct street-level outreach	Chief Executive's Department
Provide mediation between youth, residents and local businesses	Chief Executive's Department
Develop education programmes for gang-involved adults and parents	Education
Liaise directly with schools to develop 'early warning mechanisms'	Education
Assist schools in tackling gang problems	Education/Chief Executive's Department
Facilitate meetings between parents of gang members	Education/Outreach workers
Establish a 'virtual transition school' for gang-involved youth who have been excluded	Education/YOT
Establish regular information exchange between all agencies	GMP
Initiate a 'same cop, same neighbourhood' process	GMP
Engage CPS and clerks of court and establish 'community prosecution'	GMP/all agencies
Engage grass roots groups	GMP/Chief Executive's Department

Table 5.1 continued

Strategy element	Lead and secondary agency
Raise awareness of gangs and gang dynamics among all agencies and schools	GMP/Education
Enhance responsiveness to community concerns	GMP/Housing
Crackdown employing 'pulling levers' strategy	GMP/Housing, Probation and YOT
Develop a risk assessment model	GMP/YOT and Probation
Utilise anti-social behaviour orders and tenancy compliance	Housing/all agencies
Develop links with agencies in other cities to ensure continued support for relocated youth and families	Social Services
Provide intensive 'wrap around' support for youth and family	Social Services
Help youth and families access services	Social Services/Chief Executive's Department
Assist gang-involved youth to leave disorganised and/or destructive family situations	Social Services/Housing
Ensure security of young women victimised by gang members	Social Services/Housing
Provide independent and/or supported living accommodation in areas not affected by gangs	Social Services/Housing
Police/probation/YOT partnership for 'Operation Nightlight' with youth offenders	YOT/GMP and Probation
Monitor the impact of gangs on non-gang offenders	YOT/Probation and GMP
Work with incarcerated gang members and their families	YOT/Probation and Outreach workers

Implementation of the new approaches: project staffing, management, main outputs and outcomes

Cambridge staffing, management, outputs and outcomes

Staffing and management structure
In Cambridge a full-time project manager was employed in September 2000 to implement the strategy as previously outlined. This post was based at the police station. The Community Safety Manager and the Chief Superintendent oversaw the project manager. Key partners were Cambridge City Council, Cambridgeshire County Council, the colleges, and cycling campaign groups. Outputs fell into three main categories: providing secure cycle parking; implementing a registration scheme for bikes; and targeting prolific offenders.

Providing secure parking
A secure cycle parking experiment was undertaken between September 2000 and August 2001. Eight varieties of racks were selected from a range of over 120 designs considered by local cycling groups, planning officers, engineers and the disability consultative panel. The stands were selected on the basis of the following:

- *Security*: it must be possible to secure the frame of the cycle.
- *Ease of use*: stands should be placed far enough apart and not require awkward bending down.
- *Aesthetics*: stands should make an attractive contribution to the environment.
- *Variety*: there should be an assortment of stand designs as bicycles are of different shapes and sizes and each location has different needs.
- *Finish*: stands need to be durable and to have no moving parts.

Ninety-two racks were installed, the majority in May 2001. The designs for the stands selected for trial are shown in Figure 5.2.

An indoor cycle park was also established in the converted basement of a city-centre car park. This opened in March 2002. To make room for the cycle park, 24 car-parking places were removed. Cambridge City Council owns and runs the car park where the cycle racks were installed. The facility provides secure cycle parking for 285 bikes. It is open 24 hours a day, seven days a week and is covered by CCTV. It features:

- 41 vertical cycle lockers for hire at £10 per month;
- 12 horizontal cycle lockers for hire at £10 per month;
- 103 inverted U with crossbar (see Figure 5.2) (two spaces per rack) provided for free use;

Figure 5.2 Cycle racks trialled in Cambridge

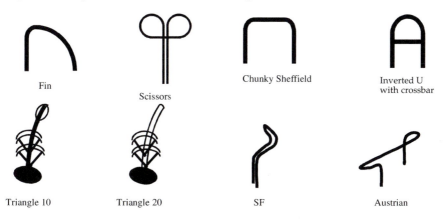

- 12 SF provided for free; and
- 7 tandem/trailer racks (two spaces per rack) provided for free.

Overall, by the end of the project a total 277 additional racks had been installed providing an additional 560 secure parking spaces.

Registration scheme
Cycle marking involves fixing a unique code number to a bicycle frame. A record of the code number, a description of the bike and the owner's details are kept in a register. In the event that a bike is lost an accurate description of the missing bike is available from the register and it can be recorded as lost or stolen. Recovered bicycles can be cross-checked with the register to return them to their owners. As shown in Table 5.2, there are two types of marks for bikes, those that are covert and those that are overt.

All the information about the bikes is maintained in a central register. This information is usually kept on computers owned by the registration company rather than by the police or other public body. This company would be responsible for keeping the information up to date and controlling access. A number of registration schemes operate in the UK, some of which are highly sophisticated. The University of Cambridge operated a relatively crude system. This involved college porters marking bikes with paint or correction fluid and making a note of the mark, the bike and its owner's details to be retained by the college. The aim in the Cambridge project was to devise more effective registration arrangements. The cycle-theft reduction project used four different registration kits. Table 5.3 shows the kits.

Table 5.2: Types of cycle-marking schemes

Overt schemes	Covert schemes
Bright mark	Hard to find
May also include the code number and who to contact to check the register	In some cases may only be read with special equipment
Usually easy to remove	Normally very hard to remove
Usually cheap	Can be high tech and quite expensive

Table 5.3: Cycle-marking technologies used in Cambridge

Kit/technique	Marking technology
Retainagroup	Bright holographic sticker with code number punched through Two covert stickers
Alpha Dot	Microdots painted on to the bike frame Presence of dot picked up by ultraviolet light Code has to be read by a magnifier
BikeRegister.com	Coded stickers Electronic transponder inside the seat tube
Datalog	Coded stickers Electronic transponders

The project manager also developed a basic scheme, as follows:

- A pack containing, among other things, pens with which to mark bikes.
- A booklet in which to record information about the bike, its owner and its code to be retained by whoever was maintaining the scheme.
- A booklet giving bike security information for the bike owner.

Overall, about 25 cycle registration events were held and several hundred bikes were marked. In addition, the project manager worked with the University of Cambridge to try to implement a more consistent and systematic scheme (previously all the colleges had been independently implementing different schemes). A questionnaire asking about bike registration was sent by the project manager to 28 Cambridge colleges in September 2002. Of these 16 were returned. The question-naire identified the registration schemes used by 15 of the colleges which replied. Five colleges replied saying they were using only the project's booklet scheme, five said they were using their own scheme and five replied saying that they were using both their own scheme and the project's booklet scheme.

The questionnaire also indicated that 682 bikes were registered in the academic year 2000/1 and that the number registered in the academic year 2001/2 had increased to 1,290.

Table 5.4 summarises the implementation status of the main elements of the project.

The bike project successfully implemented the secure bike-parking aspects of the project. It had partial success in setting up a

Table 5.4: Implementation status of the main elements of the Cambridge bike project

Specified objective	Implementation status
To trial different types of secure cycle parking racks to determine which were the most user-friendly and secure and appropriate for different locations in Cambridge	Implemented
To provide a secure car park in the basement of Park Street car park	Implemented
To identify additional locations throughout the city for installing secure cycle racking. Install extra racks and replace inadequate existing racking	Implemented
To measure the change in numbers of securely parked bikes in Cambridge	Implemented
To use a black and fluorescent 'police warning' campaign to warn cyclists of theft problems*	Not implemented
To set up a cycle squad of two police constables proactively to target prolific offenders	Not implemented
To set up a comprehensive and consistent university-wide cycle registration scheme and include publicity about racks	Partially implemented – some colleges participated

Note: *On reflection project decided it wasn't a very good idea.

comprehensive university-wide cycle registration scheme. It did not manage to establish the cycle squad to target offenders.

Outcomes

Bike theft fell in Cambridge. Figure 5.3 shows numbers of bike thefts between April 1998 and April 2002 in the three Cambridge city-centre beats. As the figure shows, the fall in mid to late 1999 preceded the start of the project and followed the apprehension, conviction and incarceration of a very prolific bike thief. The thief was sent to jail for four years in July 2000. He was known to be associated with around 16% of all bike thefts in Cambridge in 1998/9. In the 20 months prior to his charge for bike thefts in late November 1999 there were an average of 101 thefts of cycles per month in the city centre. This went down to 67 for the 29 months after his charge. In the ten months between the charge of the prolific thief and the start of the Cambridge project there were an average of 66 thefts of cycles per month, and in the following 19 months

Figure 5.3   Bike thefts in Cambridge city centre, 1998–2002

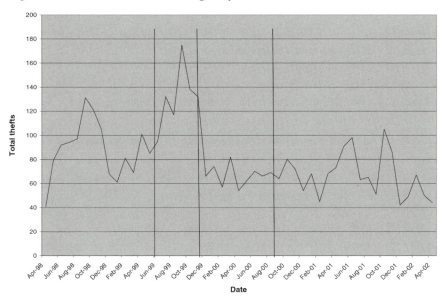

Note: The first drop line shows the arrest of a known highly prolific bike thief in possession of bolt croppers for 'going equipped'. The second drop line shows the conviction of the same prolific offender for theft of eight cycles with many other offences taken into consideration. The third drop line shows the start of the Cambridge project.

the average was 67 per month. Thus, while bike theft fell in Cambridge, it is not possible convincingly to associate this with the project.

Manchester staffing, management, outputs and outcomes

Staffing and management structure
In Manchester a full-time project manager, a police inspector, was appointed to co-ordinate the implementation of the strategy. A civilian implementation manager and a civilian information manager were also employed specifically to work on the project and were based at a police station. Practitioners were seconded from agencies or employed on short-term contracts, as shown in Table 5.5. The project was overseen by a steering group of senior representatives of the practitioners' home agencies, plus a headmaster from a local school. It was chaired by a police chief superintendent. Initially there were further meetings of a group for the line managers of seconded staff, though this did not last for long. Figure 5.4 shows the structure of the project while the managers' group met. The same structure operated in the absence of the managers' group subsequently.

Three days' training for the project staff was provided between 24 and 26 October 2001. This was attended by three members of the housing department, two members of the Youth Offending Team (YOT), one probation officer, two representatives from the education service, the two outreach workers and the implementation team. Social services had not recruited at this point. Training covered:

• presentation of the initial findings of the research into Manchester shootings;
• definitions of gangs and discussion of Manchester gangs;

Table 5.5: Staffing the Manchester multi-agency gang project

Agency	Number of posts	TPI-funded	Seconded
Youth offending team	2.0	2	Y
Housing	1.5	1	Y
Probation	1.0	1	Y
Social services	1.0	1	Y
Education	2.0	2	Y
Youth service			
Education and welfare			
Outreach workers	2.0	2	N

Figure 5.4   Manchester project structure

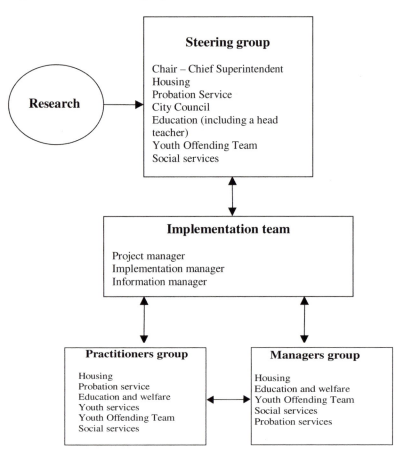

- discussion of the main interventions; and
- the implementation process.

The Manchester strategy was implemented by project staff primarily in the following ways:

- A multi-agency problem-solving group which aimed to work with 85 target individuals.
- Six multi-agency 'working groups' to focus on:
  - education;
  - diversion activities;

- mediation;
- crackdown;
- jobs bank; and
- community awareness and partnership development.

The outputs of the Manchester project were much harder to quantify than those of the Cambridge project. This is because most of the money was spent on staffing rather than on capital items, as happened in Cambridge. Nevertheless, the following is a description of the main outputs of the Manchester project.

Multi-agency problem-solving group and the target list
The implementation and information managers drew up a list of individuals to target from a total of 858 people deemed gang members, gang associates or at risk of becoming gang involved. Risk was identified, for example, from family connections with the gangs and criminal activity. Initially it was agreed at board level that 85 people should be on the target list. According to the information manager this drew in 106 individuals in all, because some responses required the involvement of more than just the target individual – for example, his or her mother and siblings.

Individuals were included in the target list on the basis of perceived or alleged involvement in firearms or gangs. The project staff conceded that there was variable evidence regarding the level of gang involvement and that there was a tendency for loosely gang-involved individuals to be included, though if there was serious doubt an individual might be taken off the list.

Other characteristics of the target list included the following:

- No one was to be 26 years old or over.

- All on the list had to be associated with south Manchester gangs.

- There was to be a mixture of males and females. (This meant there was actually a bias towards women. As few women were found to be involved, most who were were included.)

- One gang was over-represented because of the large numbers of young people in it.

- There was a skew towards those referred from a particular high school which had a large intake from gang-affected areas and a headmaster who was keen to address gang-related problems.

- No one was to be included if he or she was serving a very long prison sentence.

The multi-agency working group met once a week to discuss individuals who were on the target list. By March 2003 the team had discussed action plans for 172 individuals. Of these individuals:

- 19 were female and 150 male;
- the average age was 19 (ranging from about 12 and up to the mid-40s); and
- 65% lived in south Manchester.

The project undertook a range of actions with the people on the list, mainly providing support and preventative interventions. An assessment of needs would be made, normally related to housing, education and social services. Efforts would be made to engage the individuals – some of whom were in prison – through either existing statutory providers or through the outreach workers. Interventions would then be tailored to needs, including the following:

- Arranging counsellors.
- Providing school mentors.
- Rehousing, possibly to another part of Manchester or providing tenancy support.
- Providing support for parents, linking in with Sure Start, for example.
- Referring to diversionary schemes.

If the target was on the probation or the YOT's books, the team would look to assess suitable orders and programmes. Actions could also have related to enforcement in a number of ways including strict enforcement of bail and YOT conditions or housing tenancy agreements. Anti-social behaviour orders (or warnings) would also be considered where there was evidence that individuals were creating a nuisance.

Gang Resistance Education and Training scheme (GREAT)

A GREAT programme was developed by one of the education officers working on the project along with the civilian project implementation manager. The scheme basically attempted to teach young people and their parents the skills to avoid gang pressure and youth violence. The Manchester scheme included sessions on:

- awareness of gangs;
- consequences of gang life;
- conflict resolution activities; and
- problem-solving.

At the time of writing the programme was being trialled in a local secondary school and early difficulties were being ironed out.

Community relations
The community relations element of the strategy basically involved discussions and meetings with community groups and representatives. There were around 80 meetings as well as numerous informal discussions.

Awareness raising
A number of formal and informal meetings were held by the practitioners with members of their home agencies to try to raise awareness of gangs. There were around 50 meetings in addition to many informal discussions.

Police activity
The co-ordinated, gang-focused multi-agency crackdown, which was to follow explicitly stated and well specified targeted behaviours, was not implemented as envisaged in any of the strategy documents. The police continued to respond vigorously to incidents as they arose. The police were often not confident that they knew well enough that shootings were gang related, which gangs were involved or who were members of specific gangs. Because of this, a key element of the original strategy, the pulling levers approach, was not applied.

In all around 10 of the 31 agreed lines of work were not implemented.

Most staff time appeared to be concentrated on:

- dealing with the individuals on the target list to provide support and diversion;
- developing the GREAT programme; and
- making presentations about gangs to community groups and agency staff.

Table 5.6 shows which initiatives were not implemented along the lines envisaged in the early implementation plans. Box 5.4 shows those

Table 5.6: Elements of the Manchester gun project not implemented as originally envisaged

Strategy element	Overall status	Project explanations
Initiate a 'same cop, same neighbourhood' process	Board subsequently decided not to implement	Community beat officer system already in place
Establish a 'virtual transition school' for gang-involved youth who have been excluded	Board subsequently decided not to implement	Existing arrangements perceived to be adequate
Crackdown employing 'pulling levers' strategy	Not implemented	Practical difficulties Responding to incidents in standard way
Develop education pro-grammes for gang-involved adults and parents	Not implemented	Existing arrangements perceived to be adequate
Liaise directly with schools to develop 'early-warning mechanisms'	Not implemented	Arguably mechanism already exists via the schools liaison officers and education welfare officers
Directly intervene with youth gang members if there is a likelihood of tit-for-tat reprisal	Not implemented	No systematic implementation Possibility of some ad hoc interventions
Provide mediation between youth and residents and local businesses	Not implemented	Possibility for further work here following recruitment of more staff
Direct conflict mediation in all environments affected by gangs	Not implemented	Possibility for further work here following recruitment of more staff
Ensure employment for youth and family members in regeneration projects	Not implemented	No specific finances Arguably arrangements already exist
Develop a jobs bank	Not implemented	No specific finances Arguably arrangements already exist
Encourage local businesses to support specific projects	Not implemented	No specific finances Arguably arrangements already exist

Box 5.4: Elements of the Manchester gun project being implemented at the end of Home Office funding

---

- Assistance to schools in tackling gang problems.

- Raising awareness of gangs and gang dynamics among all agencies and schools.

- Utilisation of anti-social behaviour orders and tenancy compliance.

- Provision of independent and/or supported living accommodation in areas not affected by gangs.

- Provision of intensive wraparound support for youth and family.

- Help to youths and families in access to services.

- Assistance to gang-involved youth in leaving disorganised and/or destructive family situations.

- Improvements to the security of young women victimised by gang members.

- Development of links with agencies in other cities to ensure continued support for relocated youth and families.

- Establishment of Streetworker pilot project to conduct street-level outreach.

- Work with incarcerated gang members and family.

- Engagement with grass-roots groups.

- Facilitation of meetings between parents of gang members.

- Enhancement of responsiveness to community concerns.

- Regular home visits to identify the changing needs of youth and family.

---

elements that were being implemented at the conclusion of Home Office support through the TPI.

Finally, Table 5.7 shows those elements of the project that were still being developed following the conclusion of Home Office TPI funding.

Outcomes
Figure 5.5 shows the overall number of shootings in the two targeted south Manchester divisions. There was no fall in the number of shootings. The numbers are, however, extremely small and it was always unlikely that significant differences in the number of shootings, like those seen in Boston, would occur.

Table 5.7: Elements of the Manchester gun project still being developed at the end of TPI funding

Strategy element with ongoing development	Project comment
Establishment of regular information exchange between all agencies	Occurring informally via the practitioners groups Long term plan for shared IT systems
Development of a risk assessment model	Further work on this has been commissioned
Police/Probation/YOT partnership for 'Operation Nightlight'* with youth offenders	Superceded by ISSP – which was considered to be a focused use of resources
Engagment with CPS and clerks of court to establish 'Community Prosecution'	Ongoing consultation
Monitoring of the impact of gangs on non-gang offenders	Occurring informally via the practitioners group

Note: *Very simply, the planned Operation Nightlight in the Manchester strategy was to do with YOT and Probation (in conjunction with GMP, Social Services and outreach workers) securing tougher terms of probation for gang-involved youth and to consider developing probation officer/police officer teams to conduct home visits to adult gang offenders, especially in the evening.

Attempting to explain the difference between strategies and action

There is already a relatively extensive literature on factors that impact on the implementation of crime reduction initiatives. Hope and Murphy (1983), for example, highlighted technical difficulties, poor central control over local activity, lack of co-ordination and competing priorities.

Process lessons from the Home Office-funded Safer Cities programme highlighted problems of inadequate targeting of responses, insufficient training and poor communications between co-ordinators and others implementing the projects (Ekblom 1995; Sutton 1996). Ekblom (2002) points to a range of routine administrative factors influencing implementation such as poor project management skills, time constraints and funding issues. He also described the much more fundamental

Figure 5.5   Monthly shootings in South Manchester

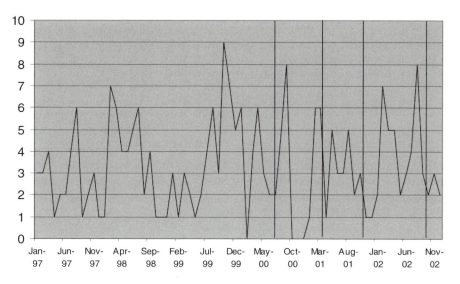

Note: The first drop down line refers to the approximate start of the research phase (June 2000). The second line refers to when the board agreed the strategy (13 March 2001). The third line refers to the start of the implementation phase (October 2001 was when most of the implementation staff were in place) and the final one to the 'formal' launch of the Project 14 October 2002.

problems of slow or non-existent organisational and cultural change in large organisations and occupational divides between organisations regarding enforcement and civil approaches. Recently, overall implementation lessons from the TPI highlighted a range of issues relating to staffing (recruitment, training and turnover), leadership/co-ordination (leverage, level of expertise) and installation of equipment (Bullock *et al.* 2002).

It is clear that in both projects, some parts of the strategies were implemented, some were partially implemented and some were not implemented at all. Some of the issues that affected the implementation of these two projects are quite prosaic. Others were possibly less commonplace and were certainly highly challenging. The following sections highlight what seem to have been the main factors lying behind the implementation patterns and problems of the projects discussed in this chapter, which centre around:

1 staffing, management and co-ordination;
2 mission drift;
3 inter-agency co-operation;
4 project concept and understanding;
5 impact of unexpected contingencies; and
6 dilemmas in targeting particular people and places.

I. Staffing, management and co-ordination

Co-ordination and management

Both the projects were facilitated by strong support at a senior level and commitment in principle to mainstreaming the projects in some form after the Home Office funding had run out. In the Manchester project especially, managers were taking some risks tackling a high-profile problem through working together in innovative ways and bringing together collaborative multi-agency teams.

The project setting in Manchester was very unusual as it involved secondment of practitioners from a range of agencies, who were to work together under a police inspector. These practitioners were not housed in the same place. Managerial responsibilities lay with the home agency, while the project was co-ordinated by a police officer. There were, un-surprising, teething problems during implementation:

> Early meetings went round in circles. This is to do with the different backgrounds from which the practitioners have come and some poor organisation (manager, June 2002).

> Communication, administration and organisation has been poor and this has not been well received. I have been especially con-cerned about the accountability of the meetings which leads to practitioners not having a clear view of what they are doing (manager, June 2002).

It took a long time to resolve some of these issues. A number of the practical problems were raised by practitioners when we conducted our first round of interviews in autumn 2001:

> The meetings are too long and loose – these are teething problems (team manager, November 2001).

> An opportunity was missed for setting ground rules, for example no mobile phones, record and minute keeping, confidentiality statements, no side meetings (practitioner, November 2001).

Communication within the team has been a problem (practitioner, November 2001).

These issues had not been sorted out by the time of the second round of interviews in spring 2002. The problems were important because they were taking up time, which should have been being spent on implementation. Box 5.5 details some of the range of challenges relating to practical and fairly mundane issues.

Staffing
In both projects dedicated staff members were appointed to deliver the strategies, and this facilitated implementation. In Cambridge, the civilian project manager ensured that the non-police elements of the strategy were co-ordinated and implemented:

A manager with responsibility for a project with the correct knowledge and contacts is important (police officer, April 2002).

The project manager's knowledge and contacts were also extremely useful (police officer, April 2002).

The dedicated project manager and project team in Manchester similarly enabled the project implementation as staff could devote themselves to the project rather than do it on top of existing duties.

Having the right people in post is also deemed important (Read and Tilley, 2000; Bullock *et al.* 2002). In both projects enthusiasm about tackling the problems was evident as was strong loyalty to the project. However, past research shows that individuals can cause problems (Foster and Hope 1993). There were some concerns raised about the Cambridge manager's experience of project management, contracting and overseeing building works though fundamentally the knowledge and dedication of the manager facilitated the implementation of the project.

In Manchester some general issues were raised about the personnel appointed or seconded to the project:

Some appointments were less than ideal (project implementation team member, June 2002).

This related in particular to the employment of one individual whose behaviour was widely perceived to have caused ongoing distractions from strategy implementation:

Box 5.5: Some practical issues in regard to the implementation of the Manchester project

Day-to-day management	• Maintaining co-ordination when not physically co-located. • Co-ordinating a range of specialisms outside the manager's sphere of competence and influence. • Use of diverse criteria for assessing performance of staff members from agencies. • Varying priorities and cultures.
Communication and IT	• Access to email. • Communication when staff not physically located near each other. • Different and incompatible IT systems.
Role of home agency managers and their relationship with the board	• Management responsibility for staff without day-to-day supervisory opportunities or powers. • Range of criteria for assessing performance and differing priorities and cultures of agencies.
Administration	• Maintenance of minutes and record of action. • Distribution of agendas/minutes and other information.
Understanding of duties and roles	• Clarity about the circumstances in which an agency can intervene. • Legal duties (and powers) to intervene. • Local procedures and practices relating to processes of intervention – especially in relation to prioritising cases. • Varying worker experience of working in a formal organisation.
Health and safety	• Possible risks associated with the nature of the serious offending. • Assorted risk assessment criteria and forms from the various agencies. • Standardising access to equipment – e.g. cars and mobile phones.
Accountability	• Information sharing and data protection. • Record-keeping. • Difference in procedures/standards of record-keeping.

A does not understand the nature of people and the person who should be reining A in isn't … A is a bit of an odd ball and doesn't have empathy with the team (practitioner, January 2002).

Person A was difficult to handle; we inherited A and A wasn't ideal. A lot of time was spent checking up on A and making sure A didn't do anything stupid (project implementation team member, June 2002).

A is like a teenage child, not an adult. On three occasions I've had to stop A doing things that would have been disastrous. We now have quite a formal working relationship. A has created some situations that were unnecessary (project implementation team member, June 2002).

A has done daft things and also not done things A was asked to do (board member, July 2001).

The impact of this individual was to create time-consuming management problems, when the time could obviously otherwise have been spent on other elements of strategy; to steer the project's agenda in a specific direction, in some ways at variance with the original strategy; and to leave undone some elements of the strategy for which they were responsible, when they left.

2. *Mission drift: expansion and contraction*

In Manchester the scope and size of the project grew as the strategy was developed and in the early stages of implementation. Basically, the implementation team expanded the remit of the project to focus more generally on gang membership rather than specifically on shootings. This was due in part to their conviction that it was necessary to focus on gang membership as in some sense the underlying cause of violence:

The objectives are to reduce firearms violence and to tackle gang culture because the two are related … Initially the project was very focused on firearms but then we realised the problem was gangs (project implementation team, August 2001).

[The objective was] to stop teenagers, young people, being shot by reducing gang membership (project implementation team, August 2001).

The Manchester project's mission slippage detached it from its roots in the Boston Gun Project, which had focused specifically on shootings rather than attempting to deal with gangs and gang members per se. Boston had shown, counter-intuitively, that it is not necessary to tackle underlying causes (which are often deep-rooted social problems) to have an impact on a problem. Indeed the social measures there prior to the crackdown element had had no discernible impact on their own.

The Manchester project became occupied with casework with the individuals on the list of gang members, associates and those at risk of becoming involved, and with servicing that list. The list became longer as referrals were taken. How the increased numbers were to be managed was unclear. The potential workload spiralled. The complex individual and family problems encountered were puzzling and it was often not clear how they could be resolved. The potentially dangerous nature of the people that project workers were dealing with was clearly stressful. Enormous resources would be needed fully to engage with all on the list:

> There is no system of referral yet the project is taking referrals … If [the project] continues in the same way the workers are going to be swamped with requests. As awareness is raised there will be more demand. We need to be clear about the aim and get the structure right (practitioner, June 2002).

> [There] may be too many to address all at once. It may be better to focus on fewer to see what can be achieved, what things are working, lessons learnt (practitioner, December 2001).

> The project started off with a target list of 85. Now it is taking referrals. This has not been worked through. How are they going to cope with the numbers? … It is just ad hoc and woolly (manager, June 2002).

In contrast to the expanding scope of Manchester's project, in Cambridge the scope shrank. Initially a significant element of the proposed strategy had been offender-focused and involved proactive efforts at detection. This part, though, was dropped. In the end, only the proposals for physical measures were implemented. This was basically because there was a shift in priorities and the local management team could not justify a dedicated team of two officers to target offenders. Both absolutely and relative to other offences the rate of cycle theft had dropped dramatically. The allocation of officers to cycle theft was not deemed appropriate, especially in view of staffing shortfalls and other competing demands:

> Obstacles to progress included the strain on resources felt by the police force. There was more police involvement in the project at the beginning. As bike theft fell, so did the amount of time the police were involved in the project (cycle theft taskforce member, April 2002).

> We were unable to provide the officers because of chronic shortage of officers caused by increased public order duties and general recruitment problems. (police officer, April 2002)

3. Inter-agency co-operation – procedures, personalities and cultural differences

Both projects involved inter-agency co-operation that brought benefits. In Manchester multi-agency work brought access to resources that would not have been available otherwise. This meant that cases could be dealt with more quickly and provided a range of specialisms that might not be available to a single agency:

> [An advantage of the project was] access to multi-agency resources – that would otherwise take a long time to provide (practitioner, June 2002).

In Cambridge a range of partners was represented on the steering group, including the Cambridge cycling campaign, the colleges and the county and city councils. The city engineers and planners were especially important in facilitating implementation. They offered advice and expertise that could not have been provided from within the police service.

Multi-agency work also brought problems. In Manchester, on top of the co-ordination difficulties already described, delays were caused by the need to attend to the agendas and concerns of representatives of all involved organisations. Additionally, there were quite marked differences between the agencies in their views on the mix of enforcement and diversion/support-type activities. This goes some way to explain the drift towards the implementation of interventions that were more diversionary and supportive than enforcement based, and explains some of the conflict between the group members:

> Advocacy alongside enforcement. This could work and it does work. Enforcement is essential and it's not happening here (practitioner, June 2002).

> There is a clash of philosophies (practitioner, June 2002).

> Where people were involved in shootings it was assumed that levers would be pulled. I thought that this would be a bigger aspect than it has been. It might be the result of the people on the group. They are more keen on why people are doing things than what they are actually doing. This is a balance. But the balance is too far on the 'why' side (practitioner, June 2002).

Certainly many of the people on the group were, on the whole, not in favour of enforcement. This caused problems in the relationship between the agencies, which had different focuses and wanted to get different things out of the project:

> You shouldn't put enforcement first. If you have tried to engage with some one then so be it. X seem to be gathering information to enforce but they should be gathering information to prevent. (practitioner, June 2002).

> I would agree that [the project] has been stronger on help than enforcement (project implementation team member, June 2002).

> People having different agendas. For example, housing are about enforcement, whilst we're about improvement, help. The two approaches come against each other (practitioner, June 2002).

> Some of the group are not so happy with the coercive approach. There is a massive amount of anti-enforcement feeling. They would all agree it is important but we can't get them to do it (project implementation team member, June 2002).

In Manchester the implementation of the crackdown, which is discussed further elsewhere in the chapter, is also alleged to have suffered from failure to engage partners – such as DVLA and the Benefits Agency – who might have played a significant part. It was anticipated that the role of these agencies would have been to check, for example, whether vehicles were taxed, whether benefits claims were legitimate and take enforcement action where necessary as part of a co-ordinated crackdown strategy against gangs participating in specified violent action:

[The project manager] claimed that the other agencies who were supposed to be involved didn't respond (practitioner, June 2002).

It is hardly surprising that there was some conflict between agencies. Research has already highlighted the potential for conflict in inter-agency crime reduction (Blagg *et al.* 1988; Sampson *et al.* 1988; Pearson *et al.* 1992). Certainly, the potential for disagreement about whether enforcement or prevention is most appropriate has been revealed in earlier research. Liddle and Gelsthorpe (1994), for example, noted variation in probation involvement in multi-agency crime prevention initiatives – stating that commitment was much more likely to be seen in social crime prevention initiatives.

4. Project concept and understanding

In the Manchester project, the relationship between the crackdown and support sides of the initiative came to take on a meaning that had not been present in the original strategy. The original strategy talked about well publicised, gang-focused, multi-agency crackdowns as a means of applying leverage to deter shootings by gang members. This, it was conjectured, would reduce the number of shootings and thus the need gang members felt they had to carry weapons to protect themselves. This in turn might then also create conditions in which there would be less gang-inspired coercion. In these circumstances services offering support to young people in difficult circumstances who were either already involved in gangs or at risk of becoming involved were, it was thought, more likely be taken up. The revised understanding of crack-down and support and their relationship to one another seemed to be as follows: that crackdowns would be targeted on individuals if they failed to respond to the offers of help or support to enable them to steer clear of gangs and gang-related criminal activity. Coercion thus became a threat faced by individuals who would not co-operate with the help on offer, rather than by groups if members behaved in prespecified violent ways.

There is nothing intrinsically incoherent about the account of the nature and role of the crackdown in relation to individual behaviour that emerged in Manchester. It is simply different from the role of crackdown as envisaged in the original strategy. In practice, the strong anti-enforcement sentiments widely held among the practitioners meant that it was deemed appropriate only as a last resort in relation to individuals. There was, thus, in practice little crackdown either as originally envisaged or as it was reinterpreted:

I don't think that there has been that much crackdown … most people have complied. I'm not aware of it happening, except for normal policing. I think we have to chat to people and if they don't play ball with us, enforcement will follow (practitioner, June 2002).

5. The impact of unexpected contingencies

In Manchester one key local event compromised the potential to deliver the form of crackdown originally envisaged. During most of the project, members of one of the gangs were on trial. The lawyers involved (and ultimately the judge) advised against formally launching the project (and the report of the original research informing the strategy), since it might be deemed to prejudice the outcome. In these circumstances it was difficult to effect the publicity that was an integral part of crackdown, as it was originally conceived. While the outcomes of the trials promised rich material for a well publicised gang-focused crackdown, in the event the project had a low profile at variance with its logic. This is not to say that the police were not responding vigorously to shootings – they were. It is only to say that the implementation of co-ordinated, highly publicised, explicitly gang-oriented crackdowns was hamstrung.

6. Dilemmas in targeting places and people

The Cambridge project was targeted on a very specific area, where the volume of cycle crimes was highest and where the availability of secure parking was poorest. Here targeting was relatively unproblematic.

The Manchester project planned to focus on south Manchester and on those aged under 25 who were vulnerable to shootings because of their association with gangs. Nevertheless determining which individuals were most at risk and thus suitable priorities for preventative interventions was difficult. This issue arose with the drift towards targeting gang membership (however defined) as the problem rather than shootings (as originally envisaged). What constituted a gang and membership of a gang was far from clear on the ground (as has also been found more generally in much of the literature, see Bullock and Tilley 2002). Moreover, some members of the group of workers, notably those who had previously been gang members themselves, felt that their colleagues did not understand gang membership and gang dynamics. Altogether, determining who should fall within the compass of project intervention was contested and fraught with difficulties:

> The dynamics of the gangs are not properly understood by others (practitioner, November 2001).

> The focus has been far too much on those on the periphery of the gangs but anyone who lives in X or Y could be considered to be on the periphery ... at the moment there are far too many people on the periphery of gangs for this to be a sensible way of prioritising (practitioner, November 2001).

> The focus has been on those on the periphery of the gangs ... We would prefer more time spent on those who are more involved ... Targeting and strategising of the list is not at all well done (practitioner, November 2001).

There was certainly disagreement in practice about whether the right people were on the list with arguments about whether people were involved enough to merit intervention. For example, one young man, in Year 11 at school, was discussed at an early case conference. The outreach workers did not consider him to be gang involved and generally there were mixed views about whether he should be included. In the end he was included because of concern that his gang-involved brother may have an impact on him.

Some project workers felt it important to target only those who were already members of gangs or at serious risk of becoming involved. Their experience highlighted the stigma that could be associated with gang membership and possible resistance from parents, who rejected the label attached to their children:

> Parents take a backward step when you mention gangs. Parents deny and resist because of stigma. Greater stigma is attached to gang membership than crime (practitioner, June 2002).

Conclusions

This chapter has described strategy development and implementation in two very different projects. We have identified a range of reasons why the interventions that were implemented often failed to match those that were originally planned. Generally, as has been noted previously, *staffing*, *management* and *co-ordination* are all important. What in these two cases was found to be especially important included:

- recruiting the right staff with the right skills;
- engaging, committed and supportive management;
- systems of co-ordination that, among other things, facilitate communication between practitioners, day-to-day administration and IT.

A sense of *mission drift* changed the size and scope of both projects. For Manchester the focus of the project shifted as practitioners' discretion enabled them to shape the initiative to accord with the ways in which they perceived and understood problems. In contrast the Cambridge project contracted as priorities changed. *Inter-agency co-operation* brought benefits to both projects – especially in access to resources and specialist skills. But it also brought difficulties for the Manchester project. The strong difference in cultures and personal values of the secondees resulted in conflict, which in turn helps explain the shift in the mission of the project. Variations in culture and personal values are also associated with the ways that practitioners came to *conceive and understand* the projects: in Manchester the project took on a meaning that was never envisaged in the strategy documents. *Unanticipated events* had an impact in Manchester: in particular, ongoing trials made it difficult to launch and publicise the project.

So to conclude, even where fairly detailed plans, based on research, are evident we cannot suppose that the plans will be fully implemented. Practical problems and unexpected events may interfere. The values, personalities and preferences of practitioners can and do intervene as they seek to make sense of problems and interpret strategies using their discretion on the ground.

References

Blagg, H., Pearson, G., Sampson, A., Smith, D. and Stubbs, P. (1988) 'Inter-agency co-operation: reality and rhetoric', in T. Hope and M. Shaw (eds) *Communities and Crime Reduction*. London: HMSO.

Braga, A., Kennedy, D. and Piehl, A. (1999) 'Problem-oriented policing and youth violence: an evaluation of the Boston Gun Project'. Unpublished report to the National Institute of Justice, Washington, DC.

Bullock, K., Farrell, G. and Tilley, N. (2002) *Funding and Implementing Crime Reduction Initiatives*. Online Only Report 10/02. London: Home Office.

Bullock, K. and Tilley, N. (2002) *Gangs, Shootings and Violent Incidents in Manchester: Developing a Crime Reduction Strategy*. Crime Reduction Research Series 13. London: Home Office.

Ekblom, P. (1995) 'Safer Cities programme phase 1: informal process evaluation'. Unpublished report, Home Office Research and Statistics Department.

Ekblom, P. (2002) 'From the source to the mainstream is uphill: the challenge of transferring knowledge of crime prevention through replication, innovation and anticipation', in N. Tilley (ed.) *Analysis for Crime Prevention*. Crime Prevention Studies 13. Monsey, NY: Criminal Justice Press/Cullompton, UK: Willan.

Foster, J. and Hope, T. (1993) *Housing, Community and Crime: The Impact of the Priority Estates Project*. Home Office Research Study 131. London: HMSO.

Goldstein, H. (1990) *Problem-oriented Policing*. New York, NY: McGraw-Hill.

Hope, T. and Murphy, J. (1983) 'Problems of implementing crime prevention: the experience of a Crime Reduction project', *The Howard Journal*, XXII: 38–50.

Irving, B. and Dixon, J. (2003) *Hotspotting*. London: The Police Foundation.

Kennedy, D. (1997) 'Pulling levers: chronic offenders, high crime settings and a theory of prevention', *Valparaiso University Law Review*, 31: 449–84.

Liddle, M. and Gelsthorpe, L. (1994) *Interagency Crime Prevention: Organising Local Delivery*. Crime Prevention and Detection Unit Paper 52. London: Home Office.

Pearson, G., Blagg, H., Smith, D., Sampson, A. and Stubbs, P. (1992) 'Crime, community and conflict: the multi-agency approach', in D. Downes (ed.) *Unravelling Criminal Justice*. London: Macmillan.

Read, T. and Tilley, N. (2000) *Not Rocket Science?* Crime Reduction Research Series 6. London: Home Office.

Sampson, A., Stubbs, P., Smith, D., Pearson, G. and Blagg, H. (1988) 'Crime, localities and the multi-agency approach'. *British Journal of Criminology*, 28: 478–93.

Scarman, Lord (1981) *The Brixton Disorders, 10–12 April 1981* (cmnd 8427). London: HMSO.

Sutton, M. (1996) *Implementing Crime Prevention Schemes in a Multi-agency Setting: Aspects of Process in the Safer Cities Programme*. Home Office Research Study 160. London: Home Office.

Chapter 6

Data and analysis for problem-solving: alcohol-related crime in pubs, clubs and the street

Mike Maguire and Matt Hopkins

Introduction

This chapter draws on evaluations of three projects funded under the Targeted Policing Initiative (TPI) which had in common the aim of reducing 'alcohol-related' crime. One, the Tackling Alcohol-Related Street Crime (TASC) project in Cardiff, was focused upon two city-centre police sectors. The other two, Operation Amethyst in Cornwall and the Nottinghamshire Alcohol Related Crime (NARV) project, each covered a whole county. They also differed in that the TASC project was aimed at preventing violence and disorder both inside licensed premises and on the city-centre streets, whereas Amethyst and the NARV project were targeted primarily at offences occurring in licensed premises. The full evaluation report of the TASC project has been published (Maguire and Nettleton 2003); those on Amethyst and NARV (Hopkins and Maguire 2003; Maguire and Swainson 2003) are unpublished.

All three projects made use of special databases constructed to keep track of incidents associated with specific licensed premises (and, in the case of TASC, of alcohol-related violence or disorder in the street). One of the main purposes of this chapter is to describe and assess the value of these databases, both as a practical aid to the work of the project and as a tool for measuring the effectiveness of the interventions. In doing so, it is necessary to consider questions around the definition of 'alcohol-related' crime and the reliability of the data sources.

The chapter begins with an overview of the nature of the problem and previous responses to it, then addresses issues of definition. This is followed by a description of the aims, approaches and interventions adopted by the three projects, in each case discussing how their databases were constructed and used, and summarising their main findings. Finally, some general comments are made about the emerging lessons from these projects regarding the collection and use of data (including the use of specially created databases) in the implementation and evaluation of problem-solving approaches to crime reduction.

Nature of the problem and previous responses

Alcohol-related crime – especially violence around pubs and clubs – is by no means a new phenomenon. On the contrary, generations of police constables cut their teeth on dealing with drunken mêlées in and around public houses at closing time. However, in recent years the problem has taken on a major new dimension with the relaxation of the licensing laws and the rapid growth of what has come to be known as the 'night-time' or '24/7' economy: the development of major entertainment areas in many city centres, based around concentrations of pubs, clubs, discotheques and fast-food outlets and catering to a mainly young clientele until well into the night (Light 2000; LGA 2002; Hobbs *et al*. 2000, 2003). On Friday and Saturday nights in some of the larger cities, well over 100,000 people may be crowded into such areas. At the same time, the number of police officers available to deal with any trouble is often surprisingly small. In fact, most of the policing is undertaken by private security staff attached to individual licensed premises – usually referred to as 'door staff' or 'bouncers'. While the situation is undoubtedly improving, such staff have themselves often been 'part of the problem'. Until relatively recently, they were subject to very little regulation and the job, poorly paid and offering little training, tended to attract people who were quick to resort to violence and in some cases engaged in drug dealing or other criminal activity (Morris 1998; Lister *et al*. 2001; Hobbs *et al*. 2002).

While it is emphasised that definitions and measurement in this area are problematic issues (see next section) and the complexities of the databases used in the evaluations have yet to be explained, a general idea of the shape of the problem can be discerned from statistics such as the following. In all three project areas:

- at least two fifths of known incidents of violence and disorder associated with licensed premises occurred between 10 pm and 3 am on Friday or Saturday nights;

- door staff were involved (as victims, offenders or both) in at least one in six of all such assaults;

- the most common form of violence used was punching or kicking, but weapons (especially glasses and occasionally knives) were used in at least 10% of known assaults; and

- most injuries were minor, but more serious injuries such as cuts requiring stitches, broken bones and concussion were apparent in at least a fifth of known assaults.

In addition to the problems associated with door staff, previous studies have identified a number of other factors that can increase the likelihood of violence, both in and around licensed premises and in the streets of the main entertainment areas of town and city centres (see, for example, Tuck 1989; Homel and Clarke 1994; Graham and Homel 1997; Purser 1997; Deehan 1999; Hobbs *et al.* 2003). In relation to individual premises, these factors may be categorised into those relating to the physical and to the social environment. The physical environment of licensed premises can promote violence if they are poorly designed (for example, have inadequate seating or lack quiet areas), overcrowded or poorly maintained. Social environmental factors that may increase risk include drug use, sexual activity, high noise levels, a lack of trained bar staff, irresponsible serving practices and a failure to keep aggressive or intoxicated patrons out of the premises.

Broader factors in the local environment that have been identified as increasing risk include allowing licensed premises and fast-food outlets to cluster within certain areas and not providing transport to move people out of the city centre quickly at peak closing times. Building on earlier work by Ramsey (1982) which advocated a 'situational crime prevention' approach to the problem, Tuck (1989) noted over a decade ago that alcohol-related violence is often generated at 'congestion' and 'cluster' points within cities. Congestion points are particularly busy spots or bottlenecks at which revellers may pass each other on public thoroughfares between pubs and nightclubs. Cluster points are areas where crowds of people may gather when waiting for (and sometimes competing for) service, such as fast-food outlets, taxi ranks and at the bars of public houses. Both offer the potential for incidents to be triggered as people jostle each other or argue over access to services.

Despite an accumulation of knowledge over some time about the nature of the problem, the implementation of strategies to prevent or reduce these kinds of violence and disorder has generally been sporadic and *ad hoc*, and there has been little rigorous evaluation of what actually 'works' in this regard. Until quite recently, too, such problems have tended to figure fairly low among the priorities of Community Safety Partnerships (Deehan and Saville 2000; SIRC 2002). A few studies in the mid-1990s produced evidence to suggest that the promotion of well managed premises and reducing congestion around them could help to reduce incidents in those specific locations (Graham and Homel 1997; Purser 1997; see also Deehan 1999), but most commentators eventually reached the conclusion that it was only through partnership working – especially between the police, local councils, licensees and the drinks industry more generally – that a more sustained grip on the problem of alcohol-related violence would be achieved (Deehan 1999; NACRO 2001).

Definitional issues

There is no obvious answer as to what should be counted as an 'alcohol-related' crime. First of all, it would be a mistake to base any such definition on assumptions about causality, in some way attempting to distinguish between cases which were or were not due to the intoxication of the assailant or victim. The consumption of alcohol is almost certainly a contributory factor in many late-night assaults in and around pubs and clubs (although even this is disputed in some research commissioned by the drinks industry: see SIRC 2002) but, as noted above, other factors in the environment or in the relationships between those involved may sometimes be as much or more important.

Secondly, while it seems reasonable to count only those cases in which one or more of those involved have been drinking, this is difficult to establish in many cases from police reports. Moreover, should the consumption of *any* amount of alcohol qualify as a case for inclusion, or should there be a cut-off point, such as two pints of beer (or the equivalent units of wines or spirits), under which people's emotional or motor responses are assumed to be unaffected? Even leaving aside the practical problem of determining how much has been drunk, it is well known that degrees of intoxication vary according to body weight and many other individual factors, so this, too, seems a blind alley to take.

An alternative, and more pragmatic, approach – variations of which were adopted in all three projects – is to base definitions not upon the physiology of those involved in individual cases, but upon the locations (and to some extent the 'ambience') in which offences occur. The main interest from the policing and community safety point of view is in reducing the numbers of violent incidents occurring in and around licensed premises, particularly during the late-night gatherings of crowds of young people in city centres. While it may well be that some of those incidents involve people who have been drinking only lemonade, they can still arguably be deemed 'alcohol related' in the much wider sense that they are associated with a location in which the consumption of alcohol is a core feature of the cultural environment. Further details on the precise definitions adopted in the three evaluations will be given later.

Overview of the projects

In this section, we describe the aims and approaches of the three TPI projects evaluated by one or both of the authors, examine and comment on their use of data, and summarise the main findings on their effectiveness.

The TASC project

When first set up, TASC was among a relatively small number of projects pioneering multi-agency work to reduce alcohol-related violence. The project offices were visited on many occasions by representatives of police forces and Community Safety Partnerships from other parts of Britain (as well as attracting some overseas interest) and it can claim some influence in the recent rapid expansion of similar schemes, some of which have also adopted the name TASC.

TASC's principal objective was to reduce the level of alcohol-related violence and disorder in Cardiff city centre and the Cardiff Bay area. Like other TPI projects, it was based on inter-agency partnership and adopted a focused, 'problem-solving' approach, seeking innovative solutions to specific forms of offending in specific locations. The lead agency was South Wales Police, and the partners included Cardiff County Council, the University Hospital of Wales and – vitally – the private sector, in the shape of the Cardiff Licensees Forum. It was staffed by a project manager (a police inspector), a training sergeant, a data analyst, an administrator and a project nurse (based in the hospital accident and emergency unit). Staff were appointed from late 1999, and the project was launched in June 2000. The initial Home Office grant ended in March 2002, but the project received extra funding to continue with reduced staffing for 12 months as a 'demonstration project'. Its interventions included the following:

- Focused dialogue between the police and members of the licensing trade, mainly through an active Licensees Forum.
- Measures aimed at improving the quality and behaviour of door staff.
- Attempts to influence licensing policy and practice.
- Measures aimed at publicising the problem of alcohol-related violent crime.
- Targeted policing operations directed at crime and disorder 'hot-spots'.
- A cognitive behavioural programme for repeat offenders (COV-AID).
- A training programme for bar staff ('Servewise').
- A programme of education about alcohol for school age children.
- Support for victims of alcohol-related assaults attending hospital.

The TASC database

Where evaluation of crime reduction outcomes is concerned, the basic approach adopted was to undertake comparisons of levels of 'alcohol-related violence and disorder' in police sectors 29 and 30 (Cardiff City and the Bay area, respectively), or in particular streets or licensed premises within these sectors, both before and after the commencement of the TASC project, and before and after specific interventions. The main instrument for these purposes was the TASC database. This was held in an SPSS (Statistical Package for the Social Sciences) data file, designed to a large extent by the evaluators and maintained throughout the life of the project by the TASC data analyst. It held detailed information about the time and location of relevant incidents, the apparent reasons behind them, any weapons used or injuries sustained, and the characteristics of victims and alleged offenders. Two key issues in designing the database, of course, were what sources of information should be used to compile it, and what exactly should be counted as 'alcohol-related violence and disorder'.

Data sources: The database combined into one file data from several police sources and an outside source. The police sources were incident records, custody handling records, crime records, CCTV logs and extra information obtained by the analyst directly from officers. These were supplemented by information from the hospital accident and emergency unit, where patients who said that they had been assaulted were asked by reception staff to give brief details on where and when the assault took place. Further detail was added by the project nurse, who systematically telephoned such patients to offer support or advice and at the same time gleaned extra information about the incident. The resulting information was passed to the analyst (in open or anonymous form depending upon victims' permission) and added to the database, where it was used to create a new incident record or to enhance existing records. In compiling the database, the analyst checked each record individually to ensure that cases from the different sources were not 'double counted'. She received sufficient information in the vast majority of cases to be confident that this had not occurred. In the few cases where she could not be sure, she did not create a new record.

In order to allow 'before and after' comparisons of patterns of crimes and incidents, the analyst entered equivalent data going back to 1 July 1999, thus providing comparable data for a 12-month period prior to any TASC-initiated interventions. As far as possible, this retrospective data collection was carried out in the same way as the prospective data collection (see below).

Definitions adopted: Incidents qualified for inclusion in the database only if they fell within the definitions of 'alcohol-related violence' or 'alcohol-related disorder' adopted by the project. First of all, in keeping with the aims of the TASC project, information was collected only on incidents which occurred on the streets or inside licensed premises or fast-food outlets: 'domestic' violence occurring within private homes was excluded. 'Violence' was deemed to include any kind of physical assault (including robbery, but not 'snatch' theft or 'theft from the person'). 'Disorder' was defined as any event classified in police crime or incident records as involving a breach of the peace, 'disturbance', 'drunk and disorder' or actions falling under s.4 or s.5 of the Public Order Act 1986.

Secondly, the definition of an incident as 'alcohol related' was based on the principles either that it was clear from the reports that one or more of those involved (as victims or offenders) had been drinking, or that it occurred in a location in which the consumption of alcohol was an important feature of the cultural environment (see the discussion on this earlier). These principles were translated into systematic recording practice by developing a few simple rules. First, cases were included if they had already been flagged in the police recording system as 'U16' (alcohol related): however, officers were not always diligent in attaching this flag and there was clearly a degree of under-recording. Secondly, reports of assaults or disorder taking place inside or just outside named pubs or licensed clubs were assumed automatically to be alcohol related. As noted above, there will be a few cases in which none of the participants had actually consumed alcohol and a few in which the named premises had nothing at all to do with the incident. However, detailed examination of samples of cases included on the above criteria revealed that such exceptions were rare (most offenders had clearly been drinking, and particular premises tended to be named in police reports only when the person concerned had been inside them or had got into an altercation with their door staff). Thirdly, incidents occurring elsewhere in the streets or, for example, fast-food premises or the railway station, were included if there was some prima facie evidence in the reports of the consumption of alcohol by offender, victim or both. And finally, in any incidents occurring in public places in which it appeared likely that alcohol had been involved (e.g. street assaults occurring in the late evening) but this was not certain from the available information, the analyst made persistent efforts to discover whether one or more of the participants had recently been drinking: most commonly, she sent a memo to the officer in the case asking for further details. Similarly, the project nurse chased up unclear cases via A & E records or through telephone calls or short postal questionnaires to victims. Both the analyst and (to a lesser extent) the project nurse carried out these inquiries retrospectively as well as prospectively, so that the figures for the pre-TASC period were based as far as possible on the same procedures as those for the period the project was in operation.

Despite the exceptional care taken in sifting and checking data (to the extent of this constituting the main duties of a full-time analyst), no claim is made that the above methods produced a full picture of 'alcohol-related' incidents of 'violence and disorder' in the targeted area. As is well known, only a proportion of potential crimes are reported to and recorded by the police. The British Crime Survey indicates, for example, that in 2000 only 45% of violent incidents were reported to the police, and that 40% of those reported ended up as recorded crimes (Kershaw *et al.* 2001). The method adopted attempted to get at as many of the 'hidden' incidents as possible, both by including hospital data and by searching incident and custody records in addition to crime records (the inter-relationships and overlaps between these different sources will be discussed later). However, not only do many cases never come to the notice of hospital or the police, but the key details of some cases in their records which may have merited inclusion as 'alcohol related' were never found despite the efforts of the analyst or nurse. More importantly, as already emphasised, whether to classify and record an incident as 'alcohol related', as 'disorder' or as an 'assault' itself involves a degree of subjective judgement on the part of the individual police officer (or member of the hospital staff), especially at the lower end of the scale of injuries sustained. Despite these obvious caveats, the method chosen was applied consistently, and the evaluators regard the resulting database as sufficiently robust for the main purposes for which it was designed.

Uses of the database: In addition to providing a means of comparing levels of alcohol-related violence and disorder before and after the implementation of the TASC project (both across the police sectors as a whole and in specific locations within them), the database proved to be of considerable practical use to the TASC team. First of all, it was used routinely to identify any specific licensed premises which appeared to be experiencing high or increasing levels of violence or disorder. These were then visited by the training sergeant, sometimes with licensing officers, in order to discuss with the manager the possible reasons for the problems and to suggest ways in which they could be tackled. Generally speaking, there was a good relationship between managers and the TASC staff, and most co-operated willingly with their suggestions: this was assisted by the success of the Licensees Forum, on which virtually all Cardiff pubs and clubs were represented and which acted as a vehicle for sharing views about the most effective policies for violence pre-vention. In most cases, the suggested changes involved relatively straightforward measures such as minor design changes, more effective CCTV coverage, more training of – and tighter control over – door staff, clearer guidance to bar staff on dealing with intoxicated people and possible under-age drinkers and so on. On occasion, however, a much larger operation was mounted, combining covert and overt police activities with more significant changes in the way that the premises were run. As described below, some of these operations appeared to have a significant and sustained impact on violence levels at these premises.

Secondly, the database was used on occasion to assist in police objections to the granting of a new licence, or as part of a more general dialogue with the city council about patterns of drinking and violence in Cardiff and the need for a more planned approach to managing them. For example, the data clearly showed that one small area of the city centre, in which several new pubs and clubs had opened within a short time, was experiencing a rapid rise in violence and disorder. The TASC team's conclusion was that this area had become 'saturated' in terms of licensed premises. The TASC manager, supported by senior officers and some members of the Licensees Forum, took the decision to oppose the granting of any new alcohol licences in this area, arguing that the city centre could not sustain any more such premises in a limited space. However, despite the high standing of TASC, and despite convincing data from the database to support their argument, the police were largely unsuccessful in convincing licensing magistrates that granting such licences increased the potential for serious disorder in this area. They were also unsuccessful in an appeal to the Crown Court against the granting of a licence to open a new club in the location. The judge decided that it was not a properly brought case and commented that the police should 'get on with the job' of policing the area. In the face of these setbacks, the TASC team concluded that they needed to intervene much earlier in the licence application process, at the planning stage. To this end, the project manager and data analyst began exploratory discussions with the Council Planning Department. Arguments were put in terms of the council's responsibilities under s. 17 of the Crime and Disorder Act 1998 (i.e. that each local authority must 'exercise its various functions with due regard to the need to do all that it reasonably can to prevent ... crime and disorder in its area'), as well as pointing out the disadvantages of creating an unattractive area in the city centre in which most premises were locked up during the daytime. They also made presentations about the distribution of violent and disorderly incidents, again using information from the TASC database. This had some impact, in the form of successful objections to an application to convert a commercial property in the street into a new nightclub. However, objections to planning permission for two other conversions in the area failed.

Main findings of the evaluation

A major problem in evaluating the overall impact of TASC (as opposed to its impact on individual premises) was that there was during the lifetime of the project a large increase in the numbers of people drinking in the city centre late at night. Over its first 12 months, there was a 10% growth in total customer capacity of pubs and clubs in the two sectors covered, as well as several large-scale sporting and cultural events. These developments clearly increased the numbers of potential offenders and victims affected by alcohol, but it is very difficult to estimate to what extent – had there been no TASC project – this potential would have been translated into reality. A 10% increase in drinkers would not necessarily be expected to produce a 10% rise in violent and disorderly incidents, although some increases might be expected. In the event, alcohol-related *disorder* continued to rise sharply, increasing by 49% in the first 12 months (most of this increase, in fact, was accounted for by incidents in the small area of the city centre in which several new clubs and pubs had opened within a short period). By contrast, incidents of *assault* fell by 4% – ostensibly quite a positive outcome (Maguire and Nettleton 2003).

The most encouraging findings, however, concern the impact of intensive police operations aimed at particular venues and undertaken in close collaboration with the managers of the premises and the Licensees Forum. The most successful of these, both targeted on large clubs, took place over an eight-week period in summer 2000. Both entailed a package of measures including regular inspections of facilities, close dialogue with managers, a greatly increased plain-clothes and uniformed presence, close examination of door staff licences and liaison with local taxi services for efficient dispersal of customers. The following 12 months saw reductions of 41% and 36% in incidents of violence and disorder in and around the two clubs. It is worth noting, by contrast, that similar operations targeted at whole streets, rather than individual premises, were less successful (Maguire and Nettleton 2003).

Despite the above successes in individual initiatives, the study found that the TASC team largely failed to persuade 'key players' in the county council, breweries or other relevant companies to adopt broader strategic approaches to the prevention of late-night violence and disorder. Its best achievements in this respect were improved registration, training and disciplinary systems for door staff. However, it made little headway in influencing planning policy or in slowing the expansion of licensed premises in 'saturated' areas of Cardiff. It also failed to secure general agreement to changes in alcohol-marketing strategies. It is argued that, while better management of individual premises is a necessary first step, attention to wider issues arising from the growth of the 'night-time economy' is vital to the long-term success of crime prevention in this field. Ideally, this requires close co-operation between the police, council, licensing authorities and senior managers from the brewing and entertainment industries, and the adoption of a more planned and managed approach to the development and regulation of late-night entertainment areas and of the infrastructure to support them.

The Nottinghamshire Alcohol Related Violence project

The principal aim of this project was to develop a co-ordinated strategy to reduce crime and disorder in and around pubs and nightclubs across Nottinghamshire. A police project manager was employed to develop the key interventions and to foster a partnership approach between Nottinghamshire Police, Nottinghamshire Healthcare NHS Trust, and Nottinghamshire Drug and Alcohol Action Team (DAAT).[1] Oversight of the project was exercised by a joint police–DAAT steering group that met every three months. After a preparatory period, the project ran at full strength for 12 months from April 2001 to April 2002.[2] The main interventions included the following:

- Proactive advice to managers on licensing issues and violence prevention, mainly through visiting premises shortly after incidents had occurred.
- Marketing campaigns aimed at those perceived to be at risk of heavy drinking and becoming involved in violence.
- Training for door supervisors across the county.
- High-visibility policing in 'hot-spot' areas.
- An arrest referral scheme where those arrested for alcohol-related violence were educated in 'brief intervention' sessions run by nurses.

These interventions generated a number of project outputs. For example, the ten licensing officers employed made over 1,100 visits to licensed premises, a total of 104 special policing operations ran over the project period, 83 door staff completed an NCFE2 (National Certificate of Further Education, Level 2) training course and 1,783 people were interviewed by an arrest referral nurse. In addition, over 130,000 project leaflets, 309,700 beer mats, 15,000 posters and 1,000 tee-shirts were distributed as part of the marketing campaign.

Data sources
Unlike the TASC project, it was not possible to develop a comprehensive database which could serve the dual purposes of providing information to guide the work of the project team and allowing the evaluators to undertake a 'before and after' comparison to assess the effectiveness of the scheme. The licensing officers used their own database, known as the 'Innkeeper' system, but this was compiled only during the project period and there was no comparable information for the previous (pre-project) year. The researchers themselves undertook some retrospective data collection, but this was based only on recorded crimes (see below).

The Innkeeper system was maintained and regularly updated by licensing officers to record all incidents known to have occurred in and around licensed premises. This was not restricted to violence and disorder, but included incidents of criminal damage, theft, drug dealing and so on. It was based not only on official crime and incident records (which the licensing officers trawled daily for relevant incidents), but on any other incidents which came to their notice from other sources: mainly reports from licensees direct to the project team. Each entry included the date and time of the incident, the crime number (if applicable), the name of the premises or street where it took place and a brief description of what happened. As the interest of the project was in remedial work with individual pubs and clubs, general 'alcohol-related' violence on the streets was not included in the Innkeeper records.

While very useful for the licensing officers, this database was of only limited value to the evaluators. In order to allow some kind of 'before and after' comparison, they constructed their own database covering a 'baseline' year (April 2000 to March 2001) and the first year of the project (April 2001 to March 2002), but it proved impossible, given the number of incidents recorded across the county, to do any more for the baseline year than identify relevant incidents from the crime recording system: in other words, to search for all recorded offences of violence against the person which had either (1) taken place inside or just outside named licensed premises, or (2) had occurred in a public place, with a specific mention of alcohol consumption. For the project year, they had access to police incident records and the Innkeeper database, which they included on the SPSS database,[3] but obviously comparisons between the two years could only be based on recorded offences.[4]

Main findings of the evaluation
In terms of crime reduction outcomes, the data collected allowed two main indicators of effectiveness to be produced. First, when the numbers of crimed 'alcohol-related' assaults (as defined above) were compared, it emerged that there had been an overall reduction across the force of 18% during the project year as compared with the pre-project year. Secondly, when short-term 'before and after' comparisons were made within the project period in terms of incidents occurring in specific pubs and clubs which had been visited by licensing officers, there were a number of encouraging findings. In particular, it was possible to identify a list of premises across Nottinghamshire that had been defined by licensing officers as having 'chronic' problems and which therefore received the most visits and were most subject to other interventions. Over the short term, trends in incidents associated with these 'chronic' premises were more positive than those in other licensed premises in the county: as a group, they experienced greater than average reductions in known incidents of assault, and smaller than average increases in other kinds of incident (disorder, drug dealing and so on) – the latter showing a rising trend across Nottinghamshire throughout the year. Responses from managers and landlords of licensed premises also suggested that the licensing officers were generally seen as effective: for example, 55% of the 54 licensees surveyed said that advice given to them after an incident had been 'extremely helpful' and 50% that it had had a direct impact in reducing similar incidents in the future.

Data collected in relation to the high-visibility policing operations show that they were on the streets for a total of 12,591 hours and during this period, 261 arrests were made for violent crimes. They were also said by the police to have produced useful intelligence. However, evidence regarding their effectiveness in reducing incidents of violence and disorder is mixed. There was little evidence of reductions in incidents in Nottingham city centre (a major late-night entertainment centre, with growing numbers of licensed premises), though more precisely targeted operations in smaller town centres such as Mansfield did appear to reduce incidents around specific premises, again over the short term. This finding echoes those on similar operations generated by the TASC project.

Findings on the effectiveness of other elements of the project were less clear, although there were indications of a lower than expected rearrest rate among people with a record of frequent arrests for alcohol-related offences who took advantage of the arrest referral services offered by the project. In addition, 80% of 58 door supervisors who responded to our survey thought that the NCFE2 training could help to reduce trouble with the police and over half thought it would help to reduce trouble with customers. However, the real test for such training courses will be if incidents involving door supervisors who have completed the course are reduced. It was not possible to monitor this during the period of the evaluation.

Operation Amethyst (Cornwall)

Operation Amethyst was launched in November 2000 with the broad aim of reducing alcohol-related violence and disorder in Cornwall and the Isles of Scilly. Like other TPI projects, it was a multi-agency initiative, in this case with Devon and Cornwall police as the lead agency, supported by the Local Authority Licensing Department, Environmental Health, Health and Safety and the Fire Service. The project team comprised a police manager with administrative support, closely linked to the force's Licensing Department for the county of Cornwall, which was doubled in strength (from three to six officers) through funding from the project grant. At the same time, the role of the Licensing Department was revised to place a much stronger focus on enhanced problem-oriented and proactive policing of licensed premises.

The project was made up of a variety of separate components, including a major arrest referral scheme. The evaluation, however, was limited to its core 'policing' element, the identification of licensed premises which experience serious or frequent incidents of violence or disorder and the implementation of problem-oriented interventions in these premises, co-ordinated by the licensing officers (in some cases in partnership with other agencies). Due to limited resources, it was also largely a 'desktop' evaluation, based on an analysis of data collected by Amethyst staff (Maguire and Swainson 2003).

The main methods adopted to achieve these aims were as follows:

- Enhanced co-operation between the police and relevant partnership agencies.

- Focused dialogue between the police and the licensing trade.

- Increased supervisory (and sometimes multi-agency) visits to premises giving cause for concern, sometimes resulting in action plans for improvement and monthly review meetings.

- Initiatives (such as training and registration) to improve the quality and behaviour of door staff, and guidance on good practice to managers and bar staff.

- Targeted policing operations, including drug test purchases, against carefully selected premises.

The Amethyst database

As with the other two projects, the key tool in the evaluation was the development of a database of incidents and interventions in licensed premises across Cornwall. The database was developed by the researchers and updated on a regular basis by the Amethyst staff. It was created by transferring information from the police licensing database (known as 'Insight') into an Excel file. This information was then 'cleaned' and maintained by a trained member of the Amethyst team. It was then possible to transfer this into an SSPS spreadsheet at a later date for in-depth analysis by the researchers (a direct transfer of information from 'Insight' into SPSS posed problems of readability).

The information in the database included data from 'L10s', which are reports by police officers of incidents that occurred inside, or were connected to, licensed premises. These contain relevant information about the incident's location, nature, time and date, any injuries sustained, the method of reporting and any action taken by officers. All L10s are forwarded by control room staff directly to Licensing to be input into the licensing database. In addition, licensing officers go through all daily incidents to identify and add to the database any that have been overlooked and which they consider should have generated an L10.

The licensing officers also recorded details of supervisory visits they made to particular premises. These could be either 'routine' or 'post-incident' (some of the latter were undertaken jointly with representatives of, for example, the Local Authority Licensing Department, Health and Safety or the Fire Service). Post-incident visits were usually made to offer advice or enforce regulations in response to an L10 report, and in the case of the more serious incidents normally took place between 24 and 72 hours after the event. However, while these were the most important visible actions undertaken by the licensing officers in terms of crime prevention, interviews revealed that a considerable amount of other contact was made with pub and club managers which was not systematically recorded.

In order to allow some 'before and after' comparisons of patterns and trends, the Amethyst team member entered data retrospectively to cover incidents that had occurred in the 12 months before the co-ordinated and proactive role of licensing officers and other agency representatives was established (i.e. prior to April 2001). As the licensing database had been less comprehensive during this period (due partly to less systematic submission of L10s and partly to less trawling of general incident records by licensing officers) it was necessary to undertake extra work in order to make the 'before' and 'after' datasets more directly comparable. This required the Amethyst team member not only to transfer data from the old licensing database, but to conduct retrospective trawls of incident records for the whole of Cornwall, seeking other cases that should have received L10s. This was an extremely time-consuming task, which involved a great deal of collation and cleaning of data. As a result, the retrospective exercise had eventually to be limited to four individual months of the 'pre-Amethyst' year – July and December 2000, and January and February 2001. The figures for these four months could then be compared with those for the equivalent months of the project period.

Main findings
Based on data from four equivalent months, comparison of the first year of Operation Amethyst's implementation with the period prior to its existence indicates that there was an overall 7% rise in recorded incidents associated with licensed premises in Cornwall. This rise was greater for fights, scuffles and other minor violence (12%), disturbances (9%) and especially drug-related incidents (58%), than it was for assaults (4%). There was also considerable variation between districts, ranging from a 26% *increase* in Kerrier to a 7% *decrease* in Penwith.

During the same year, it should be noted, there was a 7% increase in the number of new licensed premises in Cornwall, increasing the capacity for people to engage particularly in late-night drinking. In addition, certain other changes increased the likelihood of incidents being reported to and recorded by the police, at least to a small degree. These include greater use and improved central monitoring of CCTV, and the work of Operation Amethyst itself, which raised the profile of alcohol-related incidents within the police service. It also encouraged more use of L10 forms, which made it easier to identify relevant incidents than simply relying on subsequent trawls of general incident data. In other words, the overall rise in recorded incidents of alcohol-related violence and disorder could be partly an artefact of increased 'visibility' of relevant incidents.

Where incidents in *individual premises* are concerned, reliable comparisons over time are more difficult to make than was the case with the large clubs in central Cardiff, owing to the relatively small numbers of incidents involved in most Cornish pubs and clubs. The overall conclusion from analysis of ten individual cases of premises targeted by the Amethyst licensing officers was that the picture appeared very mixed. Two cases seemed at face value to suggest that the interventions had led to a reduction in incidents, two that there had been an increase and the remainder either that there had been no change (or possibly a 'slowing down') or that there was insufficient evidence even for speculation. Equally, the towns in which the premises were located (like all towns in Cornwall) varied considerably between those experiencing increases, decreases and 'no change' in their patterns of recorded incidents.

Other perceived benefits

From a police licensing perspective, the increase in personnel resources produced by Amethyst gave the team the capacity to forge better, co-operative working relations with outside agencies. The Cornish licensing officers emphasised especially the improved liaison with local authorities, establishing partnership work which has been strongly co-operative and proactive in almost all districts (with perhaps a partial exception in Carrick, where internal council regulations hindered enforcement practices). Overall, they argued, they were able to identify problems at specific premises more quickly, and to set up multi-agency visits to tackle them. They could also engage in more frequent contact with targeted premises (including monthly review meetings), keeping up greater pressure on them to improve.

As far as the licensing trade is concerned, it would seem that the aims and practices put into effect during the lifetime of the project were met with a generally positive and co-operative response. A substantial increase in numbers of reportedly active and influential local Pub Watch schemes and Licensee Forums was put forward as evidence of this. In addition, good liaison with trainers from the British Institute of Innkeeping (BII) ensured good quality door staff and bar staff training. Indeed, training is now an essential requirement for registration of all door staff wishing to work in Cornish premises which hold a public entertainment licence. A forum for regular dialogue between police and door staff ('Club Safe') has also been set up. Initial meetings were said to have met with both very good attendance and positive feedback from door staff.

Data and problem-solving: some emerging lessons

The experience of evaluating three projects aimed at reducing 'alcohol-related' crime has helped the researchers to arrive at some fairly firm conclusions as to the most appropriate sources of data for assessing the scale of this problem and measuring trends. It has also indicated the relative ease or difficulty with which the different types of data can be obtained and analysed. More generally, it has drawn attention to some important issues around the availability and use of data to assist 'problem-solving' approaches to crime prevention, especially when these are aimed at problems about which the police do not routinely record information. This section offers some brief conclusions about the strengths and weaknesses of the various forms of available data, first as means of producing as full a picture as possible of alcohol-related crime, and then as practical tools both to assist practitioners in adopting problem-solving approaches and to facilitate robust evaluations of their effectiveness.

Police and hospital data: overlaps and additions

As outlined in the project descriptions above, the four main data sources used by the projects were crime, incident and custody records generated by the police and – in the case of TASC – information specially collected from A & E patients at the local hospital. Although there are many overlaps, each of these sources paints a somewhat different picture of the problem of 'alcohol-related violence and disorder', and each varies in the ease and accuracy with which relevant cases can be identified and extracted. The hospital data are of particular interest as they raise questions currently exercising the Home Office about the reliability of police data and how much 'value' might be added by the routine collection of crime-related information from other sources (see, for example, Simmons 2000).

Table 6.1 shows, over the whole period for which the TASC analyst maintained the database, the numbers of 'alcohol-related' incidents identified from each of the four main data sources used. It can be seen that the highest number of incidents (3,431) appeared in the police incident records (i.e. the computer records compiled by staff in the command and control centre, mainly on the basis of telephone calls from the public and messages from patrol officers). Trawls of crime records and custody records threw up 2,509 and 2,164 incidents, respectively (if more than one person was arrested in relation to the same incident, only one incident was counted). Most of these were found in both sets of records, and many of them, too, had already been identified in the incident records. However, as Table 6.2 shows, the custody and arrest records together produced a further 951 cases not identifiable in the incident records, bringing the total number of incidents identified from police sources to 4,382. Finally, the grand total was boosted to 4,792 by the inclusion of another 410 violent incidents identified from the hospital data but not identifiable in any of the police records. The tables also show how many incidents from each source involved one or more actions that were eventually 'crimed' – i.e. were officially recorded as criminal offences of violence against the person or offences against public order.

At first glance, it does not appear that the hospital data added a great deal to what was already known from police records. Not only were 76% of the 1,698 cases reported by the hospital already in police records, but the 410 'new' incidents increased the total of known incidents by only

Table 6.1: Total numbers of alcohol-related incidents in central Cardiff, July 1999 to December 2001, according to the four main data sources

Data source	Type of incident				All incidents	
	Violence		Disorder			
	n	Crimed	n	Crimed	n	Crimed
Incident records	2,163	1,030	1,268	522	3,431	1,552
Crime records	1,391	1,364	1,118	1,098	2,509	2,461
Custody records	1,006	894	1,158	1,045	2,164	1,939
A & E	1,689	758	9	1	1,698	759
Total incidents	2,933	1,370	1,859	1,103	4,792	2,473

Note: The totals are smaller than the sum of their columns as many incidents were recorded in more than one data source (see Table 6.2).

Table 6.2: Overlaps between sources of data

Source of data	Number of incidents of crime or disorder	Number of violent incidents	Number of incidents with crimed assaults
Incident records	3,431	2,163	1,030
In custody/crime but not incident records	951	360	340
Total in police records	4,382	2,523	1,370
In hospital records but not police records	410	410	(potentially 410 extra crimes)
Totals of known incidents	4,792	2,933	(potentially 1,780)
% of incidents added by A & E data	9%	16%	30%

Source: Maguire and Nettleton (2003).

9% (from 4,382 to 4,792). However, it has to be remembered, first of all, that the police figures include many incidents of public disorder not resulting in injury, which one would not expect to result in visits to hospital. If we look only at incidents resulting in assaults (see column 2 of Table 6.2), the hospital data add 16% to the police-derived total. This figure rises to 30% if the comparison is made only with incidents involving at least one crimed offence of assault (column 3). In other words, if every one of the 410 'new' incidents identified by the hospital was reported to and recorded by the police as an assault, the official crime figures for this type of offence would rise by around 30%.[5]

The above analysis suggests that, all things being equal, if one wants as accurate a picture as possible of 'alcohol-related violence and disorder', it is necessary to trawl all four data sources – incident records, crime records, custody records and hospital data. Among these sources, it is clear that the fullest picture is provided by police incident records, which were found to capture 72% of all incidents known from all sources: other police records captured a further 20% and data from the hospital added 9%. However, going beyond the experience of the three projects discussed here, it is also worth considering a variety of other possible sources of data to assist in 'profiling' the phenomenon of alcohol-related crime. Tierney and Hobbs (2003) list a number of such sources which they suggest would be of value to those undertaking local crime audits, including CCTV incident logs (which were used in the TASC database, although in almost all cases the incidents also appeared in the police incident records), ambulance service records, and bus and taxi incident forms. However, while these may well provide some new insights, and while they may add some previously unknown cases to a body of data such as the TASC database, none appears to provide a *comprehensive alternative picture* to that created by police incident and crime data. It might be also argued that victimisation surveys could make a substantial contribution. However, the British Crime Survey produces valid data at force level at best, and at present does not distinguish between 'alcohol related' and any other forms of street violence, nor does it collect data on 'disorder'.

The practical importance of good data

The availability of good data about problems such as alcohol-related violence is not merely of academic importance but can be vital to effective practice in a number of respects. In the context of problem-oriented policing, it is important at all four stages of the 'SARA' process (explained in Chapter 1).

'Scanning'

First of all, reliable data are needed to ensure sound decision-making and rational prioritisation of the use of resources, by allowing effective 'scanning' for problems. To take a simple example, the projects described in this chapter all originated from bids to the Home Office for funding, in which they claimed to offer sound strategies to reduce a particular set of problems identified within their area. This assumes that they had undertaken some initial kind of 'scanning' in which alcohol-related violence was identified as a growing problem within specific areas of the force. However, it is evident that such scanning was based on data that were relatively unsuited to this purpose. First of all, the forces were reliant upon 'violence' data rather than 'alcohol-related violence' data. Indeed, the Nottinghamshire bid relied entirely upon recorded offences of violence against the person for the force area. This identified a number of 'hot-spots' for violence, but no acknowledgement was made that such data could possibly be a gross misrepresentation of the actual picture of alcohol-related violence across the county. Thus, there was no mention that many incidents of the kind they were interested in might not come to police notice; that even if reported, they might not be 'crimed' as violence against the person; and that many recorded offences might not have been alcohol related.

In other words, the initial 'scanning' for alcohol-related violence problems was largely based on a mixture of proxy measures and speculation, rather than reliable empirical evidence. While, in this case, specially created databases later confirmed that the initial concerns about alcohol-related violence were in fact justified, the experience draws attention to the general problem that police records often contain insufficient data on specific types of incident or are not 'research friendly' in the sense of allowing quick electronic trawling to identify cases with specific characteristics (such as being 'alcohol related', or occurring in particular kinds of locations). As a result, funding could potentially be channelled towards 'problems' which are in reality less widespread than believed, while others more deserving of attention fail to come to light.

'Analysis'

Scanning provides some confirmation that a problem of some magnitude exists. To identify a response to these problems there has to be further in-depth analysis of the conditions giving rise to these problems. Here two important factors have to be present. First, the problem has to be set within some kind of analytical framework and, secondly, robust data are required to inform that framework.

The problem analysis triangle or 'PAT' (Hough and Tilley 1998; Leigh *et al*. 1996, 1998) has often been used as an analytical framework to help analysts visualise problems, to consider the key elements of the problem and to analyse the relationships between these elements. Its key elements are outlined in Figure 6.1 in relation to alcohol related violence.

Here the problem analysis triangle asks what it is about the victim, location and offender that help to generate alcohol-related violence.[6] Therefore, further analysis of the underlying conditions that generate such incidents would require data to shed light on:

1 the key characteristics of the victim that may attract violence;
2 the key features of the location/situation that may help to generate violence;
3 the key characteristics of the offender.

Readily available police sources of data are not very informative about any of the above questions. For this reason, the projects all made some attempt to 'dig deeper' by creating special databases. These varied in sophistication, to a large extent depending upon how much effort could be put into 'trawling' other police databases, contacting investigating officers and so on. The main data sources used to inform the projects

Figure 6.1   The problem analysis triangle and alcohol related town centre violence.

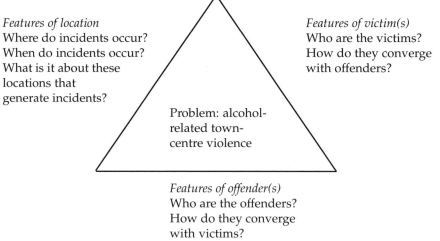

Features of location
Where do incidents occur?
When do incidents occur?
What is it about these
locations that
generate incidents?

Features of victim(s)
Who are the victims?
How do they converge
with offenders?

Problem: alcohol-
related town-
centre violence

Features of offender(s)
Who are the offenders?
How do they converge
with victims?

about each of the three core elements of the triangle are outlined in Table 6.3.

However, information on the above features should only be a starting point if any deeper understanding of the problem is to be achieved. In addition, it is important to explore the nature and immediate genesis of the incidents themselves: for example, what are the most common types of relationship between offenders and victims? What precisely 'triggered' the incident? (e.g. being refused drinks? The attitude of security staff? An argument over a partner?). While some information about the circumstances of assaults was available in crime reports and (to a lesser extent) incident reports, this was usually in free-text form and

Table 6.3: Data sources to allow further problem analysis

Key element of problem analysis triangle	Data sources used to inform projects
Features of location	Police data (most importantly, incident data). Beat level, mapping data
Characteristics of victims	For example, innkeeper data on licensed premises. Hospital data
Characteristics of offenders	Custody records/arrest referral data

to code it for analysis in any but the crudest way would have been a very time-consuming task. In the event, although the coding provided some 'clues' as to the most common reasons for fights occurring (such as the frequency of the entry, 'altercation with door staff'), a great deal remains unknown about the circumstances that triggered most incidents.

'Response'

The day-to-day use of information to guide interventions has been described in outline earlier in the chapter. All three areas had some arrangements by which relevant issues were brought quickly to the attention of the project staff, although these were by no means always followed. In Cardiff, incident reports were supposed to be flagged by the attending police officers with a 'U16' code if they judged them to be alcohol related, while in Cornwall, an 'L10' report form was supposed to be completed and sent to the licensing officers. In both areas, project staff also regularly trawled other databases to pick up cases where these procedures had not been followed. In Nottinghamshire, the onus was on licensing officers to conduct their own daily searches of command and control messages and crime reports. The end result was the capacity in all three cases to identify premises and areas that were experiencing high or increasing levels of violence and thus where resources should be targeted. Most importantly, being able to flag incidents and quickly identify patterns allowed a quick response to incidents. The main responses included the following:

- In Cornwall and Nottingham an incident in a named pub or club would result in an automatic visit from a licensing officer.

- In all three areas, meetings were set up with premises that were identified from the databases as having ongoing problems or to be developing problems. At these meetings, project staff or licensing officers were able to use information from the databases to highlight precise patterns of incidents in those premises, providing them with a strong 'lever' to persuade managers that they had a real problem and should take urgent remedial action.

- Police patrols could be directed towards areas where problems appeared to be particularly prevalent, in some cases at certain times of the day or week.

- In Cardiff especially, several major operations were set up on the basis of detailed data analysis.

As noted earlier, the data were also used on occasion in the TASC project to assist the police in objecting to the granting of a new licence, and to attempt to persuade the council to avoid further growth of licensed premises in an area regarded as 'saturated'.

However, although the databases were a valuable resource for identifying where problems had occurred, there were times when they were not utilised to their full potential. For example, in Nottinghamshire there was evidence that alcohol-related violence was becoming a problem in certain untargeted beat areas while targeted patrols in other areas were having little impact in terms of reducing violence. Further analysis of the problems suggested that high-visibility policing might be an appropriate option for the non-targeted areas. Despite this, police managers persevered with operations that were not particularly successful and did not respond to new problems identified. Again, there was evidence that patrols in some areas were highly successful, though these operations ran only intermittently. Here the evidence suggested that regular patrolling of these areas might have produced further reductions in alcohol-related violence, but no action was taken to respond to the suggestion.

'Assessment'
In addition to providing valuable data for the external evaluations, the databases were used by project staff to monitor and assess their own progress. Regular reports on apparent trends in violence and disorder were prepared for senior officers and for partners on steering groups or Community Safety Partnerships. However, while a fair degree of confidence could be placed in trends apparent from the TASC database, owing to the consistency and thoroughness of the trawling of data sources, the databases in the other two areas were primarily geared to facilitating the day-to-day work of licensing officers, rather than to evaluation, and were less rigorously constructed and maintained. This highlights a general problem that unless, as was the case in Cardiff, people with close knowledge of evaluation methods are closely involved in the design of such a database and in developing and monitoring its 'operating rules', it is likely to become unreliable for the purpose of evaluation.

Final comments

The overall conclusion concerning the kinds of data needed to sustain an effective 'problem-solving' response to alcohol-related crime and disorder (or indeed, any kind of crime problem which is perceived to be significant in scale, but about which there is little routinely collected evidence), is that it is well worth the investment of appointing a dedicated data analyst to produce and maintain a special database, if necessary by manually trawling other sources of information. It is also sensible to start such a database in advance of any significant set of interventions (such as a funded project) in order to create a baseline against which to measure the impact of the interventions – this can, of course, be undertaken retrospectively, although the task then becomes much more difficult. In the long term, of course, the data collection task would be made very much simpler if officers were persuaded to 'flag' relevant incidents in a consistent manner, or if more thought were given to the recording of incidents so that they can be searched electronically, as opposed to manually, for the presence of specific factors such as the consumption of alcohol or location in or outside licensed premises.

Notes

1   Other partners included local universities, transport companies, sports clubs and the local council.
2   Since the Home Office funded project ended, the scheme has become part of mainstream approaches to crime reduction in Nottinghamshire, funded by police and other partners, and the licensing officers and arrest referral workers are now permanent employees.
3   Some attempts were also made to get a local A & E department to record details of alcohol-related assaults, but this proved unproductive as staff were overstretched and often forgot to log basic details.
4   In addition to the database, evaluation data were collected through interviews with or questionnaires to 54 licensees, 58 door supervisors and 27 arrested people who took part in the arrest referral scheme.
5   It has to be remembered that in the present study the comparison being made is with a very specific subgroup of violent incidents – those involving alcohol-related assaults occurring on the street or in licensed premises in two police sectors. It may well be that the 'dark figure' for other types of violence such as domestic assault is larger, and that hospital data would reveal a greater proportion of hidden offences of these kinds. This would be consistent with findings in Bristol by Shepherd *et al.* (1989).
6   Similarities have been noted here to routine activities theory (Cohen and Felson 1979). This postulates that for a crime to occur, motivated offenders and suitable targets have to converge in time and space in the absence of capable guardianship.

References

Cohen, L. and Felson, M. (1979) 'Social change and crime rate trends: a routine activity approach', *American Sociological Review*, 44: 588–608.

Deehan, A. (1999) *Alcohol and Crime: Taking Stock*. Policing and Reducing Crime Unit Research Series 3. London: Home Office.

Deehan, A. and Saville, E. (2000) *Crime and Disorder Partnerships: Alcohol Related Crime and Disorder in Audit and Strategy Documents*. Briefing Note 9/2000. London: Home Office.

Graham, K. and Homel, R. (1997) 'Creating safer bars', in M. Plant *et al.* (eds) *Alcohol: Minimising the Harm – What Works?*. London: Free Association Press.

Hobbs, D., Hadfield, P., Lister, S. and Winlow, S. (2002) ' "Door Lore": the art and economics of intimidation', *British Journal of Criminology*, 42(2): 352–70.

Hobbs, D., Hadfield, P., Lister, S. and Winlow, S. (2003) *Bouncers: Violence and Governance in the Night-time Economy*. Oxford: Oxford University Press.

Hobbs, D., Lister, S., Hadfield, P., Winlow, S. and Hall, S. (2000) 'Receiving shadows: liminality, governance and the night-time economy', *British Journal of Sociology*, 51(4): 701–17.

Homel, R. and Clarke, J. (1994) 'The prediction and prevention of violence in pubs and clubs', in R.V. Clarke (ed.) *Crime Prevention Studies. Vol. 3*. Monsey, NY: Criminal Justice Press.

Hopkins, M. and Maguire, M. (2003) 'Reducing alcohol related violence in Nottinghamshire'. Unpublished draft report to Home Office.

Hough, J.J.M. and Tilley, N. (1998) *Auditing Disorder: Guidance for Local Partnerships*. Crime Detection and Prevention Series 91. London: Home Office.

Kershaw, C., Chivite-Matthews, N., Thomas, C. and Aust, R. (2001) *The 2001 British Crime Survey*. Home Office Statistical Bulletin 18/01. London: Home Office.

Leigh, A., Read, T. and Tilley, N. (1996) *Problem-oriented Policing: Brit Pop*. Crime Prevention and Detection Series 75. London: Home Office.

Leigh, A., Read, T. and Tilley, N. (1998) *Brit Pop II: Problem-oriented Policing in Practice*. Police Research Series 93. London: Home Office.

LGA (2002) *All Day and All of the Night? An LGA Discussion Paper*. London: Local Government Association.

Light, R. (2000) 'Liberalising liquor licensing law: order into chaos?', *New Law Journal*, 23 June: 926–9.

Lister, S., Hadfield, P., Hobbs, D. and Winlow, S. (2001) 'Accounting for bouncers: occupational licensing as a mechanism for regulation', *Criminal Justice*, 1(4): 363–84.

Maguire, M. and Nettleton, H. (2003) *Reducing Alcohol Related Violence and Disorder: An Evaluation of the TASC Project*. Home Office Research Study 265. London: Home Office.

Maguire, M. and Swainson, V. (2003) 'Reducing violence associated with licensed premises: Project Amethyst and the role of licensing officers'. Unpublished draft report to Home Office.

Morris, S. (1998) *Clubs, Drugs and Doormen*. Crime Detection and Prevention Series Paper 86, London: Home Office Police Research Group.

NACRO (2001) *Drink and Disorder: Alcohol, Crime and Anti-Social Behaviour*. London: National Association for the Care and Resettlement of Offenders.

Purser, R. (1997) *Prevention Approaches to Alcohol Related Crime – a Review of a Community Based Initiative from a UK Midlands City*. Birmingham: Aquarius.

Ramsey, M. (1982) *City Centre Crime: A Situational Approach to Prevention*. Research and Planning Unit Paper 10. London: Home Office.

Ramsey, M. (1989) *Downtown Drinkers: The Perceptions and Fears of the Public in a City Centre*. Crime Prevention Unit Paper 19. London: Home Office.

Shepherd, J., Shapland, M. and Scully, C. (1989) 'Recording of violent offences by the police: an accident and emergency department perspective', *Medicine, Science and the Law*, 29: 251–57.

Simmons, J. (2000) *Review of Crime Statistics: A Discussion Document*. London: Home Office.

Social Issues Research Centre (2002) *Counting the Cost: The Measurement and Recording of Alcohol-related Violence and Disorder*. London: The Portman Group.

Tierney, J. and Hobbs, D. (2003) *Alcohol-related Crime and Disorder Data: Guidance for Local Partnerships* (www.homeoffice.gov.uk/rds/onlinepubs1.html).

Tuck, M. (1989) *Drinking and Disorder: A Study of Non-metropolitan Violence*. Home Office Research Study 108. London: Home Office.

Chapter 7

Theory into practice: implementing a market reduction approach to property crime

Charlotte Harris, Chris Hale and Steve Uglow

... if there were no receivers there would be no thieves (Colquhoun 1796).

Introduction

There has been increasing interest among criminologists in the role of handlers or 'fences' in the distribution chain of stolen property and the potential of research into this illicit market structure to inform theft prevention strategies. There is 'compelling logic to the idea that disrupting the distribution chain, and the market, for stolen ... goods will reduce the motivation for stealing such items'.[1] Research articles published around the world have discussed the possible impact on rates of burglary and theft of disrupting the markets thieves use to dispose of the property they steal. These works have been mainly descriptive and limited to recommendations as to what could be done to disrupt these markets. There had been no sustained attempt to put the suggested interventions into practice and measure their actual impact on property crime levels.

Such an attempt was started in 1999 when two Crime and Disorder Partnerships were funded under the Targeted Policing Initiative (TPI) to test out what former Home Office researcher Mike Sutton had called the 'market reduction approach'. This was a 'strategic, systematic and routine problem-solving framework for action against the roots of theft' (Sutton *et al.* 2001). We were appointed as independent evaluators to the two projects and what follows draws on this involvement. The chapter will describe the theory of the market reduction approach (MRA) and some of the work done by others in the same area before describing how the two projects used these ideas to develop their interventions and some of the issues that arose about implementation. The chapter concludes with a discussion about any disparity between the 'compelling logic' of the MRA and what was achieved and the likely reasons for this – is the theory flawed or did the projects fail to implement their chosen tactics fully?

Theory

Overview of research on the role of receivers of stolen goods

As the quotation at the beginning of this chapter from the eighteenth-century English law reformer, Patrick Colquhoun, shows, the idea of the importance of the fence to the thief's activity and productivity is not new.

This neat concept becomes more problematic when practitioners planning to target the handling of stolen property have to unpick what they actually mean by a 'receiver'. The type of interventions thought likely to be effective would necessarily be different dependent on the 'type' of receiving involved. Colquhoun (1796) himself distinguished between the 'Innocent Receiver', for whom for example 'rule setting' marketing measures (Sutton 1998) might work, and the 'Careless Receiver' (who, as the name implies, does not care about the origins of the goods bought), for whom tactics aimed at increasing the perceived risks of handling – their arrest and charge or the arresting and charging of similar offenders – might be more appropriate.

Subsequent writers also discriminated between types of receiver. American law reformer, Jerome Hall (1952), in his seminal study on theft focused on the more knowing of these receiving types. He developed a threefold typology of 'Lay', 'Occasional' and 'Professional' receivers. The first who 'knowingly buys stolen property for his own consumption' is similar to the English workplace entrepreneurs of Henry's (1975) study of 'the property crimes committed by ordinary people in legitimate jobs'. The professional receiver has more in common with the full-time fences who are the subjects of Klockars' (1974) and Steffensmeier's (1986) ethnographic case studies, 'Vince' and 'Sam' being businessmen who both owned successful second-hand shops through which they knowingly bought and sold stolen goods.

The magnitude of the influence of the role of the fence in the thief's motivation, from 'innocently' encouraging theft of certain items by their willingness to buy, to 'ordering' particular goods, to identifying victims who own the right property, is discussed in Walsh's 1977 study documenting interviews with 115 fences known to the American police. Walsh advocates a reconceptualisation of the theft problem as a 'stolen property system' in which the theft is only the first stage, but stops short of identifying interventions based on this system.

In a theoretical article, Roselius and Benton (1973) propose looking at the workings of stolen goods markets in the same way as you would legitimate markets and using marketing theory to suggest interventions. They argue that the 'promotional aspects' of the business, such as the use of classified advertisements in newspapers to sell goods, provide the greatest opportunities for law enforcement officers to block traffic.

Cromwell et al. (1993, 1994) undertook similar research with potential consumers of stolen goods. This suggested that 'direct marketing' to the ultimate consumer and to part-time amateur fences is common. While, unsurprisingly, the opportunity to buy stolen goods correlates directly with the frequency of doing so, thieves were said purposefully to choose prospective buyers in the same fashion they chose victims.[2] Cromwell et al. offered another typology of fences – including the 'Associational Fence' (for example, police officers and defence attorneys whose legitimate occupation places them in close association or interaction with thieves) and the 'Neighbourhood Hustler' (who makes a marginal living wheeling and dealing outside the conventional economic system).

Ways of tackling the market for stolen goods

In the late 1990s following two initial articles by Mike Sutton (1993, 1995) exploring the potential for tackling theft by addressing the stolen goods markets, the Home Office published three substantial works containing recommendations for practitioners.

The first of these (Kock et al. 1996) analysed data on the theft of desirable electrical goods. In 1996, when the study was published, these were VCRs, TVs and hi-fi equipment. The study included interviews with police officers, with business representatives, such as insurers and manufacturers, and with offenders. They devised 'Operation Circuit Breaker', a schedule of tactical interventions to disrupt each stage of the stolen electrical goods distribution chain. These included such short-term options as, for example, 'Install tracking devices on selected lorry loads of electrical items' and 'Carry ultraviolet lamp on all dwelling searches and examine all electrical goods'. Longer-term options in-cluded initiatives such as 'Develop easily accessible cross-force records of identifiable stolen electrical goods' and 'Liaise with manufacturers of electrical goods to get better property marking especially re future aspirational goods'.

The second study, Clarke (1999), suggested that just as there are locations where crime is more likely to happen – 'hot-spots' – and people who appear more vulnerable to victimisation – 'repeat victims', some goods – 'hot products' – are more likely to be stolen. In Clarke's study these goods included jewellery, videos, cash, stereos and televisions as well as frequently shoplifted stock such as cassettes, cigarettes, alcoholic drinks and fashion items. Such lists would be subject to local variation; in America they would probably include guns (see Cromwell et al. 1993). All these items share characteristics that Clarke summarised in the acronym CRAVED: concealable, removable, available, valuable, enjoyable and disposable. His analysis used data on reported thefts – accepting that such data do not necessarily reflect exactly what thieves most crave but what they are able to steal. His recommendations addressed both tactics focused on the markets for stolen goods and more traditional crime prevention concerns aimed at preventing the original offence. They centre on the identification of existing and future local hot products and the development of interventions designed to make these items less vulnerable to theft and more difficult to dispose of. For example, he suggests the use of technology such as ink tags to stain clothing when stolen and the deactivation of digital equipment. He also suggested trying to engender an attitude change among manufacturers so that security and retainability become a selling feature as much as exclusivity. Clarke also advocates 'removing excuses' from people marginally involved in the stolen property distribution chain who seek to 'neutralise' (Cromwell et al. 1993) their involvement from real criminal behaviour, by targeting them with 'a publicity campaign focused on the harmful effects of buying stolen goods'.

The third and most influential of these studies for the projects discussed below was Sutton (1998) which first introduced the 'market reduction approach' – 'attempting to reduce demand and supply to criminal markets as a new method of crime control'. He stressed the approach was not aimed at specific thieves in specific theft situations but at 'the market and the players in it who affect many situations and many thieves by providing incentives and inducements for theft'. He questioned the unidirectional thief–receiver relationship that previous writers had espoused, suggesting that these markets should be seen as both a downstream consequence of theft and as an underlying motivational force driving much acquisitive offending.

Sutton interviewed a sample of 45 thieves, burglars and handlers of all ages from around England. He asked about how they operated, how they stole, what they stole and what they did with the property they stole. He also analysed data from the 1994 British Crime Survey that had included questions to half the respondents about whether they had ever been offered or bought stolen goods.

From this Sutton identified yet another typology of fences. Unlike Cromwell's typology based on the professional status of the subject's handling activity (how it fitted into the way they made their living) and Clarke's based on the commodity being hawked, Sutton's was based on the nature and location of the transaction, who was involved and where it took place.

He identified five types of chain within the distribution of stolen goods. From:

1 thief to commercial outlet;
2 commercial outlets to consumer;
3 thief to consumer (hawking);
4 thief to network of friends or acquaintances (network sales); and
5 thief to residential fence.

Within these Sutton focused on a number of specific findings, which could influence choice of intervention tactics. For example:

- Small business owners are frequently offered stolen goods by people they have never met before.

- Property marking did not deter thieves from stealing or handlers from buying marked goods.

- For the novice thief the experience of success or failure to convert stolen property into cash appears to play an important part in whether he or she continues to offend.

- Disputes over stolen property negotiations cannot be passed to legitimate channels of redress and are therefore liable to be settled with violence (so, Sutton suggests, it might be worth following up otherwise unexplained violent attacks to see if they are property related).

- Taxis (and black bin bags) are commonly used to transport burglars and stolen goods, but such goods were not sold at car-boot sales.[3]

Sutton highlighted a number of factors which predisposed people to *buy* or *be offered* stolen goods – being a young male, being poor, living in an area categorised as having a drugs problem, being unable to cope on the family income and having no household insurance. Overall 10% of the BCS sample questioned admitted that within the last five years they had bought goods they knew or believed to be stolen.

Addressing the five particular markets identified, Sutton suggested a number of specific interventions, which are described in Box 7.1.

Sutton proposed attacking all five of the marketplaces he identified simultaneously, in order to prevent displacement from the more visible to the more secretive locations.[4] He also endorsed longer-term measures designed to consolidate the effects of enforcement and 'price offenders out of the market' by developing ways to make certain luxury goods

Box 7.1: Specific market reduction interventions and possible implementation problems

A transaction register to disrupt theft to commercial outlet sales
Second-hand shopkeepers would record details of sellers (backed up by some form of identification) and the items sold. Sutton identified potential problems with this. Customers selling stolen property might quite easily also provide false forms of identity such as stolen driving licences or households bills. Furthermore dealers might use the scheme to *facilitate* their purchase of illicit goods if they believed that by showing that correct procedures had been followed their risk of arrest would be reduced. Because of this, Sutton suggested the onus should be placed on the shopkeeper to require a higher degree of proof of ownership – such as a receipt, original packaging or even a document supplied by the police to say that expensive goods offered for sale had not been reported stolen.

Property marking to disrupt the commercial outlet to consumer sales
In the commercial sales environment, the consumer is deemed innocent. Sutton recommended the use of property-marking schemes to reduce the value of marked second-hand goods to sellers and to alert buyers to the likelihood of such goods being stolen. Given the low take-up of such schemes generally, he suggested liaison with manufacturers to encourage property marking at source, but acknowledged current legal difficulties with the validity of warranties on goods deemed to have been altered.

Publicity to disrupt hawking sales
Sutton advocated publicity schemes to increase the awareness of the less-than-innocent purchaser of the links between buying cheap items of questionable origin and the original theft. He suggested these could work in a similar way to the 'Don't drink and drive' campaigns which are credited with considerable success in reducing alcohol-related car crashes.

'Rule setting' to disrupt network sales
Sutton suggested 'rule-setting' schemes spelling out what is and is not acceptable behaviour. These would emphasise that stealing-to-order markets thrive within network sales and stimulate theft. Precisely what mechanisms would operate to change behaviour is not clear and Sutton admitted that 'these sales take place in what is likely to be one of the most difficult markets to police'.

Targeting residential fences to disrupt neighbourhood sales
Sutton proposed focusing more police resources in 'identifying and arresting residential fences'. Again precisely what should be done to operationalise this is not clear, but the idea stems from some of his subjects who told him that the arrest of their fences deterred their thieving. However, Sutton notes that it would be unlikely that such deterrence would be felt by those offending to sustain a drug habit. Because of the prevailing links between acquisitive crime and the need to buy drugs, Sutton suggests developing a strategy to reduce illicit drug markets at the same time as reducing stolen goods markets.

---

affordable legitimately for low-income groups. For example manufacturers should be encouraged to lower the initial prices of new products by prolonging the period over which they seek to recover their investment. These ideas are expanded in the second of Sutton's major publications on the topic, published in 2001, midway into the implementation period of the two TPI projects (Sutton *et al.* 2001 p. 91).

This work, based as it was on growing experience, was a more practically focused report. Since illegal trading frequently breached administrative regulations affecting health and safety, the environment, planning, income tax and VAT, the authors suggested that stolen goods markets can usefully be tackled through inter-agency groups. These might involve the police, local authorities, the Benefits Agency, housing associations, Customs and Excise, the Department of the Environment, Inland Revenue and Trading Standards.

They devised the acronym ERASOR (extra routine and systematic opportunistic research) to describe the process to obtain detailed local information about stolen goods markets. This involves using traditional and 'extra' crime analysis and mapping to identify 'hot products' and stolen goods markets, prioritising markets to target, devising a strategy and specific tactics to undermine the targeted markets, and continuous monitoring. A number of tactics were put forward to address each of Sutton's specific marketplaces (see Box 7.2). The ERASOR information

Box 7.2: Interventions for tackling marketplaces for stolen goods

---

Commercial fence supplies and commercial sales markets
- Using existing intelligence and ERASOR information to identify which shops and businesses thieves visit in order to sell stolen goods.

- Seeking to implement local legislation requiring traders to keep records of the name and address of anyone who sells them second-hand goods.

- Utilising inter-agency support to crack down on any irregularities committed by businesses known to deal in stolen goods.

For residential fence supplies markets
- Using existing and ERASOR information to find out who the drug dealers and fences are, whom they deal with and how they operate.

- Using mobile CCTV cameras and surveillance teams to gather evidence by observing the homes of known or suspected residential fences.

- Utilising inter-agency partners such as local authority housing departments to evict those illegally trading out of residential addresses.

Hawking markets
- Surveillance.

- Analysing ERASOR information and existing criminal intelligence to identify the housing estates and pubs where hawkers frequently sell stolen goods.

- Setting up special telephone hotlines or work with Crimestoppers to invite the public to inform on pubs where hawking is taking place.

- Arresting hawkers and their customers.

---

was to come from interviews (undertaken by both police and social scientists) with offenders, police officers, prisoners, informants, shop-keepers and the public, particularly victims of burglary and neighbours of fences.

The authors also discuss 'consolidating' the successes of each crackdown by addressing the underlying causes of the crime problem. They suggested:

- recycling recovered, but unclaimed, stolen goods retrieved from crackdown operations or other police forces;

- seeking to reduce shoplifting (since research has shown that this type of offending often serves as an entry point in criminal careers); and

- working with the business community to design and implement competitive marketing strategies to undermine stolen goods markets.

At around the same time as Sutton and his colleagues were publishing these studies, similar work was being undertaken in Australia. An article by Freiberg (1997) explored the possibilities of regulating the market for stolen goods by treating it as any other market with its own suppliers, distributors and purchasers. One of the interventions Freiberg described was a 'sting operation' involving the setting up of a pawnbrokers by the New South Wales police 'in order to attract persons wishing to sell stolen goods' (1997: 243) that resulted in numerous arrests. Stevenson et al.[5] built on the work of Sutton interviewing 267 imprisoned burglars in New South Wales about how they disposed of the property they had stolen. Because of the numbers interviewed, this work was able to investigate particular elements of the stolen goods market in more detail. It looked, for example, at the links between types of thief – such as casual, drug addicted – and preferred method of disposal of goods, and the frequency with which thieves used particular outlets – i.e. the relative importance of each avenue for them. The most common methods of disposing of goods overall were through a drug dealer or selling to family and friends, fences, pawnbrokers and second-hand shops or other local traders. Because of the extensive links between drugs and stolen goods exchange, in the long term there needed to be increased co-ordination between drug law enforcement and property crime control strategies, particularly as regards the exchange of criminal intelligence.

In the majority of the literature on stolen goods markets, the criminal is viewed as a rational operator (see also Ladouceur 1993) whose offending behaviour is a matter of choice, even if that choice is where to sell stolen goods to maximise money available for drugs. From this assumptions are made about the effect of enforcement in particular areas. If the thief makes a rational decision to steal in order to make money and if elements in the choice equation alter – for example it becomes more difficult to sell goods – then he or she may desist and try something else, perhaps non-criminal. To make these links, it is necessary to ignore some of the other factors mentioned in the research about why people buy, and probably sell, stolen goods and how this illicit marketplace fits into local economies and lifestyles. Few of these factors – such as 'perceived economic necessity, freedom from the fear of threat to valued relationships and goals' – '[lend themselves] easily to policy aimed at reducing stolen-goods purchases, and therefore, thefts' (Sheley and Bailey 1985: 412).

It is therefore no surprise that of all the sorts of interventions suggested in the research above, the projects – whose activities are outlined in the next section – tended to choose those with a more discrete focus.

Practice: operationalising the market reduction approach

The two projects funded by the Crime Reduction Programme – one in the north and one in the south of England – were each given just over £400,000 over three years to implement proposals to reduce acquisitive crime by tackling the markets for stolen goods. As with a number of the other projects outlined in this book the bids were put together in a relatively short timescale. One consisted of quite bare outlines while the other had a lengthy list of plausible-sounding tactics.

South Town

Background
The South Town project began first. Its structure and logic were heavily influenced by Mike Sutton who was personally involved in the early stages. The basis of the project strategy was Sutton's typology and the project was managed and led by the police. Many other agencies were initially invited to contribute ideas – from the Fire Service to retail organisations. These were soon reduced to an executive board of representatives from the police, local authority and the Chamber of Commerce and a tactical group involving agencies with enforcement potential such as housing, planning, Customs and Excise, and Trading Standards whose level of attendance also varied. On a day-to-day level, specific interventions were devised by a succession of police sergeant project managers who reported to the executive board. Limited resources meant the project tackled Sutton's types of markets sequentially rather than simultaneously as he suggested.

From thief to commercial outlet and commercial outlet to consumer

Combining the first two of Sutton's marketplaces (from thief to commercial outlet and commercial outlet to consumer), considerable time and resource were initially devoted to setting up and running a voluntary recording scheme with local second-hand shops and pawnbrokers. They were encouraged to keep records of all their buying transactions including names and addresses of the sellers and a detailed description of the goods. Some shopkeepers took proof of identity, made a note of the time of transactions and took photographs of the sellers.[6] Many displayed a project poster publicising the project's intention to 'Stamp out the markets for stolen goods'. Once officers were dedicated to the task of visiting and liaising with the shops, a steady flow of stolen property was identified and burglars and thieves arrested. If intelligence suggested that those not co-operating were trading in stolen goods, surveillance operations were mounted. Although a number of raids took place, no handling convictions ensued, although enforcement action was taken against some of these individuals by Trading Standards, Customs and Excise, and local authority planning.

From thief to consumer

South Town then moved to Sutton's third market 'type' (from thief to consumer) and attempts were made to set up a similar voluntary scheme involving pub licensees. They encouraged them to register with the project and report any suspicious activity. This had very little success. Another tactic was to search the second-hand advertisement press, using Internet versions and scanning technology, to locate suspiciously repetitive advertisers. However, there were few repeat advertisers who were anything but innocent and of just three cases meriting follow-up, none was pursued. Finally, despite Sutton's findings that car-boot sales were not used by offenders or their associates to sell stolen goods, they were briefly targeted. The project was influenced by the oft-stated conviction by members of the public, particularly second-hand shop-keepers subject to increased attention, that this was so. However, they found little robust evidence of the selling of stolen goods. Nevertheless there was a benefit for one of the partners – Trading Standards – in a number of cases of counterfeit goods being discovered.

Network sales and residential fences

In the latter months of the project, attention was turned to the fourth and fifth types of marketplace – network sales and residential fences. This involved the collection of information on people dealing in stolen goods from home or in other premises not part of a legitimate business. Their home addresses were mapped and 'clusters' of them targeted. However, as Sutton had predicted, this did prove to be 'one of the most difficult markets to police' and no handling prosecutions followed. The project developed a number of intelligence packages but these were to be subsumed by a larger police undercover operation. This infiltrated the stolen goods markets in an identified stolen property hot-spot, where known fences operated and large numbers of burglaries took place. The idea of a sting operation setting up a second-hand shop as in the New South Wales study was not pursued as previous experience suggested all this might do was generate new markets rather than provide intelligence and evidence on existing ones. Instead they placed undercover officers into the area. Because of the nature of the networks unearthed, stolen goods markets became a lower priority and the bulk of the ensuing arrests and charges related to drugs.

Marketing and property identification
The project also got involved in activity relating to marketing, property identification and a number of other discrete initiatives. A substantial proportion of project funds was spent on marketing activity. These were used in tandem with a number of the different strands of activity described above but also had the more general aim of telling the public the police were 'doing something'. Activities ranged from attending supermarket roadshows to the distribution of posters and postcards targeted at those in the lower socioeconomic groups (those frequenting job centres, DSS offices, sports centres, social clubs and pubs and living in certain areas). These spelt out the risks of handling stolen goods and the links between the original theft and buying stolen goods. A website was set up to inform the public about the project's activities.

At various times during the project's lifetime the police attempted to enhance the ease of identification of property. They looked at improving the recording of the details of stolen property by central call centre staff and crime scene officers. They tried increasing the extent of property marking by targeting the most vulnerable homes and encouraging retailers to mark at the point of sale. Finally they tried to ensure that any marked property was immediately recognised by equipping all patrol cars with torches that detected ultraviolet markings.

Other interventions
South Town employed several other initiatives influenced to varying degrees by Sutton's ideas:

- They investigated the possibilities of recycling recovered items of stolen property to uninsured victims of burglary.

- They entered discussions with a local taxi firm to gather intelligence on the transporting of property.

- They devised creative methods of collecting lost intelligence – for example, employing a 'case file reader' who reviewed crime investigation files. These often contain a wealth of information about subjects peripheral to the substantive inquiry but which can be useful in compiling a network chart of associates and those who do business with one another.

- They also undertook some work in stemming the supply flow to stolen goods markets by investing in burglary prevention initiatives such as alleygating.[7] It could be said – and we did say – that this work was outside the scope of a market reduction project and more in line with traditional crime prevention. However, when the Sutton 'manual' describes similar interventions it can be a difficult position to sustain.

What can be said about the impact of these interventions?

The project collected aggregate figures on property stolen, property recovered, numbers of acquisitive crimes of various types reported, numbers of acquisitive crimes of various types detected and hot property types per week. While it became increasingly better at gathering input and output data (examples of the latter include numbers of posters produced and numbers of visits to second-hand shops), it did little close analytical work on the data available about thefts and the recovery of certain types of property. This is possibly because the project 'action researcher' left in the early months and was never replaced, in part because of a skills deficit in that it proved difficult to find someone else with the necessary experience to undertake research and make practical recommendations.

Outcomes

Analysis of the aggregate reported crime statistics proved disappointing in the sense that there were not huge drops in reported acquisitive crime or rises in detected acquisitive crime over and above what was going on in any other area of the force. Looking at key acquisitive crimes individually, the evaluation examined figures of monthly recorded 'burglary in dwelling' and 'burglary other' for 66 months covering periods both before and after the introduction of the MRA. The same data for the rest of the force area were also examined as a benchmark. There was a significant reduction in average monthly recorded 'burglary in dwelling' in the period after the tactics were adopted. However, the force as a whole saw similar reductions making it questionable as to whether the successes in South Town were attributable simply to the MRA. It should be mentioned here, however, that the Chief Constable was so pleased with the scheme that at quite at early stage many of the project ideas were rolled out to all other areas. For 'burglary other' there was a significantly larger fall in average monthly rates in South Town as compared with the wider force. However, it proved impossible except in very general terms (i.e. the area had been focusing on property crime and rates went down) to link this drop to specific project activity, which had not particularly targeted property stolen in 'burglary other' offences. The property types being stolen remained fairly static – cash always being top with jewellery a close second – with only seasonal variations such that, for example, the theft of garden equipment went up each spring.

North Town

Background

The second project was less influenced by Sutton's typologies and there was more emphasis on the identification of local problems and closer day-to-day working with the local authority. The civilian project manager arranged early brainstorming sessions among its multi-agency membership to discuss strategy and tactics. Some of the first options explored were aimed at gathering intelligence about the illicit distribution of local 'hot property' – computers and pedal cycles. The project investigated the possibilities of installing tracking devices and property marking these items.

Early operations involved a number of local agencies. Within the first six months of the project a day of raids following the identification of targets thought to be involved in the illicit economy by the partners saw prosecutions by Trading Standards and the Benefits Agency for safety offences and benefit fraud. A later target – a suspected handler in receipt of benefit – was also prosecuted for fraud but not eventually for property crime. There were disagreements about the boundaries of the project – could the project fund an operation against a suspected handler who turned out to be dealing drugs? Where were the parameters of market reduction to be drawn and who was to be targeted – handlers or their customers? How was information gleaned from custody interviews or informants to be acted upon?

Marketing/rule setting
As at South Town, this project undertook numerous publicity campaigns, each one aimed at eliciting information from target groups. There was a poster and radio advertisement aimed at young people featuring a teenager who had had his DVD stolen; a poster for pubs showing a suspect transaction with the woman involved in a cell; a poster designed through a children's competition; and car stickers. Each piece was designed to emphasise the risks of being caught handling stolen goods (with the maximum sentence of 14 years highlighted); to make explicit the link between the 'misery' of theft and buying a bargain in suspicious circumstances; and to ask for any information relating to stolen goods markets.

Intelligence gathering
After the project employed a full-time police inspector in charge of inter-vention, a number of operations were undertaken against increasingly sophisticated targets. These targets were chosen on the basis of the type of crime that was feeding the market rather than on the basis of one specific hot product. For example, initially the project wanted to impact on 'domestic burglary' figures. As a police performance indicator these were important to the police and justified the use of police resources on the project. Information was sought on those handlers who bought the types of goods stolen in house burglaries. Enforcement information was gathered through a number of the traditional sources identified by Sutton – informants, members of the public, custody interviews, police officers – but this was not done routinely but purposively for each target or target group. Surveillance was also undertaken on a number of targets both in residential settings and elsewhere. Resource-intensive property-viewing days were organised for the public to identify some of the property seized in raids, though with limited success unless items had particularly identifiable features – one victim identified a sander which he had had stolen from him from the colour of his home-made sandpaper.

Research information was collected by the project researcher who undertook a number of interviews with offenders about stolen goods markets. However, these sessions were periodic rather than regular and were eventually discontinued. These interviews had suggested that local offenders used taxis to transport stolen property. As taxi firm call-outs have to be recorded for Trading Standards, the project sought to map the records of one taxi firm against reported burglaries. Trading Standards also set up a visiting regime to second-hand shops, which under local legislation were obliged to keep records of transactions in contrast to the voluntary scheme in the South Town project. The agency was also involved in attempts to scan in the local second-hand advertisement press.

Links between stolen goods markets and drug use

Recognising the links between stolen goods markets and drug use and dealing, the project wanted to incorporate some element of drug treatment work within its remit. This would have formed some kind of longer-term consolidation to stem the motivation to supply stolen goods markets by theft. They contracted a prison link worker to work with prisoners serving less than 12 months for acquisitive crime, for whom previously there was no support provision. This worker had difficulty in contacting local prisoners who were moved around the prison system away from the prison local to the area.

Monitoring

Much of the project manager's monitoring activity was concentrated on input and output measures, what was being spent, by whom and examining whether what had been promised was being delivered.

Outcomes

Aggregate figures for reported crime were supplied but again analysis proved disappointing in that the project area showed no more decrease in rates of acquisitive crime than elsewhere in the force. Again looking at key crimes individually, figures for reported domestic burglary showed no evidence of substantially reduced levels following the onset of the project compared with the rest of the force. Similarly there is no evidence of any impact on the 'burglary other' figures. There is, however, one point worth noting. If June 2001, the date the full time police interventions officer arrived, is taken as the point at which the project began to function effectively then the following months showed a 9.4% reduction in average recorded figures for 'burglary in a dwelling' compared with 7.1% force wide. Although weak this suggests the co-ordination of intelligence gathering was beginning to have an impact.

Empirical divide between theory and practice: discussion

The data that we have suggest that the interventions in neither North Town nor South Town had as much of an impact on crime reduction as the intuitive logic of the theory would imply. Why was this?

- Is the theory flawed? Does disrupting markets for stolen goods have no effect on rates of acquisitive crime?

- Did Sutton and others underestimate the problems of enacting their recommendations?

- Were the implementations selected not suited to particular local conditions?

- Were the data available just not sufficient to detect impact?

Is the theory flawed?

The problems encountered by the projects all related to operationalising the theory. Talking about property marking in the first of his books, Sutton quotes a Swedish researcher saying 'the actual theory ... is reasonable but that reality turns out to be other than the theory assumes' (Knutsson 1984). While implementation has been difficult there is certainly not sufficient evidence from the two projects to suggest that the compelling logic of the theory of market reduction is unsound.

Is the theory too difficult to implement?

There is also no doubt that it is easier to describe stolen goods markets in general and suggest what could be good ways to tackle these markets than actually to implement these tactics and monitor their effectiveness. Some of the problems were underestimated. Initial discussions in groups like the North Town's 'Fagin' group involving intelligence officers from a number of local agencies came up with lengthy lists of potentially good ideas. But not all these 'good ideas' proved feasible, actionable or good value for money (in the face of competing priorities for resources). Many required a considerable infrastructure that may be either time-consuming to construct or prove ultimately undoable within the time frame of a small-scale project. Some examples illustrating these points will be expanded upon before the last two questions posed at the beginning of this section regarding local implementation and data are addressed.

Feasible

In a number of cases, the theorists suggested specific interventions which proved particularly problematic when attempted. Kock et al.'s (1996) suggestion that tracking devices should be inserted into hot property sounds feasible. North Town explored this in relation to their local hot property product – computers – which were being stolen in large numbers from schools. But:

- they couldn't locate a tracking device small enough to go into a suitably desirable computer;

- arranging resources available for tracking the computer whenever it got stolen proved difficult; and

- no suitable 'victim' was willing to act as bait.

Similarly Sutton *et al.*'s (2001) suggestions about recycling recovered and other property to try to 'price offenders out of the market' was investigated. South Town explored this in relation to their plan to recycle recovered items of property to uninsured victims of burglary. But:

- there were issues of consumer safety – if the police sold such goods would they be liable if they malfunctioned; and

- there were issues of how such sales would fit into the marketplace – how would local sellers of new goods react to being undercut, and would buyers want what they happened to be offered by the police or would they want the latest version which they could order from a fence?

On a more general level, Sutton *et al.* suggest the use of surveillance to target both hawking markets and residential fences. In practice both North Town and South Town found such locations very 'tight' – it was difficult to install any kind of camera (or stranger) without drawing attention to it. Targets were often surveillance aware and there were occasions where they did become aware of surveillance. There were also occasions where the owner of the property in which the camera was placed was deemed at risk because the evidentiary footage, which would be shown during any court case, could only have been shot from one place.

Actionable

Though some ideas were feasible, they proved not to be actionable. Some targets were identified by the theorists as generic locations for the sale and transport of stolen goods, such as pubs and taxis. Suspecting or even knowing that stolen goods trade does take place through these media does not make these places actionable – does not make them a realistic point of intervention. Problems of surveillance in pubs have already been mentioned. The pub licensee scheme in South Town, whereby licensees would inform the project of any suspicious behaviour, also failed. There was no real incentive or leverage to encourage licensees to take part in such a scheme – they do not commit an offence by allowing shady deals to take place in their pub, and they could lose custom if they report it. It was similar with taxis – the North Town project produced promotional car stickers for taxis to display only for taxi drivers to refuse to use them because two were threatened by some of their customers for being 'grasses'. Encouraged in one sense by this, North Town subsequently tried to map the call-out of taxis against reported burglaries in order to be able to target suspicious taxis. However, the numbers of taxi call-outs involved mapped against the timescale within which burglaries could have been committed proved to widen the net to an unactionable load. One imagines, though neither project tried it, that a similarly large data set would be produced should agencies take up another Sutton suggestion to track incidents of unexplained violence in case the attacks were linked to disputes about stolen property that could not be resolved in any other way.

Value for money (in the face of competing priorities for resources)
The two projects had external funding and to some extent were able to spend money on experimenting. However, much of the staff costs was met by matched funding arrangements within the agencies involved. Project targets as regards staff time therefore had to meet with agency targets in competing for resources. This meant for example that while Sutton and others had emphasised the importance of shoplifting to the markets for stolen goods – particularly hawking and network sales – and also to the beginning of criminal careers, the projects themselves were loath to put resources into this because efforts in this direction would not be reflected in reported instances of the key crimes of burglary and auto theft and thus be deemed effective. Other suggestions by the theorists, though not tried out, also look not to be cost-effective – such as the Sutton suggestion that people obtain a document from the police before selling items to second-hand shops to state that no item matching its description has been reported stolen. Quite aside from the identification issues, which will be gone into in more detail below, the level of work involved for what level of result would need to be considered.

The projects spent quite large amounts of money on non-human resources such as publicity. A number of theorists had expounded on the considerable scope for aiming publicity – particularly at Colquhoun's 'Innocent Receiver' type – at the close links between theft and buying goods of questionable provenance. However, this is based on quite scanty evidence of the decision-making of these consumers (Sutton and Cromwell's research suggested there was more than just bargain hunting going on). It is questionable whether even a series of posters can produce the major cultural change in some social circles that would be needed to reduce the demand chain to the market. While Sutton compared these measures to the successful drink drive campaign, this was done on a national basis, included prime-time TV footage, and was accompanied by a change in the law. It seems unlikely that small-scale projects can hope to inspire the kind of widespread mindset change, which would result in measurable changes in people's willingness to buy potentially stolen goods.

It should also be noted under this heading that Sutton and others suggested that all marketplaces should be attacked simultaneously in order to minimise displacement effects. Neither project managed to do this because of resourcing issues, which means that this part of his theory has not been tested.

Infrastructure

The theorists tend to take for granted a number of infrastructural requirements that are necessary to implement a market reduction project successfully and which proved substantially problematic to the projects in practice. These include:

- the gathering and collation of intelligence by both the police and project researchers;
- the sharing of intelligence within a multi-agency environment; and
- the identification of property.

Police intelligence gathering and collation

Although Sutton et al.'s (2001) publication repeatedly spoke of 'using existing intelligence' on stolen goods markets to tackle the various disposal avenues, the gathering of intelligence about stolen goods markets represented a new focus for the police in the two areas. In this scenario, the mere collation of known intelligence on handlers is likely to result in a concentration on the 'usual suspects' of property crime, those already known to the police for burglary who may also handle and are therefore easy targets, rather than exploring further afield. South Town officers said gathering new intelligence was more problematic than in other areas of criminality in that thieves, while having no reason not to tell police about other thieves, are likely to be protective or even fearful of their fence.

There were also issues about the sharing of intelligence internally within the police. As centrally funded projects, initially the teams tried to 'go it alone' collecting information for a stolen goods project pool without reference to other units within the organisation. This proved ineffectual as handling networks do not operate in isolation from other areas of criminality that other police units may have information on. This was demonstrated during the undercover operation in South Town when, after it was decided to widen the scope of the infiltration to drugs networks, more handling offenders were identified due to the close links between the two.

The prospect of routine information gathering of the general state of stolen goods markets from a number of sources as suggested by Sutton's ERASOR mechanism also seems problematic. Officers working with informants said that if they are to be paid or tasked for information, it needs to be seen to be used. The researcher in the North Town project was questioned by some of his respondents currently serving probation orders who wanted to know exactly what he was doing with the information he got from them – even though he had repeatedly emphasised that he, as a social scientific researcher, did not want identifying names but only information about the types of selling that they used. They suggested that he might be at risk from offenders should it become known that he was asking.

Sharing of intelligence and multi-agency working

It may be that multi-agency working is an ideal situation. The experiences of both projects, however, have shown that it cannot be taken for granted by the police that other agencies with a more tangential interest in those who deal in stolen goods will be able to devote resources to a multi-agency project of this kind, though it may be true that those involved in stolen goods marketplaces may also be the same people that the Benefits Agency, Inland Revenue and Customs and Excise are likely to be interested in. Their involvement and their sharing of information with one another have to be on a case-by-case basis under the auspices of an agreed protocol in line with the provisions of the Data Protection Act. The North Town project partners failed to agree a data-sharing protocol by the end of the funded period and this caused considerable unease among agency personnel (South Town had one already from pre-existing multi-agency work).

Property identification

The identification of mass-produced items of property necessary to prove a handling charge is likely to be time-consuming and difficult. This is because of three reasons. First, records taken by the police when a property crime is reported can be scant because the victim is not quite sure what had been taken. The person taking the report has not traditionally been that interested in taking an exact a description as possible of the goods. Ensuring sufficient details are routinely logged into an accessible database would need to be addressed at force or even national level in order for thorough checking of recovered items to take place. This process is likely to take longer even than the two years allowed for by Kock *et al.* (1996). On an area basis North Town introduced a new stolen property form including spaces for pertinent details such as serial numbers.

Secondly, identifiable features on property are rarely noted and victims often do not know the identifiable features – such as serial numbers – that manufacturers do put on items. Property-marking schemes have a low take-up rate and it is difficult to market them to improve this when so little property is recovered. Property marking at point of sale was arranged with shop managers by South Town but each arrangement lasted for only short periods because of shop staff turnover. Very little property-marked property is recovered – so little in fact in South Town that the torches distributed to patrol cars to check recovered property for ultraviolet pen marks were allowed to run out of power and not used. Property-viewing days involving inviting victims of theft to view recovered property can result in individual pieces being recognised but are costly to organise.

Thirdly, the situation is exacerbated when trying to track property across borders. Although research suggests many thieves operate reasonably locally, they can easily cross police borders either intentionally or because of geographical proximity.

Local context

In neither of the two projects described here was it known that there was a particularly serious problem relating to stolen goods markets. Instead the MRA was suggested by Home Office staff as a solution to a general hypothesised situation – namely, that markets for stolen goods must exist as thieves do not use all they steal themselves. Because of this, there were fewer data relating to local stolen goods markets prior to the beginning of the project than would have been the case if the projects were trying to reduce a particular local problem that they were already aware of and had been able at least provisionally to measure by instances of reported crime. This meant that, lacking many local data beyond anecdote, the projects were heavily reliant on theory and theorists' recommendations, which were only later translated into local interventions. This was particularly the case for the South Town project which stuck to Sutton's typologies quite rigidly with little regard to local circumstances and the input of other agencies. The locational emphasis of Sutton's typology did not allow for individuals who may cross between shops and operating in pubs, for example – the marketplaces that were eventually identified by the North Town project were networks of individuals who operated in a number of different arenas.

Data – were there enough to show impact?

Measurement issues – identifying markets
As suggested above, the two projects did not have a full picture of the stolen goods market when they put their bids into the Home Office – indeed with the nature of the activity it is unlikely they ever would have. Instead they had discrete pieces of data about stolen goods markets – the odd character who was 'known' to be a fence, the odd shop with a reputation, a number of people with convictions for handling, but who may or may not be a fence in the way we have been describing and more likely to be a burglar caught in possession of stolen property but against whom the police could not prove a case of theft. They had little idea of what part of the picture these bits of information represented. In other words, they had no real baseline data to describe the situation pre-implementation and against which to monitor any effects of interventions on the marketplace.

Measuring issues – detecting impact
This uncertainty became magnified in trying to measure impact. Recognising that aggregate property crime figures could be masking movement within markets and thefts of different types of goods, not to mention the effect of other initiatives and offenders in the area, the evaluation team worked with the projects to establish a matrix of effectiveness of each set of interventions hoping to disaggregate the myriad elements in the equation. For each set, the projects identified the following:

- The nature of the intervention.

- Inputs and outputs and resources used.

- The manner in which it was expected to work (the 'mechanism', to use Pawson and Tilley's (1997) term).

- The outcomes it was expected to achieve.

- The outcomes it did achieve.

- Any contextual features working across the whole matrix affecting the whole project in a general manner, for example policing styles and demographic statistics, or affecting a single tactic – for example, with

South Town's commercial outlet scheme, the number and quality of second-hand good shops and police relationships with them.

The completing of this matrix proved extremely complicated due to the multiple sometimes conflicting outcomes that could be envisaged and the difficulties of measuring desired outcomes beyond hearsay and anecdote. To take a relatively simple example, with the policing of the second-hand shops in South Town various outcomes (positive and negative) were identified:

- Changed attitudes of dealers.
- Reduced purchase of stolen goods.
- Increased intelligence on disposal of stolen goods.
- Reduced use of commercial outlets to dispose of stolen goods.
- Increased intelligence on those thieves who dispose of goods using commercial outlets.
- Recovery of stolen property.
- Displacement of the market into other markets.

These were to be measured by

- survey of dealers;
- impact on businesses – numbers closing down and their reasons according to Trading Standards records;
- monitoring of transaction records;
- monitoring of intelligence forms;
- survey of offenders; and
- amount of property recovered from outlets compared with elsewhere.

The immediate problem in measuring 'change', 'reduction' and 'increase' was that there was, as said above, little baseline data against which to measure what was happening – previously there had been little or no intelligence about dealers because they had not been focused on before. On a very simple level, there had been no transaction records to collect. But even counting from zero, few of the identified desired outcomes were quantifiable in any meaningful way. Without being able to read every intelligence form, it was difficult to discriminate between large numbers of forms merely reporting a visit to a dealer and a form with useful intelligence on it.

Trying to measure attitude change was even more challenging. By the time the evaluation team were in place this intervention was already in operation so it was too late for a pre-implementation survey of dealers.

In attempting to measure attitude change by behaviour, there was no way of knowing how many shady transactions went on before entry into the scheme. There was no way of knowing if any supposed reductions in known burglars going into the shop were because they were no longer going in and therefore no longer selling property there, no longer going in but selling property to the dealer elsewhere or still going in but not going in the book. There was no baseline of the numbers of second-hand dealers that could be expected to shut down in any one year. It was difficult to create a causative link between a dealer shutting down and a suggestion that this was because of the project's demands – though anecdotally one dealer was repeatedly said to have told an officer that he was shutting down to move to an area without the project! The most difficult outcome to pin down was the displacement to other markets when a sequential targeting of markets meant absolutely no information was known about other marketplaces.

It was also attempted to try to disaggregate the reported crime data by looking at any fluctuations in the levels of theft involving the types of property stolen within one Sutton-identified marketplace but the results proved inconclusive due in part to the overlap between marketplaces for certain types of goods. Most of the positive data relating to impact rest in the realm of anecdote and hearsay of the words of confidential sources. South Town, for example, told us that their informants had told their intelligence officers that thieves would no longer go into commercial outlets (we are not sure if that was the precise vocabulary used). Higher-level criminal organisers in North Town were reputedly wary of increased arrests among their circle but not realising the true focus of the crackdown.

Conclusions and discussion

The emphasis in this chapter has been fairly negative regarding what the two 'market reduction' projects achieved in terms of crime reduction. Encouraged by the intuitive logic of theory we were expecting the projects to follow the simple steps to arrest lynchpin handlers whose demise would cause rates of theft to plummet as thieves were left floundering with nowhere to sell their booty. While the steps described in the theory did not prove so simple either to implement or measure, a number of positive results were achieved.

The South Town project developed a change in emphasis to property crime intelligence gathering – something akin to Walsh's reconceptualisation of the theft problem into a wider focus on the stolen property system – which has influenced the rest of the police force. Even if substantive tactics from the project have not been rolled out at least the importance of exploring stolen property markets and how they operate has been more widely accepted. Intelligence is now routinely gathered and collated, not just on the original theft but also on what happens to property after it is stolen. A new post has been established within each area intelligence unit to co-ordinate this information and target offenders. Local legislation regulating the second-hand trade and making compulsory some of the provisions of the voluntary scheme has been taken through Parliament and is now being routinely enforced. These new foci are expected to produce long-term benefits.

The North Town project committed a dedicated team of officers to look in depth at marketplaces and unearthed high-level links with organised criminality.[8] The project was instrumental in improving the level of custody interviews and intelligence exchange in the police basic command area and the quality of property-recording systems generally throughout the force. The police area in which the project took place has routinised its system of interviewing arrested individuals, with a cadre of specialised officers identifying and contacting potentially useful informants. It has also developed a secure system of passing confidential information to other areas via police headquarters – it is now the most active division in this regard. An early activity by project analysts was to upgrade the computer system in order for recorded property details to be entered in searchable fields. While this was intended initially to help the project create a detailed picture of what was being stolen in the area, the new system has benefited the entire force.

Both projects achieved a level of multi-agency co-operation that they said improved relationships across the board and both projects certainly learnt more about the marketplaces operating locally and the potential for intervention.

Addressing the marketplaces for stolen goods in a systematic way represented an innovative way of tackling crime problems. These projects are perhaps best seen as forerunners, and others can draw on their experiences. Perhaps in this light, progress should be viewed less in terms of the crime reduction outcomes but more in terms of lessons about the processes through which market reduction approaches should be implemented. Lessons highlighted here include the importance of the following:

• Proper identification of specific local problems – theft of a particular item type (e.g. computers); theft of a particular type (e.g. domestic burglary).

- An analysis of the agreed elements of the project – a market reduction project could be defined as widely as supply and the motivation behind the supply (which would include burglary prevention and drug/consolidation schemes) through to transportation and distribution and retail (which is what we would actually call the marketplace) to eventual sale to the consumer (the potential targets of rule-setting marketing).

- The establishment of a base line – property stolen, what type of property, where stolen, where recovered.

- The development of appropriate tactics – e.g. targeted operations, second-hand shop scheme, publicity.

- The establishment of methods of monitoring activity and evaluating impact – bearing in mind that relying on traditional sources of monitoring, such as reported crime statistics and prosecutions, may not provide the level of detail necessary to measure performance.

Notes

1   Foreword to one of a series of studies addressing aspects of the stolen goods marketplace published by the Home Office (Kock et al. 1996).
2   Both the Cromwell and McElrath 1994 article and Sheley and Bailey (1985), which also looks at consumer motivation to buy stolen property (and the cost of theft to society), provide discussion on survey design to elicit this information.
3   Sutton also identified a number of strategies aimed at traditional burglary prevention such as working on the idea that burglars often ring the doorbells of houses they intend to burgle and if they are answered ask if X is in. Sutton suggests that residents should be encouraged to report such false callers to identify where a burglar may be operating. Another idea – working on the information that people living in neighbourhoods don't like the people they know burgled while new residents are seen as fair game – was that estate newcomers should be introduced to respected members of the community so they would not appear to be without allies.
4   As reported as happening in Japan in Miyazawa (1992: 48).
5   Summarised in Stevenson et al. (2001) but with more methodological detail, including survey design, in Stevenson and Forsythe (2001).
6   In interviews with the evaluation team all shopkeepers laughed at the idea of asking for receipts or original packaging.
7   Erecting a gate at the end of an alleyway linking the vulnerable back entrances of terraced property in order to prevent unobtrusive exit by burglars.

8 It is not possible to give details of these links because court cases are still ongoing.

References

Clarke, R.V. (1999) *Hot Products: Understanding, Anticipating and Reducing Demand for Stolen Goods*. Police Research Series Paper 112. London: Home Office.

Colquhoun, P. (1796) *A Treatise on the Police of the Metropolis*. London: C. Dilley.

Cromwell, P. and McElrath, K. (1994) 'Buying stolen property: an opportunity perspective', *Journal of Research in Crime and Delinquency*, 31(3): 295–310.

Cromwell, P., Olson, J. and Avary, D. (1993) 'Who buys stolen property? A new look at criminal receiving', *Journal of Crime and Justice*, XVI(1): 75–95.

Freiberg, A. (1997) 'Regulating markets for stolen property', *Australian and New Zealand Journal of Criminology*, 30(3): 237–58.

Hall, J. (1952) *Theft, Law and Society* (2nd edn). Indianapolis, IN: Bobbs Merrill.

Henry, S. (1975) 'Stolen goods: the amateur trade'. PhD thesis, University of Kent at Canterbury.

Klockars, C. (1974) *The Professional Fence*. New York, NY: Free Press.

Kock, E., Kemp, T. and Rix, B. (1996) *Disrupting the Distribution of Stolen Electrical Goods*. Crime Detection and Prevention Series 69. London: Home Office.

Knutsson, J. (1984) *Operation Identification: A Way to Prevent Burglaries? Research Report* 14. Stockholm: The National Council for Crime Prevention.

Ladouceur, C. (1993) 'Ecouler la merchandise volée, une approche rationnelle?', *Canadian Journal of Criminology/Revue canadienne de Criminologie*, 35: 169–82.

Miyazawa, S. (1992) *Policing in Japan: A Study in Making Crime*. Albany, NY: State University of New York Press.

Pawson, R. and Tilley, N. (1997) *Realistic Evaluation*. London and Thousand Oaks, CA: Sage.

Roselius, T. and Benton, D. (1973) 'Marketing theory and the fencing of stolen goods', *Denver Law Journal*, 50: 177–205.

Sheley, J.F. and Bailey, K.D. (1985) 'New directions for anti-theft policy: reductions in stolen goods buyers', *Journal of Criminal Justice*, 13: 399–415.

Steffensmeier, D.J. (1986) *The Fence: In the Shadow of Two Worlds*. Totowa, NJ: Rowman & Littlefield.

Stevenson, R.J. and Forsythe, L.M.V. (2001) *The Stolen Goods Market in New South Wales: An Interview Study with Imprisoned Burglars*. Sydney: NSW Bureau of Crime Statistics and Research) (http://www.lawlink.nsw.gov.au/bocsar1.nsf/pages/pub_qtot#stolen_goods).

Stevenson, R.J., Forsythe, L.M.V. and Weatherburn, D. (2001) 'The stolen goods market in New South Wales, Australia', *British Journal Criminology*, 41: 101–18.

Sutton, M. (1993) 'From receiving to thieving: the market for stolen goods and the incidence of theft', in *Home Office Research and Statistics Department Research Bulletin* 34. London: Home Office.

Sutton, M. (1995) 'Supply by theft: does the market for second-hand goods play a role in keeping crime figures high?', *British Journal of Criminology*, 35(3): 400–16.

Sutton, M. (1998) *Handling Stolen Goods and Theft: A Market Reduction Approach.* Home Office Research Study 178. London: Home Office.

Sutton, M., Schneider, J. and Hetherington, S. (2001) *Tackling Theft with the Market Reduction Approach.* Crime Reduction Research Series Paper 8. London: Home Office.

Walsh, M. (1977) *The Fence: A New Look at the World of Property Theft.* Westport, CT: Greenwood Press.

Chapter 8

Problem-oriented evaluation? Evaluating problem-oriented policing initiatives

Mario Matassa and Tim Newburn

> The stronger the hold of involved forms of thinking, and thus of the inability to distance oneself from traditional attitudes, the stronger the danger inherent in the situation created by people's traditional attitudes towards each other and towards themselves. The greater the danger the more difficult it is for people to look at themselves, at each other and at the whole situation with a measure of detachment (Elias 1987).

Evaluation within criminology has recently been experiencing something of a boom. The budget set aside for evaluation of the government's Crime Reduction Programme (CRP) represented the single largest investment in a programme of criminological research ever initiated in the UK (Morgan 2000). For cash-hungry universities and criminological research units this represented a significant opportunity to undertake research in what promised to be some potentially innovative projects to reduce crime. New Labour's avowed commitment to evidence-based policy and practice offered an opportunity for interested criminologists to contribute directly to the policy-making arena.

Our involvement in this programme, on which this chapter is based, concerned three separate but related evaluations of initiatives designed to tackle hate crime. The evaluations, all part of the Targeted Policing Initiative (TPI), conformed to the general pattern for such studies established by the Home Office. During the course of the work a number of very significant problems were experienced and it is some of these that we examine here. In particular, we wish to explore the role of the evaluator in relation to problem-oriented policing (POP) initiatives. We examine the ways in which the role of the evaluator has generally been understood, both in government guidance and contracts, as well as more generally within the evaluation literature. We suggest that the lack of clarity which can surround the evaluation enterprise creates an arena (both real and perceived) in which conflicting purposes and interests exist. We examine the often unclear, sometimes conflicting roles evaluators are asked to play and argue that a more nuanced under-standing of the multiple purposes of evaluation, and the role the evaluator may be called upon to play, would produce both better evaluations, and potentially better practice on the ground. In the context of POP, we argue that a more explicit recognition and acceptance of the 'involved' role of the evaluator will not only aid evaluation in this difficult area, but also has the potential to help overcome some of the difficulties currently experienced in POP initiatives – not the least of which is implementation failure.

The Targeted Policing Initiative and tackling hate crime

On 11 December 1998, the Home Office Minister of State, Paul Boateng, wrote to all 43 chief constables in England and Wales inviting them to submit applications for developmental projects to reduce crime under the first round of the TPI, part of the government's CRP. One year later a second invitation announced the second round of the initiative. A total of 59 projects were ultimately funded, at a cost of approximately £32 million, of which 20 were evaluated. These development projects attempted to tackle a wide range of problems including hate crime, the stolen goods market, street violence, vehicle crime and alcohol- and drug-related crime.

The rationale behind the TPI generally was to help the police, in conjunction with local Crime and Disorder Partnerships, to understand better and to develop a problem-solving approach to tackling crime. The popularity of this approach stems from previous Home Office research, building on Herman Goldstein's original thesis (1990), which suggests that such an approach – analysing problems and devising solutions to tackle the underlying causes – is more likely to have an impact than traditional reactive policing (Leigh *et al.* 1996, 1998). The primary objective of the TPI, in keeping with the underpinning logic of the CRP, was to develop cost-effective interventions to reduce crime, and to improve the evidence base about what works in reducing crime.

This chapter draws from experiences in the field in conducting three evaluations of projects designed to tackle hate crime.[1] Two of these initiatives were implemented in London: the four boroughs Racially Motivated Crime Programme (RMCP) and the Southwark anti-hate crime project – Police, Partners and Community Together in Southwark (PPACTS). The third, the Brighton and Hove Anti-victimisation Initiative (AVI), was sponsored by Sussex Police in addition to Home Office funding.

These projects were established not long after the publication of the report into the police response to the murder of Stephen Lawrence. On 22 April 1993, 18-year-old Stephen Lawrence was stabbed to death in Eltham, south London. He was by no means alone in being subject to a vicious racist assault. There were numerous other cases at the time and, of course, they continue (Bowling 1999). However, partly because of the way in which the case was handled, and partly because of the public campaign that was subsequently mounted by family and supporters, the case focused attention on racist victimisation and, once again, on the attitudes and behaviour of the police. The Macpherson Inquiry, which reported in February 1999, was highly critical of the Metropolitan Police, identifying not only professional incompetence but also, notably, 'institutional racism'. The then Home Secretary, Jack Straw, laid special emphasis on the need for the police service, and other agencies, to improve markedly their response to racist and other forms of hate crime. At the time of the establishment of the CRP there was, therefore, a particularly keen interest in improving police responses in this area.

The tactics and interventions employed in the anti-hate crime initiatives varied significantly, across and within programmes and between the three sites. All the projects were delivered within a partnership framework, although the initial conceptualisation and subsequent evolution of 'partnership' differed significantly in each (see Table 8.1). Likewise the focus of the individual programmes varied but broadly a number of common themes or foci of attention emerged. These included enforcement, education and awareness raising, victim support, community development and (potential) offender identification, deterrence and rehabilitation.

In keeping with the ethos of the TPI the interventions across the sites (actual and proposed) involved a combination of both innovative and more traditional methods for addressing the problem. Among the more innovative, for example, were much needed work in relation to identifying actual and potential hate crime offenders through risk assessment, coupled with a proposal to develop programmes directed at challenging such offending behaviour. Equally innovative, and inevitably challenging, were mechanisms designed to encourage and

Table 8.1: The three anti-hate crime initiatives in the TPI

Initiative	Objectives	Mechanisms		
		Offender strategies	Victim strategies	Community development strategies
(RCMP) four boroughs Racially Motivated Crime Programme (Merton, Hounslow, Tower Hamlets and Greenwich)	• To achieve a long-term re-duction in the true incidence of racially motivated crime • To increase confidence in the Metropolitan Police Service's (MPS) commitment to deal effectively with racially motivated crime • To identify areas of good practice and promulgate the lessons learnt throughout	Adult offender programme; young persons' offender programme; education pack; outreach work (enforcement strategies – reactive (police oriented, e.g. high-visibility policing, surveil-lance, race crime car)	Physical security; target hardening; third-party reporting; victim link line; mediation; chaperone scheme; victim visits	Community witness scheme; community grants; mobile bus project; community development workers
PPACTS (Police, Partners and Community Together in Southwark)	• A sustained and long-term reduction in the true incidence of hate crime across the borough • An increased confidence across the borough in the MPS's commitment to deal convincingly with hate crime • The creation of sustain-able structures that will provide a bulwark against	Enforcement strategies – multi-agency teams – problem oriented; intelligence-led; proactive and reactive operations; dedicated hot-spot team (with extended multi-agency family)	Dedicated victim support worker; language line; mediation referrals; enhanced police service overtime budget (victim and witness visits); victim caseworker; target hardening; police–victim reassurance model	Virtual neighbour-hood watch co-ordinator; community development worker; schools education programme

intolerance across the community

| The AVI (the Anti-victimisation Initiative) Brighton and Hove | • The overall aim is to reduce incidents within the ambit of the unit primarily by increasing the level of prosecutions for domestic violence, homophobic and racist incidents through encouraging victims to report them

Secondary objectives included:
• Build confidence in the criminal justice system
• Increase reporting of incidents to the police
• Reduce domestic murders and serious assaults
• Reduce repeat victimisation
• Assist partners in taking forward the Community Safety and Crime Reduction Strategy
• Ensure statutory partners have greater clarity of responsibilities and powers and take appropriate action
• Increase capacity of partners to develop services and support victims | Enforcement strategies – mostly reactive (police oriented): seconded probation officer; risk assessment panel | Victim liaison officers (×3); community advocates (×2); intimidated witness support service (domestic violence advocacy); anti-victimisation unit (secondary investigation of hate crime) | Community forum co-ordinators |

enable community involvement in strategy design, implementation and monitoring. Simultaneously, more traditional policing enforcement tactics were combined with intelligence-led and problem-oriented approaches to attempt to reduce or prevent hate crime within identified 'hot-spots'. Finally, tried and tested mechanisms were combined with more innovative approaches to support victims and engender greater trust and understanding.

The four boroughs Racially Motivated Crime Programme

The RMCP was sited in the London boroughs of Merton, Tower Hamlets, Greenwich and Hounslow. The design of the strategy was underpinned by Sibbitt's (1997) research, which suggested that racially motivated crime can most effectively be tackled through a holistic approach – effective action against perpetrators, diverting potential perpetrators and addressing the perpetrator community's general attitude towards ethnic minorities. Funding restrictions inhibited a holistic strategy in all four sites. Merton's leading role in the original project design meant that it alone would attempt to implement the 'Sibbitt model' in its entirety. Each of the remaining three sites was to focus on a specific programme of activity, addressing a particular aspect of the problem. The strategies were as follows:

- Hounslow – developing services to support victims of racially motivated crime, to explore community attitudes to the problem and to build informal secondary controls within the community.

- Greenwich – developing strategies to address offending behaviour in partnership with the Probation Service and to divert likely offenders from offending through detached youth outreach work.

- Tower Hamlets – utilising a problem-oriented methodology to develop more effective enforcement practices, with emphasis placed on detecting offenders and educating potential offenders.

- Merton – developing a holistic approach by employing all the above methods in addition to developing strategies that empower communities to formulate local strategies.

PPACTS

The PPACTS project originated within the partnership unit in Southwark police. The aim of the PPACTS project was to pilot a range of interventions aimed at tackling and reducing the high incidence of 'hate crimes' in the London Borough of Southwark.[2] The project was heavily victim oriented and there was an explicit recognition from the outset that strategies would be problem-oriented and intelligence-led. The proposed strategy involved a holistic multi-agency/inter-agency approach consisting of three concentric strands, namely:

1   The victim strand – providing a bespoke raft of services tailored to the individual needs of victims.

2   The community strand – raising the profile and awareness of issues of diversity and tolerance and constructing sustainable structures that will provide a bulwark against intolerance in the community.

3   The policing strand – a sustained campaign focused on the perpetrators of hate crime.

All the proposed interventions were linked to one or more of the theoretical principles underpinning the strategy and to intended outcomes. A dedicated core support team (including a project manager, dedicated information officer, victim caseworker and Virtual Neighbourhood Watch co-ordinator) provided close scrutiny and operational oversight of the various strands at all stages. In addition, the team was responsible for ensuring that weaknesses and strengths were identified, shortcomings addressed and opportunities for development and mainstreaming were realised.

The Anti-victimisation Initiative

At the heart of the AVI was the development of a holistic infrastructure to support the victims of hate crime in Brighton and Hove.[3] Strategic oversight was provided through an advisory group attended by a mix of project partners including representatives from each of the three community forums: minority ethnic communities; the lesbian, gay, bisexual and transgendered (LGBT) community; and women experiencing domestic violence. Other partners included representatives from the local authority, the Probation Service and Victim Support. The group was chaired by a senior officer from Sussex Police. The structure developed sought to ground strategic development and accountability within the communities that the project sought to support.

The project was victim oriented with an emphasis on encouraging victims to report hate crime. The proposed infrastructure was based around a bipartite combination of policing and community-based structures/interventions. The former revolved around the establishment of the Anti-victimisation Unit (AVU). The unit was dedicated to the investigation of hate crimes and supporting the victims of those crimes. The AVU comprised 12 officers and was supported by a seconded probation officer, an analyst and three victim liaison officers. An independent project manager, to oversee the administration and development of the project and to act as a conduit between the statutory and community representatives, was also housed within the unit. The purpose of the unit was to provide a dedicated resource for the secondary investigation of all 'hate crimes'. The addition of civil liaison officers within the unit was to ensure that victims were supported and updated on case progress and to provide a source of 'outside' expertise for officers conducting hate crime investigations. The unit's remit was both reactive and proactive, although in practice the volume of cases meant that the former took precedence.

On the community strand a number of posts were created to provide mechanisms and opportunities to report crimes and to support victims. These included two advocate posts – one for the LGBT community and one for minority ethnic communities. Advocacy support for victims of domestic violence was provided through the Women's Refuge project's 'Intimidated Witness Support Service' (IWSS). The advocates provided an alternative reporting opportunity for those victims who did not feel sufficiently confident to report crimes directly to the police. Additionally, three co-ordinators provided a strategic link between all project interventions and strands and the three community-led forums. The aim was to provide administrative support for the forums and to promote the services of the AVI within public services and across the community.

It is not our intention here to comment in detail on the success or otherwise of the respective programmes.[4] In summary, the results of the programmes were at best somewhat mixed. There were some indications of developing good practice and in one of the sites, Southwark, some apparent reductions in racist crime. However, there were also considerable difficulties and problems. All the projects were ambitious; indeed, in retrospect they were perhaps too ambitious. In at least two of the projects, the RCMP and AVI projects, the fundamental problems experienced could be subsumed under the rubric of 'implementation failure'. Long identified as a problem in relation to the evaluation of crime reduction and prevention initiatives (see, for example, Hope and Murphy 1983) once again the ability of agencies on the ground to deliver what was promised at the outset was extremely limited. Not only does this of course have serious repercussions for evaluation, it also raises significant questions about the role of the evaluator in 'observing' unfolding implementation failure. In exploring this question, and its particular relevance to POP, it is the experience of the RMCP that we will focus on primarily here.

Evaluation and the role of the evaluator – in theory

The growth in the 'evaluation industry' over the past 20 years has been paralleled by considerable debate and dispute over methodology, methods and purpose. The debate has been conducted, for the most, along bifurcated lines of competing paradigms. The 'paradigm wars', as they became known, between experimentalists and non-experimentalists, quasi-experimentalists and realists, advocates of quantitative or qualitative methods, dominated this debate (in criminology see, for example, the debate between Farrington 1997, 1998, and Pawson and Tilley 1998a, 1998b). Their origin lies in the history and development of evaluation and the near hegemony enjoyed in the early years by experimentalists and quasi-experimentalists (Oakley 2000). Methodological preference dominated these debates, the result being that 'whatever the technique, whatever the strategy, two camps of a basically opposite persuasion seem to foregather and glare at each other, with the result that methodological choices seemed forever framed in mutual hostility' (Pawson and Tilley 1997: 153).

Little value is served in rehashing this debate and it is not our intention to do so. It is probably fair to say, however, that the debates have waned slightly in recent years, some commentators going so far as to suggest that they are all but dead (Stern 1995). While Stern's prognosis is undoubtedly somewhat premature, there is certainly increasing recognition and acknowledgement that evaluation is a broad enterprise in which methodological pluralism is a positive attribute (Newburn 2001). In addition to continuing questions about appropriate method-ologies, there also remain a number of other issues that affect how evaluation is undertaken. The two we wish to focus on here, and arguably two of the most important, concern the *purpose* of evaluation and the *role* of the evaluator.

Much of the difficulty experienced in evaluation research is, we think, a product of a lack of clarity as to the purpose(s) of particular studies. All too often the purpose of evaluation is considered to be self-evident. However, in our experience, rarely is it the case that all parties to the enterprise – the funding body, the evaluators and those being 'evaluated' – have an explicit agreement as to the precise purpose(s) of the work being conducted. Indeed, even the primary parties – the funder and the evaluator – may not always have shared views as to the purpose of the evaluation. There are a number of reasons for this. First, it cannot always be assumed that the funding body will have a clear or uniform idea about why a particular evaluation is to be conducted (Newburn 2001). Thus, for example, it is perfectly possible for the research arm of a government department to have goals which differ somewhat from the policy arm of the same department (see Crawford and Newburn 2003). This is not necessarily problematic, but may become so either if the goals are in some way incompatible or, even when compatible, they are not fully or properly spelled out at the outset. The second reason is that, even in cases where a funding body is clear about its goals, it is possible for the evaluator to undertake the work with contrasting objectives in mind. Thirdly, there may well be cases in which the funder and the evaluator have a clear, explicit and shared idea of the purpose of the evaluation but this is either not communicated clearly to the organisations on the ground subject to the evaluation or, despite clear communication, those on the ground continue to hold contrasting 'hopes' for the evaluation. At the very least, therefore, defining the purpose of an evaluation, and getting explicit agreement to that definition, is a necessary if not sufficient condition for developing a framework that will adequately serve the interests of all stakeholders.

In thinking about the purpose of evaluation, a useful starting point is provided by Eleanor Chelimsky (1997). She defines three broad conceptual frameworks of evaluation, namely:

- *Evaluation for accountability* (concerned with outcomes, measuring results or efficiency).

- *Evaluation for development* (concerned with processes, providing evaluative help to strengthen institutions).

- *Evaluation for knowledge* (knowledge focused, obtaining a deeper understanding in some specific area or policy field).

Chelimsky's framework[5] helps focus attention on the scope of evaluation and begins to suggest a multiplicity of aims and a multiplicity of stakeholders. In addition to serving the goals of the funding agency, which in the case of the research discussed here was government, evaluation has a wider audience that potentially includes the programme management, steering groups, practitioners, recipients and the evaluators themselves. The view of the purpose of the evaluation that each holds will play a large part in their sense of, and response to, such research.

In addition to the purpose of evaluation, an area in which further disagreement and confusion may arise is in relation to the role of the evaluator. Traditional views of evaluation hold that the role of the evaluator is a 'neutral' one observing, in an unbiased manner, the matter being evaluated. Thus, the Home Office guidance for the CRP (1999b: 12) instructed that: '... evaluators must not be closely involved in the running or designing of programmes (other than the evaluation framework). This ensures that those evaluating programmes do not have a conflict of interest. This is a Treasury requirement.' Though less clearly specified, this view of evaluation also permeates the Treasury's influential 'Green Book' (HM Treasury 1997: 31) in which it is suggested that there is a 'strong case for normally maintaining the independence of evaluators from the day to day management of the project, programme or policy'. And, further, that 'There will also be a problem for independent evaluators of gaining sufficient confidence from management to be able to gain access to records and technical support, yet maintaining sufficient distance from that management to be able to exercise independent judgement'.

And, yet, in many forms of evaluation it is clearly accepted that evaluators may (have to) adopt a significantly more 'hands-on' role. There is, as numerous commentators have noted (see, for example, Patton 1997), a continuum of evaluator roles, ranging from traditional social scientific 'objectivity' and distance at one end to a form of activism which is close to advocacy (Lincoln 1991). What we take from this is the message that there are multiple possible roles for evaluators, and the one selected will depend primarily on the needs of the evaluation and the circumstances in which it is being undertaken. In this, we are with Patton (1997: 125) who argued that 'neither more nor less activism ... is morally superior'. While evaluator activism isn't to everyone's taste, in our view in the area of POP it is very nearly impossible to avoid.

The Targeted Policing Initiative: evaluation and the role of the evaluator – in practice

Put crudely, the central argument we wish to put is that the existence of multiple 'purposes' for the evaluation, and the resultant confusion about which 'masters' were being served, and with what ends in mind, problematised, and potentially compromised, the position of the evaluator. The 'role' of the evaluator in these circumstances is far from the straightforward 'objective outsider' often presented in the literature. For example, there was on the one hand an assumption within regional government offices and, to a lesser extent, within the Home Office that information from the evaluation would be available for 'development' purposes. On the other hand, there were numerous occasions where senior police managers approached the evaluation team for advice about the work of their own programmes in order to check upon progress against targets – i.e. for use as an 'accountability' mechanism. These and other reasons – the fact that the programmes and the evaluation were government funded together with the suspicious and defensive nature of police culture – led to evaluators being perceived as 'agents' of the government on the one hand, and of senior police management on the other. This situation was further complicated by the police service's limited ability to engage in 'problem-oriented policing'. These limitations, in short, meant that in practice the programmes often fell far short of what had been anticipated. The very real prospect of 'implementation failure' presented a series of challenges for the engaged evaluator, most obviously, how deeply involved to become in the design and running of programmes? In practice, it appeared to us that there was little choice other than to become engaged, often quite heavily so, in order to maximise the likelihood that there was *something* to evaluate. Becoming engaged in this way opened up a further set of 'roles' for the evaluator. These roles, and the continuing confusion over the purpose of the evaluation, led to misapprehensions on the part of the police about the nature of the relationship between themselves and the evaluation and subsequently, when critical evaluation reports were either anticipated or delivered, to a highly defensive and sometimes overtly hostile response.

Rosenbaum (2002) suggests that there are five major obstacles to evaluation of multi-agency crime partnerships. These are:

1   the complexity of interventions (both horizontally and vertically);
2   the complexity of contextual variables;
3   the dynamic, changing nature of interventions;
4   the diversity of intervention processes and outcomes; and
5   the lack of optimal conditions for traditional experimental research.

All these five factors were present in the TPI evaluations which form the basis of this chapter. It was a sixth, and oft-noted, obstacle that we wish to focus on here: implementation failure (and its variant implementation breakdown).

The TPI evaluations were subject to fairly clear guidelines. However, it was acknowledged that the initiatives being evaluated were generally complex and that, therefore, the evaluations themselves were also likely potentially to be tricky. The understanding was that TPI initiatives contained diverse elements and that this should be reflected in the framework of the evaluation. The framework, though not spelling this out, included elements of all three of Chelimsky's evaluation perspectives – accountability, development and learning – as the following Home Office (1998) explanation indicates:

> The development projects will be subject to in-depth monitoring ['accountability'] and independent evaluation. Lessons learned will be fed back to police forces and their partners nationally through the central support team, so as to promulgate and consolidate the development of good practice ['development']. The aim of the projects is not simply to identify what works in particular circumstances ['learning'] but to foster the development of a general problem solving capacity within police forces and their partners.

In order to accomplish this, projects were to receive central support provided by a team established by the Home Office. To this end it would provide:

- consultancy advice on targeted policing;
- technical support (including IT advice);
- oversight of the independent evaluation, including feedback to avoid implementation failure; and
- targets and performance monitoring.

In practice, the extent to which this support was provided (or a structure was put in place to facilitate this) was somewhat limited. In our experience, programme teams were more inclined to approach the evaluators for support, advice and technical assistance. This is perhaps understandable in a number of respects. The reluctance to approach the funding body, and thereby expose limited competencies, or lack of progress, is under these circumstances likely to be perceived as a high-risk strategy. The possibility that funds could be withdrawn is hardly likely to entice programme managers to expose their own organisational failings. Also, as we explain in greater detail below, uncertainty surrounding the funding decision-making process may also have worked to mitigate the likelihood of such transparency among certain partners.

The nature of an evaluation potentially has a profound effect on the role of the evaluator. A study that conforms to what is often thought of as the 'classic' form of evaluation – one primarily concerned with impact or outcomes – requires something different from the evaluator than does a study that is primarily concerned with 'development' where the ongoing feedback of results, usually about outputs, in order to guide and influence the development of a service, is the primary motivation. A study which combines all three of Chelimsky's major forms, particularly where these were not fully specified at the outset, potentially considerably complicates the evaluator's role.

Fieldwork is an unpredictable business. Funding bodies, other stake-holders and evaluators often have different and sometimes conflicting priorities. The expectations of evaluators, the role they are expected to play, may change from day to day, depending upon the nature of the 'audience' (Goffman 1971). Questions such as who defines the nature of 'success', how interim evaluation reports relate to future funding decisions and the nature of the protocols that govern the relationship between evaluator and practitioner, constitute an arena in which conflicting expectations and interests inevitably collide and coalesce. In the hate crimes evaluations the range of roles played, or expected to be played, by the evaluator, at times seemed legion. In attempting to bring some order to this we have identified 11 of the key 'roles' occupied by, or attributed to, the evaluator in this study. The categories are not mutually exclusive, nor is the list necessarily exhaustive. However, it is these 11 roles that we take to have been the most visible within this particular evaluation and which, on the basis of experience in other government-funded studies, we believe are by no means confined to this evaluation. The 11 are as follows:

1 *Project 'author'* – in which the evaluator is invited to take an active role in designing aspects of the project being evaluated.

2 *Product champion* – in which the evaluator seeks to persuade others of the importance of the initiative being evaluated.

3 *Data analyst* – in which the evaluator takes responsibility for providing data in a form that will aid POP.

4 *Policing 'consultant'* – where the evaluator provides specialist advice about policing tactics and approaches.

5 *Inter-agency facilitator* – where the evaluator takes responsibility for attempting to find solutions to problems that have arisen in partner-ship working.

6 *Home Office 'agent'* – in which the evaluator is perceived to be, and may actually be, acting on behalf of the government department.

7 *Home Office 'spy'* – in which the evaluator is perceived to be using evaluation as a 'screen' behind which to check up on the work of those being evaluated.

8 *Project spy* – where the evaluator is asked to report on the actions of implementers by other, generally senior, members of his or her organisation.

9 *Watchdog* – a more active role than 'spy'; formally reporting to the government department and to senior police management.

10 *Amateur therapist* – a 'listening ear' allowing others to voice their worries, their concerns and other feelings.

11 *'Scapegoat'* – when things are not going to plan, and where such difficulties are likely to be exposed, evaluators may be used as a means of deflecting criticism.

The purpose of this typology is to begin to unpick some of the reasons that the role of the evaluator can be experienced as a relatively messy and chaotic one to occupy. Some of the 'roles' described above are relatively unproblematic; others much more obviously so. In our view, the fuller the understanding, and the greater the potential anticipation, of the range of expectations potentially attaching to the job of 'evaluator', the higher is the likelihood that attendant problems can be mitigated or even prevented. In the evaluations on which this chapter is based, there were three primary sources of difficulty. The first was confusion over the purpose of evaluation. The second, a lack of clarity over the role expectations of the evaluators. The third set of problems concerned the implementation of the programmes themselves and, more particularly, the limited capability of the police service to work in a problem-oriented manner. In large part, it was the emerging difficulties associated with the implementation of the POP programmes, and how to respond to these difficulties, that highlighted (indeed, in some cases gave rise to) the problems over the purpose of the evaluation and the role of the evaluator. It is to POP in theory and practice that we turn next.

Problem-oriented policing – in theory

POP was conceived by an American academic, Herman Goldstein, in the late 1970s (Goldstein 1979, 1990). The basic idea is that police officers seek to identify recurring problems, as opposed to reactively responding to single incidents and then to devise appropriate solutions. Goldstein identifies 11 basic elements of POP (see Chapter 1):

1 Grouping incidents as problems.
2 Focusing on substantive problems as the heart of policing.
3 Effectiveness as the ultimate goal.
4 The need for systematic inquiry.
5 Disaggregating and accurately labelling problems.
6 Analysis of the multiple interests in problems.
7 Capturing and critiquing the current response.
8 An uninhibited search for a tailor-made response.
9 Adopting a proactive stance.
10 Strengthening the decision-making processes and increasing accountability.
11 Evaluating results of newly implemented responses.

In summary, effective problem-solving requires the analysis of data to establish the existence and extent of a problem, to examine its nature and source, to plan intervention measures to reduce it, and to monitor and evaluate the effectiveness of the selected response. It also entails drawing on findings from existing research to inform data analysis and choice of responses (Read and Tilley 2000).

Problem-oriented policing and hate crimes – in practice

Relatively early on it became clear to us that the ability of the police service to undertake a problem-solving approach, at least in two of the three initiatives, was extremely limited. This limited capacity has been noted in previous research (Read and Tilley 2000). In these initiatives the limitations seemed to us to be visible in at least ten separate, but linked, ways:

1 Limited understanding of the theory of POP.
2 Limited experience of POP in practice.
3 Little experience of responding strategically to racist harassment and crime.
4 Inadequate data capture.
5 Inadequate data analysis capability.
6 A very limited desire to utilise data.
7 Limited ability/capability to organise a strategic policing response

on the basis of data analysis.
8. Inadequate or problematic relationships with partner organisations.
9 Limited understanding of the essentials of the hate crime reduction projects within the police service and partner organisations.
10 Inability/unwillingness to focus on substantive problems.

These shortcomings were exacerbated by a number of structural features of the TPI which were, to a degree, somewhat in conflict with the needs of POP. These were as follows:

11 The timetables imposed for initial bids.
12 The timetables for implementation.

We now take each of these in turn and explore the realities of POP as they were experienced in the three TPI anti-hate crime initiatives.

Limited understanding of the theory of POP

Though we encountered exceptions, by and large relatively few officers involved in the three anti-hate crime initiatives appeared to grasp the principles of POP. This could be seen in two main ways. First, it was visible in officers' approach to the collection, analysis and use of data/ intelligence (discussed in greater detail below). Secondly, all three of the original bids for anti-hate crime projects made by the police to the TPI failed to include any form of integral enforcement strategy, suggesting a limited understanding of both the TPI and POP.

Limited experience of POP in practice

During the course of the programmes, and with approval from government officials, we began to explore and discuss with the programme management appropriate policing strategies. This responsibility was then delegated to staff within operational units. Within some of these units, it soon became apparent that their understanding and appreciation of what is entailed by a problem-solving approach were seriously lacking. One officer suggested to us that POP requires a change of mindset away from the quasi-military mentality they are used to. POP can be extremely difficult in practice and the tendency within the police service is to resort back to what they know best. As one chief inspector said when confronted with a particularly thorny problem by an officer, 'I don't give a fuck, Jeff. Get it sorted.'

Little experience of responding strategically to racist harassment and crime

In terms of a holistic multi-agency response to racist crime, there was little evidence of problem-solving at the programme management level or, indeed, below. The tendency was to resort to highlighting the deficiencies of partners, attributing blame and resorting to traditional enforcement methods. Policing tactics involved 'high-visibility patrol' and surveillance, and were all offender focused. One of the major problems was that the Community Safety Units (CSUs) did not have a proactive capacity. Furthermore, they rarely communicated with sectors or core teams and were never consulted in the original discussions surrounding the project. Policing is compartmentalised and fragmented, with different 'silos' having their own distinct responsibilities and tending to be concerned with meeting their own targets.

Inadequate data capture

This is probably the least important of the barriers to POP. In most cases it appears that many of the data required are collected by the police. The major problem, as we discuss below, is that the data are rarely used for strategic problem-solving. While routine data collection is relatively unproblematic, that undertaken specifically in support of POP is less straightforward. During these initiatives local area surveys were to be undertaken to help guide interventions, target resources and measure impact. The Metropolitan Police, including its specialist consultancy arm, appeared to have little experience of such data collection.

Inadequate data analysis capability

Detailed analysis of the target sites did not precede submission of at least two of the bids. In part, as we describe below, this was influenced by the tight timescales (data could not be found and analysed quickly). Thereafter, any data collection/analysis was usually at the behest of the evaluation team. In two out of the three initiatives, a common factor was an absence of dedicated analytical support. Previous Home Office research has noted that the ability of analysts is variable (Read and Tilley 2000), and in only one of the six areas in which we conducted research did we come across a skilled analyst. When the existence of this person was discovered by the police in other London boroughs, they sought access to her skills. Her borough commander refused.

A very limited desire to utilise data

The ACPO guide to combating hate crime (2000) states that use should be made of a range of data to tackle hate crime. On no occasion throughout the programmes was use made of any data other than police crime data – and this was solely for operational purposes. The Project Information Officer (PIO) in the RMCP was never asked to collate any data for strategic or monitoring purposes. Indeed, programme managers could see no role for the PIO other than to serve the needs of the evaluation. As the Programme Manager said at one point: 'I do think that the [PIO] ought to understand the full extent of their role and so a lot of this is really about how and where you [the evaluators] would like to use them. So ... to that extent they'll be working for you.' The consequence of this was that strategies were being implemented with little or no understanding of the extent or nature of the problem on the ground. Evidence throughout that information/intelligence and data were being used to inform or steer strategic or operational decision-making was scant. As one officer put it: 'we're constantly playing catch up here. We're just managing to cope rather than trying to solve the problems at source. Management here has a tendency to hide problems rather than dealing with them.'

*Limited ability/capability to organise a strategic policing response
on the basis of data analysis*

Organising a response to hate crime was seriously inhibited by capacity. Even when data/intelligence were collated, which was not frequent, it was rare for action to result from it. As one example, the Race Crime Intelligence Officer (RCIO) in one of the London boroughs designed an intervention known as the Cell Cultivation Project. This entailed interviewing all suspects charged and detained at the police station to provide information about racist incidents. This was arguably the best example of small-scale anticipatory problem-solving. The idea was to collect intelligence and then act upon it. However, the initiative failed because once the information had been collected, the RCIO did not have the resources to act upon it. The Project Manager, in the closing report, noted that 'the capacity to conduct low-level surveillance, arrests, intelligence meetings and interviews was confined to times when volunteers could be found amongst CSU staff'.

Inadequate or problematic relationships with partner organisations

The focus of this part of the chapter has been on the limitations that appear to characterise police attempts to problem solve in the area

201

of hate crimes. Many of the observations apply equally to partner organisations such as the Probation Service and local authority community safety departments. In addition to such limited organisational capabilities, POP was hampered by problematic relationships between partners. These concerned different working practices and cultures, differing interpretations of the purpose of initiatives and differing levels of commitment to programmes (the police service, notwithstanding the problems identified, often tended to be the most committed of the organisations involved), all exacerbated by the absence of effective inter-agency reporting structures and a consequent lack of accountability.

Limited understanding of the essentials of the hate crime reduction projects within the police service and partner organisations

The understanding within the CSUs of the various strands and components of the project within the individual sites was at best limited. In fact, the CSU in two boroughs in the four boroughs initiative had not been consulted about the project prior to meeting with the evaluators. The only policing input up to this point had come from the borough liaison officer's office, where the project was being managed. This limited understanding at 'ground level' made it especially difficult to develop working strategies that would operate in synergy with other strands and interventions within the programme. In one of the initiatives, at a steering group meeting, a sector inspector announced that his team would be conducting a crackdown in a target area in which local detached youth workers had been attempting to work for some time. The high-profile policing operation effectively undermined the longer-standing youth work programme – even though both were undertaken under the umbrella of the anti-hate crime project. The local area co-ordinator, a police sergeant, later commented: 'what we didn't want in [this borough] was a scenario where youth workers are engaging with these youths and our people putting in place operations that'll put them in jeopardy. We all needed to be singing the same tune. But that never happened.' This absence of joined-up working, of an 'holistic' approach to problem-solving, was common.

Inability/unwillingness to focus on substantive problems

All too often in these programmes there was little attempt to understand the underlying conditions of a problem; the tendency instead was to address the immediate, presenting issues. In Hounslow, in the very early stages of the RMCP, a group of youths were identified as perpetrating the majority of crime in the target estate. The response was to install surveillance equipment with the aim either of deterring the young offenders or collecting evidence which would support prosecution. There was no attempt to understand the problem. Similarly, in Tower Hamlets in the same programme, detailed analysis identified the problem as rival gangs, segregated by race, competing for territorial dominance. The consequence was running battles and repeated calls for police assistance. No attempt was made to confront and address the attitudes of those involved; the police response was to resort to traditional enforcement methods using regular high-visibility policing. In both cases, the result appeared to be the displacement of the problem to surrounding neighbourhoods.

As we suggested earlier, these barriers to POP which, we think, are more common than a reading of the literature on contemporary policing might suggest, were stimulated, and in some ways exacerbated, by the timetables under which these programmes were initially established and then conducted.

The timetables imposed for initial bids

Bids for funding within the TPI by police forces were prepared under very short deadlines. As one senior police officer put it, 'it was a question of suddenly becoming an enthusiast and an expert in a particular piece of work to somebody else's timescale'. This was especially unfortunate given that the TPI was established ostensibly to help forces in conjunction with local Crime and Disorder Partnerships to develop a problem-solving approach to tackling crime. Yet, according to the Police Service, the timescales imposed by the bidding and application process did not allow for the form of detailed analysis that was expected within a problem-oriented approach. In two sites in which our research was based, and to a lesser extent in the third, research and analysis were conducted retrospectively, once funding approval was received. This was after key partners had been identified and had become involved. To paraphrase Crawford's (1998) analogy, this is akin to buying a suit and then seeing if it fits. This problem of timetable was recognised, if not entirely resolved, in the second-round bidding process. In a letter to chief constables announcing the second-round of the TPI, the Home Office stated that: 'one of the lessons learnt from Round 1 was that some forces appeared too preoccupied with a particular tactic or apparatus and did not properly assess the problem itself and how to tackle it in the most cost-effective manner'.

The problem of timescales had adverse implications in another important way. That is, there was significant slippage between the receipt of applications and final ministerial approval from the Home Office. For example, following an expression of interest, the application for the RMCP was submitted early in June 1999. Clarification was requested by Government Office for London on a number of issues resulting in a revised bid being submitted in September. However, delays in gaining ministerial approval meant that the overall programme was not officially approved until March 2000.

While rigid timescales influenced the quality of the original submissions, the apparent lack of urgency thereafter had a number of negative consequences. These included difficulties in relation to the advertisement for and recruitment of staff, the commissioning of surveys and the scheduling and allocation of internal resources to meet project demands. In one site provisional approval was requested to begin recruiting key personnel on the basis that tacit approval had already been gained. In the absence of ministerial approval, however, officials were unable to agree to this. Moreover, project steering groups, advisory bodies and consultative groups had been pre-established on the assumption that funding would become available and was imminent. Yet prolonged delays meant that these groups were often convened without either the mandate or the resources to commence work.

The timetables for implementation

The assumption, and expectation, as one project manager put it, was that projects would be prepared to 'hit the ground running' once monies were agreed. However, this failed to take into consideration the logistical difficulties presented by implementing new innovative projects (and the already existing problems of the bidding timetable). In the natural early life of any development project there is an initial period of learning during which problems and pitfalls are the norm, not the exception. Often, and in a number of the cases on which this chapter is based, the period of funding was insufficient to progress beyond the initial developmental phase. This is a by no means uncommon problem in government-funded initiatives where political timetables and implementation timetables are not easily squared. As Tilley (2001: 83) reminds us, 'elections create a periodic imperative for politicians to show results, which is liable … to lead to policies and practices offering relatively quick fixes to take precedence over measures whose effect is only likely to be felt in the longer term'.

Problem-oriented evaluation?

As will be clear by now, in our view the Home Office stipulation that 'evaluators must not be closely involved in the running or designing of programmes (other than the evaluation framework)' was somewhat unrealistic. This was the case, we have argued, for two primary reasons. First, because the 'development' and 'accountability' functions that were built in to the research from the outset required a greater degree of engagement than the stipulation allowed. Secondly, and more importantly in this context, the reality of POP – at least in these cases, though we suspect more widely – significantly increased the 'development' and 'accountability' functions and of necessity drew researchers into a more engaged or involved role. In the remainder of this chapter we want to explore in slightly greater detail some of the aspects of this more engaged role – i.e. elements of the 11 'roles' we identified above – some of the problems and pitfalls therein, and the consequences for 'trust relations' that can ensue.

Many of the difficulties in the programmes stemmed from weaknesses in the initial bids that were submitted. Pawson (2002: 160) reminds us that 'programme design is often a research free zone'. The weakness of the bids, together with the limited capacity of the police to problem solve as outlined above, resulted either in very little action at all on the ground or in activities being undertaken that, in our view as evaluators, bore little relation to what had initially been proposed. Partly as a consequence of this we were progressively drawn into the programmes in a number of ways. In the first instance, we were requested to help clarify and resolve outstanding ambiguities in two of the programme proposals. In one particular case project goals, aims and objectives were not clearly defined; roles and responsibilities remained unspecified; strategies and project location remained undetermined; lines of communication, management and co-ordination were not clarified; and insufficient, if any, attention had been given to the linkage between intended strategies and objectives. As evaluators we were very concerned about this. In our view, without specification of, at the very least, the particular strategies to be used, it would not be possible to identify the 'theory' that was supposed to link particular interventions and stated objectives. To put it crudely, little thought had been given to how particular interventions might lead to particular outcomes. Without this it was nigh impossible to take strategic decisions about the data it was important to collect, and why. In other words, it was simply not possible to construct an evaluation framework. As a consequence we took the decision, encouraged by professionals on the ground, to play a much more active role in guiding the design of the initiatives we were contracted to evaluate. In our terms above, to a degree, we became *project authors*.

Had this more engaged role been confined to playing a greater part in the design of the interventions it might have been relatively (though not entirely) unproblematic. However, in several parts of the programme it became clear early on that the very limited capacity within the police organisation to analyse data, and use them in support of police and/or multi-agency responses to identified problems, was likely to result in little or no activity within the programme. Under these circumstances evaluators are faced with what appears to be a stark choice between programme failure and attempting to stimulate and promote activity. We chose the latter – in the main with the knowledge and support of the Home Office. We acted as *data analysts* – analysing data, for example, in support of funding bids for extra policing resources – *product champions* – promoting the programme among partner agencies and within the police service – and *policing consultants* – providing examples of policing initiatives, introducing officers to colleagues working on similar problems in different forces and advising on the nature and design of various elements, especially policing elements, of the programmes. Each of these roles, in different ways, served further to blur the boundaries between the police, the Home Office and the evaluation team. Acting as 'policing consultants' and 'project author' illustrates the point. The lack of an integral policing component to the original RMCP became a focal concern in an early evaluation report. The report prompted the Metropolitan Police to prepare and submit a bid to the Home Office for additional funding to support a policing strategy. Shortly after this we received correspondence from the programme steering body requesting support in preparing the application. It outlines the dilemma for the evaluation and is worthy of lengthy quotation:

> A key point in your recent interim report on the progress of the project evaluation highlighted an apparent gap in the project in respect of police enforcement ... The importance of this omission has only begun to be fully apparent. We had hoped to be able to make our contribution from existing resources. It is becoming clear that increasing demand and competing priorities for diminishing resources mean that we will not be able to re-deploy police officers in the manner originally intended ...We need to fill this gap. The most effective way of doing so is for the MPS to make a request to the Home Office, via [Government Office for London] GOL, for a further grant to fund additional policing activity. Informal

enquiries suggest that such an application would be sympathetically received but it will need to be based on a sound business case. I see your involvement as *central to this process*, and would be grateful to have your views on what sort of additional activity should be supported and how much of it might be required in order to make a quantifiable difference capable of satisfactory evaluation. Most importantly, I would like to know to what extent you feel that an additional bid is necessary for the project to achieve its overall objective (project correspondence June 2002, emphasis added).

The letter raises a number of issues. First, it illustrates the lack of clarity surrounding the nature and purpose of targeted policing development projects – something that would, in principle, need to be recorded for use in future evaluation reports. Secondly, the letter is an explicit invitation to become a 'project author'. It arises out of a lack of clarity about the role of the evaluator, itself partly the product of a blurring of the boundaries between the police service and the evaluator. The request was therefore based on the assumption that it was perfectly reasonable and unproblematic. Refusing the request was likely potentially to compromise the relationship between the evaluator and those responsible for implementation and, at worst, could have led to implementation failure.

Engaging in 'product championing' poses similar conundrums. Early in the RMCP we attended a number of steering group meetings in Hounslow where plans for the programme were to be established. During these meetings it became clear that the key local authority representative either did not understand the nature of the proposed programme, or wilfully wished to ignore what had been agreed in the contract with the Home Office. The police representative did not appear overly concerned about this and certainly did not appear likely to resist proposals to make very substantial changes to the programme – changes that would have left it unrecognisable. Faced with what we perceived to be the imminent breakdown of this part of the programme, we acted as 'product champions', reminding all parties of the nature of the proposed programme and that this had been detailed and agreed in the contract with government. Engaging in such a role undoubtedly blurred the distinction between the evaluation team and the Home Office in the eyes of some parties. In a similar manner, acting as 'authors', 'data analysts' and 'police consultants' undoubtedly blurred the boundary between the police and the evaluation team in the eyes of the police. We return to this below when discussing the issues of 'trust' and 'blame'.

A variant on the role of 'product champion' was that of *inter-agency facilitator* in which the evaluator works to find solutions to problems that have arisen in the relationship between partners within the programme. As one example, in one of the sites visited regularly mediation services had been funded through the project and made available to officers as one of the resources in their arsenal for resolving cases and disputes. Direct mediation services were particularly suited to persistent low-level cases where an offence had not been committed but where there was felt to be a risk of more serious problems developing. However, the initial take-up of the service within the CSU was poor. Officers confided that they were reluctant to make referrals for two reasons. First, as they had no previous experience of working with the service they were reluctant to promote it to (potential) victims with whom they were in contact. In addition, some officers expressed an inherent organisational reluctance to promote a service that might undermine their professional primacy. The consequences of this for the project would have been low output and partial implementation. However, our relationship with the mediation service, project management and CSU staff placed us in a position to put forward remedial action. As an initial solution we suggested that the mediation service conduct a familiarisation visit to the CSU to outline their aims and methods and to share some of their experiences with officers. In addition, we suggested that a mediation worker could be seconded to the CSU office one day per week, thereby enabling officers, where appropriate and on the agreement of the victim, to refer a case directly to the mediation worker. Take-up on the service increased significantly. It did so because acting in the capacity of *inter-agency facilitator* our intervention helped to demystify the service and enabled officers and mediation workers better to realise mutual goals.

Much social research and evaluation research requires quite close engagement with the concerns and needs of the subjects of study. This is most frequently related to the need to establish and maintain relationships so that access to subjects and to other data sources is first made possible and then maintained. In the arena of POP – and no doubt in others – it is potentially somewhat more complicated than that. In the case of the RMCP, many of the skills the evaluators possessed were precisely those that appeared to be in short supply within the police service. From our experience across the three TPI initiatives, this is likely to be true in POP more generally. The consequence, as we have described briefly, is that it is almost inevitable that evaluators will get drawn more heavily into the fabric of the programme they are evaluating than is often thought to be ideal. We do not view this as being, of itself, problematic. Rather, what is required is role clarity – an explicit understanding – between evaluator and others, if the major difficulties are to be avoided. As one example of such problems, the existence of blurred boundaries may make the reporting of findings, especially critical findings, more difficult than would otherwise be the case. It is to this we turn next.

Reporting, distance, trust and blame

In particular, ethnographers of the police have largely been silent on the difficulties they encounter, implying that their entry into the field and relations with police officers were unproblematic (Brewer 1993: 126).

Much of the preceding discussion has concerned the circumstances under which, and the reasons why, evaluators may 'get involved' in various practical aspects of the initiative being evaluated, particularly where POP is concerned. This involvement potentially comes at a cost. That cost, we would argue, is not in practice the one it is often assumed to be: the independence and integrity of the evaluator/evaluation. These can be protected and maintained under circumstances of engagement (though we return to this in the conclusion). In practice, the major cost, or at least one of the major costs, is that 'trust relations' between the evaluator and the evaluated implicitly change. As we outlined above, confusion about the purpose of evaluation, together with the 'role conflict' that can ensue, serve (further) to blur boundaries between key stakeholders in such programmes. In some situations this would not be especially problematic. In our view, however, the nature of the police organisation, and certain aspects of police culture, mean that attention to 'trust relations' is especially important, and that confusion about the nature of such relations may result in a particularly defensive, and potentially hostile, response.

The confusion surrounding our role as evaluators was further compounded, and to some extent driven, by the fact that we 'attended' the various programme steering groups set up to oversee implementation. We went to considerable lengths to explain our presence in such forums – our role, in our view, was to observe the decision-making process. Our desire to act simply as non-participant observers was extremely difficult to maintain. In particular, we were frequently asked for our views on progress, to give a sense of what forthcoming priorities were and, on more than one occasion, whether or not a bid for further funding should be supported. We should acknowledge here that although it was primarily the police service that failed to 'understand' this 'observer' role others, including the Home Office themselves, also did so. In practice, responding to these requests became a question of judgement. It was unrealistic, we felt, not to respond to a direct request from the chair of a steering group for information. Refusing all requests to participate would undoubtedly, and possibly rightly, have been perceived to have been evidence of a lack of co-operation and of the operation of double standards; a refusal to feed back information to those from whom we expected so much information.

Providing feedback was far from unproblematic in these and other forums. As we have already noted, the evaluations had multiple purposes including developmental aims, as well as the assessment of impact. We were contracted to provide the Home Office with regular updates in the form of interim and process reports. These reports were made available to steering groups:

> The Home Office does not place any restrictions on the circulation of interim evaluation reports to the project management or the advisory/steering groups. Indeed, we would actively encourage them all to consider the interim findings with an eye to improving the impact of the initiative. Circulation of the report to other project team members and stakeholders must be handled sensitively by the management and advisory groups (project correspondence December 2001).

Such reports, depending on the progress that is being made on the ground, may simultaneously serve the three masters of 'knowledge', 'development' and 'accountability'. Moreover, even the most benign and positive of reports may draw a degree of defensiveness from organisations subject to evaluation. The issue of 'accountability', however, is a highly problematic one for the police service. In part, this results from the hierarchical, quasi-military structure of policing which tends to focus on individual, rather than group, successes and failures and results, in our view, in the existence of a 'culture of blame'. Young (1991: 30), in his ethnography of police work, quotes the following observation from a police officer in North Wales: 'Serving officers who attempt constructive criticism of the police, risk being labelled traitors and put their promotion prospects in jeopardy. If internal criticism is unwelcome, the views of outsiders are even more likely to be seen as hostile and derogatory.'

Any evaluator, therefore, may be thus labelled. This is not in itself problematic and, indeed, is well worn territory for the evaluator working in many different walks of life. It becomes more problematic, however, when the circumstances of the research require the evaluator to occupy a more 'involved' role – a role that we have argued is almost de rigueur in relation to POP. This is related to the second relevant factor which is the 'internal solidarity' of the police service (Cain 1973). As Reiner (1985: 93) notes: 'internal solidarity is a product not only of isolation, but also the need to be able to rely on colleagues in a tight spot, and a protective armour shielding the force as a whole from public knowledge of infractions.' The tendency, consequently, is for police officers to view the world in terms of 'us' and 'them' (while allowing for distinctions to be made between types of 'us' and types of 'them').

The more engaged role which we occupied – having been required, in effect, to act as 'project authors', 'product champions', 'data analysts', etc. – led, to put it crudely, to a shift in which we moved from 'outsider' to 'insider' status (not literally of course) – from 'one of them' to 'one of us'. In our eyes, our more involved role did not impact on our ability or willingness to be critical of what we observed. Clearly, however, criticism, when delivered, was then perceived by police colleagues as akin to 'treachery':

> [It is] ironic, [be]cause it's one of the biggest criticisms this organisation has, [is of] evaluators dropping in one year after a project has started, they don't know what's going on or what it took to get there. But you didn't do that so we should've been thankful. But that isn't how they [senior officers] think. They're so far up their own arses these managers that for someone to come in, like you, that's great but don't dare say a word against us. Your first report, because it didn't glow, because it had picked up on issues which were relevant, was a bombshell. Because you're working *with* them they weren't expecting to see you put down anything in black and white which would criticise. Now that was a shock for them (field interview, emphasis added).

And the inevitable response to this 'unanticipated' criticism:

> The phones were ringing. Funny that because then they did talk to each other. You know, it's 'we're working with [evaluator] and he's a really good guy, we can talk with him, he gives us advice and support and the next minute he's stabbing us in the back' ... Up to then they felt they had you on board, and you'd be writing about all the good things they were doing, you know, 'everything is fine even if it isn't, I mean we can talk about it behind closed doors' but don't bloody write it down. [Borough commander] said, 'oh

you've gotta watch [name] now, don't involve him anymore' but I'm saying 'I'm sorry, but it [evaluation report] was really helpful'. But you've got to realise that it wasn't seen like that and that's the problem … To be honest it was appalling the way they treated you. But if you ask any of those project managers if they had a problem with it [the evaluation report], they'd say they thought it was well justified, in fact we felt you didn't go far enough. But management were never going to see it that way. They're so dismissive. Arrogant in fact. You can't tell them they're wrong, they're the Borough Commanders for God's sake (field interview).

The 'us' and 'them' element of police organisational culture meant that if we were critical then we somehow must have disguised our main purpose; we had deceived those we were working with, and had shifted from 'author', 'analyst', 'consultant', even 'amateur therapist', and were perceived as a 'Home Office agent', 'Home Office spy', 'project spy' or even 'watchdog'. In part, the degree to which this is a problem is contingent upon the 'success' of the initiative being evaluated. In the one case in which we were involved in an evaluation of a TPI project that appeared to be having some successes the criticisms included in interim reports and other feedback, though sometimes provoking a fairly defensive response, did not lead to any serious threat to the relationship between the evaluation team and the police service responsible for the initiative. However, in the projects which exhibited significant levels of implementation failure, criticism was taken quite differently. The reasons for this, in our view, relate to the nature of the way in which credit and blame tend to be apportioned within the police service.

Police culture, as is often noted, is characterised by relatively high levels of solidarity (Skolnick 1966). Accepting this, however, should not disguise the fact that the policing organisation is also characterised by a considerable amount of conflict. This can be seen in a number of ways, for example between CID and uniform officers, between 'street cops' and 'management cops' (Ianni and Ianni 1983) and between officers competing for credit within the organisation. In this arena – taking credit for success – the police organisation is highly individualised. It is particular officers rather than particular shifts or squads or basic command units (BCUs) that tend to be given credit for success. The reverse is also true. When things go wrong – or are perceived to go wrong – the consequence, frequently, is the search for an individual scapegoat. For the savvy police officer the solution is to attempt to ensure that someone outside the organisation takes the flak. In multi-agency initiatives the most obvious candidates are partner organisations and their staff. In an initiative being evaluated the bearer of any 'bad news' is also a prime candidate for scapegoating. The evaluator – particularly the evaluator who is perceived at one time to be 'one of us' rather than 'one of them' – is especially at risk. This, naturally, can quickly serve to undermine the relationships so important to successful evaluation. If lines of accountability and reporting structures – between funding body, evaluation team, police and other agencies – are clear, then much of this can be avoided. Where the nature of the relationships has been allowed to blur, more fundamental breakdown is likely.

Concluding comments

> Evaluators have a stake of their own in the evaluation. They obviously have a professional interest in doing a good study and getting professional recognition and appropriate compensation for it. They usually also have an interest in satisfying the study sponsor. If they are on the staff of a government agency, program organization or research institute, they want to please their boss and colleagues and thus advance their careers. If the study sponsor is an outside funder, the evaluator may be interested in pleasing that organization so that it will send more work and funds her way (Weiss 1998: 110).

We concur entirely with Weiss' view of evaluators' interests. We would add, however, that in order sometimes to maximise the possibility of what she calls 'doing a good study', the evaluator may have to get involved in many of the design and operational aspects of the initiative being evaluated. To put it at its bluntest, if they didn't the chances are there would be nothing to evaluate. This, we think, is not an unusual occurrence in criminal justice-based initiatives. Moreover, we believe it to be an almost endemic part of the evaluation of POP initiatives, particularly given the current low skill levels in problem identification and analysis within the police service (Cope forthcoming) and the parlous state of much partnership working in criminal justice.

Though there are risks in this more involved role, as we have described in some detail, we believe that this is a legitimate role for the evaluator. No doubt, however, this more active evaluator role may be viewed by some as undermining the integrity and credibility of such evaluations. The assumption is that they cannot be 'objective'. This assumption is, in our view, wrong. There is no reason, in principle, why the 'active evaluator' cannot apply just as much intellectual distance and rigour to his or her task as any other. And there are many sound professional and ethical reasons to believe they should do so. The major problem, therefore, is likely to be the *perception* that such evaluations cannot be 'trusted'. The challenge, consequently, is 'to create appreciation for such diversity [in evaluator roles] among both those within and outside the profession who have a single narrow view of evaluation and its practice' (Patton 1997: 125). POP strikes us as an interesting place in which to take up this challenge.

Notes

1   The term 'hate crime' is used here to include racist and homophobic crime as well as domestic violence. Each of the three projects addressed one or more forms of hate crime.
2   PPACTS sought to tackle both racially motivated and homophobic crime/ violence.
3   The AVI sought to tackle three forms of hate crime: racist and homophobic crime/violence and domestic violence.
4   These will appear in summary form in forthcoming Home Office publications. A detailed account of the history, development, politics and operation of all three initiatives will appear in our forthcoming book: *Policing Hate Crime: Cultures, Partnership and Organizational Conflict* (2004).
5   For the purposes of this chapter we prefer this simple formulation to more complicated typologies such as the five-point classification proposed by Owen and Rogers (1999).

References

ACPO (2000) *Guide to Identifying and Combatting Hate Crime: Breaking the Power of Fear and Hate*. London: Association of Chief Police Officers.

Bowling, B. (1999) *Violent Racism*. Oxford: Clarendon Press.

Brewer, J.D. (1993) 'Sensitivity as a problem in field research', in C.M. Renzetti and R.M. Lee (eds) *Researching Sensitive Topics*. London: Sage.

Cain, M. (1973) *The Policeman in the Community*. London: Routledge & Kegan Paul.

Chelimsky, E. (1997) 'Thoughts for a new evaluation society', *Evaluation*, 3(1): 97–118.

Cope, N. (forthcoming) 'Intelligence led policing or policing led intelligence: integrating volume crime analysis into policing, *British Journal of Criminology*.

Crawford, A. (1998) *Crime Prevention and Community Safety*. Harlow: Longman.

Crawford, A. and Newburn, T. (2003) *Youth Offending and Restorative Justice: Implementing Reform in Youth Justice*. Cullompton: Willan.

Elias, N. (1987) *Involvement and Detachment*. Oxford: Blackwell.

Farrington, D.P. (1997) 'Evaluating a community crime prevention program', *Evaluation*, 3(2): 157–73.

Farrington, D.P. (1998) 'Evaluating "communities that care": realistic scientific considerations', *Evaluation*, 4(2): 204–10.

Goffman, E. (1971) *The Presentation of Self in Everyday Life*. Harmondsworth: Penguin.

Goldstein, H. (1979) 'Improving policing: a problem-oriented approach', *Crime and Delinquency*, 25(2): 234–58.

Goldstein, H. (1990) *Problem-oriented Policing*. New York, NY: McGraw-Hill.

Grimshaw, R. and Jefferson, T. (1987) *Interpreting Policework: Policy and Practice in Forms of Beat Policing*. London: Allen & Unwin.

HM Treasury (1997) *Appraisal and Evaluation in Central Government: 'The Green Book'*. London: HM Treasury.

Home Office (1998) *Targeted Policing: Prospectus for Developmental Projects*. London: Home Office.

Home Office (1999a) *Reducing Crime and Tackling its Causes: A Briefing Note on the Crime Reduction Programme*. London: Home Office.

Home Office (1999b) *Programmes for Offenders: Guidance for Evaluators*. Crime Reduction Programme – Guidance Note 2. London: Home Office.

Hope, T. and Murphy, D. (1983) 'Problems of implementing crime prevention: the experience of a demonstration project', *Howard Journal*, 22(1): 38–50.

Leigh, A., Read, T. and Tilley, N. (1996) *Problem-oriented Policing: Brit Pop*. Crime Prevention and Detection Series Paper 75. London: Home Office.

Leigh, A., Read, T. and Tilley, N. (1998) *Brit Pop II: Problem-oriented Policing in Practice*. Police Research Series Paper 93. London: Home Office.

Lincoln, Y.S. (1991) 'The arts and sciences of program evaluation', *Evaluation Practice*, 12(1): 1–7.

Macpherson, Lord Justice (1999) *The Stephen Lawrence Inquiry. Report of an Inquiry by Sir William Macpherson of Cluny. Advised by Tom Cook, The Right Reverend Dr John Sentamu and Dr Richard Stone*. Cm 4262-1. London: HMSO.

Morgan, R. (2000) 'The politics of criminological research', in R. D. King and E. Wincup (eds) *Doing Research on Crime and Justice*. Oxford: Oxford University Press .

Newburn, T. (2001) 'What do we mean by evaluation?', *Children and Society*, 15: 5–13.

Oakley, A. (2000) *Experiments in Knowing*. Cambridge: Polity Press.

Owen, J.M. and Rogers, P.J. (1999) *Program Evaluation: Forms and Approaches*. St Leonards, NSW: Allen & Unwin.

Patton, M.Q. (1997) *Utilization-focused Evaluation*. Thousand Oak, CA: Sage.

Pawson, R. (2002) 'Evidence-based policy: in search of a method, *Evaluation*, 8(2): 157–81.

Pawson, R. and Tilley, N. (1997) *Realistic Evaluation*. Newbury Park, CA: Sage.

Pawson, R. and Tilley, N. (1998a) 'Caring communities, paradigm polemics, design debates', *Evaluation*, 4(1): 73–90.

Pawson, R. and Tilley, N. (1998b) 'Cook-book methods and disastrous recipes: a rejoinder to Farrington', *Evaluation*, 4(2): 211–13.

Read, T. and Tilley, N. (2000) *Not Rocket Science? Problem-solving and Crime Reduction*. Crime Reduction Research Series Paper 6. London: Home Office.

Reiner, R. (1985) *The Politics of the Police*. Brighton: Harvester Wheatsheaf.

Rosenbaum, D.P. (2002) 'Evaluating multi-agency anti-crime projects: theory, design and measurement issues', in N. Tilley (ed.) *Evaluation for Crime Prevention. Crime Prevention Studies. Vol. 14*, Monsey, NY: Criminal Justice Press.

Sibbitt, R. (1997) *The Perpetrators of Racial Harassment and Racial Violence*. Home Office Research Study 176. London: Home Office.

Skolnick, J. (1966) *Justice without Trial: Law Enforcement in a Democratic Society*. New York, NY: Wiley.

Weiss, C.H. (1998) *Evaluation* (2nd edn). Upper Saddle River, NJ: Prentice Hall.

Young, M. (1991) *An Inside Job: Policing and Police Culture in Britain*. Oxford: Clarendon Press.

Chapter 9

Assessing cost-effectiveness

Janet E. Stockdale and
Christine M.E. Whitehead

Context

Use of economic evaluation in the assessment of Targeted Policing Initiatives

Towards the end of 1999, teams of independent evaluators were appointed by the Home Office Policing and Reducing Crime Unit (PRCU) to assess the Targeted Policing Initiatives (TPIs) funded under the Crime Reduction Programme (CRP). The task of the evaluation was to identify what works, where and most cost-effectively.

The evaluators' key tasks were to:

- identify and cost resource inputs;
- identify outputs and outcomes;
- conduct process and outcome evaluations;
- carry out cost-effectiveness analyses;
- provide relevant data to the Home Office for the conduct of cost-benefit analysis and comparative assessment of projects; and
- identify good practice worthy of dissemination and application elsewhere.

While evaluators were expected to comment on the benefits and/or drawbacks associated with the TPIs, a formal cost-benefit analysis was not within their remit. This was to be undertaken at the centre. But the identification and costing of inputs, the identification and measurement of outputs and outcomes, and the assessment of cost-effectiveness all played a pivotal role in the evaluation of the TPI demonstration projects.

The requirement to quantify both costs and consequences and to assess returns on investment reflects an increasing emphasis on economic evaluation in the assessment of police activity and its impact. Traditionally, the police have allocated resources in line with their perceived priorities and associated operational requirements. Most resources have been distributed in response to demand and, in some instances, on the basis of likelihood of success rather than on the basis of cost or value. But, over recent years, this position has begun to change for a variety of reasons. There is a statutory duty to ensure best value in service delivery, together with increased stress placed upon internal and external accountability and on making resource allocation decisions transparent – especially when resources are scarce. Moreover, there is a growing ethos throughout the public service of business harmonisation, performance measurement and benchmarking to ensure improvements in performance and to support the promulgation of good practice. All these factors have led to an increased interest both in cost assessment and in relating project activity and impact to costs – either through cost-benefit or cost-effectiveness analyses.

Chapter outline

The aim of this chapter is to clarify the role of economic evaluation, to exemplify the cost-effectiveness approach used in the five TPI assessments conducted by our team and to place this in the broader context of cost-benefit analysis. Cost-effectiveness has three basic stages:

1 Identifying, measuring and valuing resources used.
2 Identifying and measuring outputs and outcomes.
3 Relating the two to derive cost-effectiveness estimates.

The first two stages are illustrated by reference to all five TPI projects. A case study comparing the two TPIs directed at vehicle crime is used to clarify the assessment of cost-effectiveness. The final sections look at the rather different demands of cost-benefit analysis and its potential for future use, and recommend where economic evaluation, notably cost-effectiveness, can make a contribution to resource allocation in the context of problem-oriented policing (POP).

Evidence base

The chapter draws on the experience of evaluating five rather different TPI demonstration projects. Two of the TPIs aimed to tackle vehicle crime: Operation Arrow – implemented in three London boroughs (in receipt of £597,500 CRP funding) – and the Calderdale initiative in West Yorkshire (£180,000 CRP funding). These TPIs drew on a portfolio of interventions including intelligence-based targeted action – typically using focused teams – and publicity to encourage the public to take preventative action. The Dalston Partnership Policing Project – known as DP3 – in the London Borough of Hackney (£760,000 CRP funding) aimed to tackle drug use and drug-related crime by the use of drug arrest referral workers, outreach activity, work with the business community, diversionary and other local projects and action against drug offences and street crime. The remaining two TPIs addressed local problems in specific localities. The Tynedale initiative (£40,300 CRP funding) was designed to address problems involving crime, disorder and fear of crime in rural towns and remote villages in southwest Northumberland. The Bransholme project (initially £393,000 CRP funding) aimed to reduce crime and disorder on a large public housing estate in Hull and to assist the community in maintaining their own social order. Both projects employed mobile police offices, although of very different types. Southwest Northumberland also used CCTV.

Economic evaluation

Economic evaluation provides an analysis of different courses of action in terms of both their costs and consequences, an input into decisions about resource allocation and a mechanism for assessing the value of these decisions (cf. Stockdale *et al.* 1999: 8). It is of potential value, therefore, to the police service which faces difficult decisions about how to allocate its limited resources.

Before undertaking a particular initiative, decision-makers should estimate its likely costs and consequences. Post-implementation, they should assess the actual costs and consequences to determine whether the results were as expected and whether the use of resources was worth while. In a simple market system, where prices reflect both the value of the resources when assigned to their next best use (opportunity costs) and the value of the outcome to society, all that is required is to identify inputs and outcomes, estimate their prices and measure the difference between benefit and cost. Resources are then applied to a particular initiative wherever benefits outweigh costs. Additional resources are allocated to the activity until the value of the outcome from the application of these additional (marginal) resources falls below their cost.

But, in the context of policing, economic evaluation faces a number of potential problems (cf. Stockdale *et al.* 1999: 9). There may be problems in delineating the activity and in identifying inputs and outcomes. More importantly, there are likely to be difficulties in valuing these inputs and outcomes or in specifying the decision rule. This means that a full economic assessment, such as that provided by a cost-benefit analysis, may not be achievable. But the use of another, more viable, economic evaluation technique, such as cost-effectiveness analysis, can inform the learning/feedback cycle and thereby contribute to effective resource allocation.

The choice of technique should be determined largely by the aim of the evaluation exercise, the nature of the project activity, the capacity to identify and value project inputs and outputs/outcomes and the availability and reliability of relevant data. But it should also take account of the costs of conducting the evaluation relative to the usefulness of the guidance provided (cf. Stockdale *et al.* 1999: 11).

Cost-effectiveness analysis within the TPI programme

Basic approach

Cost-effectiveness analysis relates specified outputs and/or outcomes to the costs of achieving those outputs/outcomes. It can be used to compare competing options on the basis of the input costs per unit of output/outcome. Such options might be interventions within a project or different projects. In the simplest form of cost-effectiveness analysis only one output per intervention and one project outcome are specified. More complex measures weight different outputs or outcomes to produce an overall cost-effectiveness measure. The decision rule is to choose the option with the least cost per output or outcome.

Undertaking a cost-effectiveness analysis makes the decision process more transparent by organising information about inputs, outputs and outcomes in a single comparative framework. The analysis essentially involves:

- identifying, quantifying and valuing (i.e. costing) all project inputs;
- identifying and quantifying all outputs and outcomes; and
- relating outputs/outcomes to resource costs.

Practical guidance was provided to assist evaluators in carrying out these tasks and the key principles adhered to in each stage are outlined below (more detail is provided in Dhiri and Brand 1999; Legg and Powell 2000).

Inputs and costs

The first steps in the cost-effectiveness process were to identify and quantify all the inputs to each of the initiatives and to measure the costs associated with each of the constituent interventions and with the project as a whole.

Evaluators were asked to identify all physical, human or financial resources used in implementing each project and to assign them appropriately to each constituent intervention. In some cases inputs pertained to only one intervention but in many cases a given input had to be allocated across a project's constituent interventions. This allocation was done by the relevant project team using its knowledge of the project's activities. The inputs encompassed both additional resources assigned to the project and resources which had been diverted to the project from other, unrelated activity. The inputs included all start-up and recurrent activity covered by CRP funding and 'levered-in' resources (i.e. additional resources), such as inputs from public sector sources, necessary for project implementation.

All projects were required to be costed in economic terms – i.e. for each input the opportunity cost was to be calculated, irrespective of whether any financial cost was incurred. In most cases the market value of a resource was assumed to reflect its opportunity cost and inputs were valued accordingly.

These data were collated using the data collection tool which had been commissioned by the Home Office. The data collection tool, in principle, permitted the entry of relevant inputs and their costs and the production of summary reports. Where available, local costs were used. All the personnel costs contain adjustments for employment overheads and office use (where appropriate) in accordance with the instructions contained in the data collection manual. Standard discounts were automatically applied to equipment purchases by the data collection tool. As highlighted earlier, all costs were necessarily financial rather than strict opportunity costs.

Table 9.1 shows the total cost estimates for each of the five TPIs under consideration. The most expensive projects were Arrow (£2.8 million) and DP3 (£1.6 million). The least expensive project was Tynedale (£175,000). Cost data (not shown here) were also collated for the different stages of the project – set-up, implementation and exit – for each constituent intervention and for each source of funding – the CRP, levered-in funds from the police and levered funds from elsewhere. (The CRP component in the cost estimates was typically less than the CRP funding allocation where monies were spent on equipment because of the effects of annuitisation.)

Table 9.1: TPI total estimated costs

TPI	Estimated total cost £
Arrow	2,781,110
Islington	1,129,340
Camden	454,300
Southwark	1,197,470
Calderdale	420,670
DP3	1,625,580
Tynedale	175,310
Bransholme	650,890

Outputs and outcomes

The next step in the cost-effectiveness analysis was to identify outputs for a project's constituent interventions and outcomes for the project as a whole. A primary output measure (P) was specified for each intervention as required by the data collection tool. Some interventions had additional, subsidiary output measures (S). The constituent interventions for each of the five TPIs and their associated outputs are summarised in Table 9.2.

Outcomes were typically specified only at the project level as, in general, it was not possible to assign outcomes to specific interventions. Each project had a number of outcomes: some were quantifiable, others were not. Obviously, in many cases, the reduction in the targeted crime(s) is the key benefit. Typically, this is measured using recorded crime figures, with appropriate recognition of all the inadequacies of such data. Even then, as the case study will illustrate, the size of any reduction in recorded crime will depend upon the assumptions made about the appropriate baseline against which changes in the number of offences should be measured. However, the main focus of the Tynedale TPI was fear of crime and several of the initiatives had subsidiary aims relating to community cohesion and involvement in combating disorder. Therefore, attention was also paid to other – often less tangible – outcomes. The key outcomes and their associated measures for the five TPIs are shown in Table 9.3.

Analysis of the project outputs and outcomes produced a mixed picture. Although several projects were successful in output terms, there were some clear instances where interventions were implemented less

Table 9.2: TPI interventions and outputs

Operation Arrow and Calderdale

Interventions	Outputs	TPI
Use of analysts	Number of reports/ products prepared	Arrow – all three boroughs
Specialist intelligence unit – VCRAT	Number of intelligence packages generated	Calderdale
Focus team	Number of operations/ taskings undertaken	Islington and Southwark
Targeted action	Number of operations/ taskings undertaken	Camden and Calderdale
Publicity/informing the public	Number of people contacted/informed	Arrow and Calderdale
Target hardening	Number of target-hardening devices installed	Islington
Decoy operations	Number of operations conducted	Arrow – all three boroughs
Bullseye (communication system)	Number of calls out	Islington
Youth initiatives	Number of young person hours covered	Arrow – all three boroughs

DP3

Interventions	Outputs
Drug arrest referral scheme (DARS)	Number referred for drug treatment following assessment (P) Number assessed but not referred (S)
Drug outreach work	Number of contacts (P)
Business crime reduction initiatives	Number of businesses advised (P) Number of newsletters distributed (S) Number of personal safety courses delivered (S) Number of visits to businesses by police team (S)

Table 9.2 continued on facing page

223

Table 9.2 continued

Community interface	Number of community members contacted/ involved (P) Number of newsletters distributed (S) Number of participants in surveys/focus groups (S)
Youth activity	Number of young person hours covered (P)
Initiatives against street robbery	Number of operations undertaken – with a proactive tasking (PAT) form (P) Number of high-visibility patrols (S)
Initiatives against drugs	Number of operations undertaken – with a PAT form (P) Number of high-visibility patrols (S) Number of taskings (S)

Tynedale and Bransholme initiatives

Interventions	Outputs	TPI
Mobile police office	Number of hours those staffing the office are available to the public – in the office or on local patrol (P)	Both Tynedale and Bransholme
	Number of visitors (S)	Both
	Number of visits made (S)	Tynedale only
	Number of different locations visited (S)	Tynedale only
Movable CCTV	Number of times CCTV system is accessed for purposes of monitoring/ interrogation	Tynedale only
Use of analysts	Number of reports/products produced	Bransholme only
Publicity/educating the public	Coverage achieved, i.e. number of leaflets distributed/ number of people receiving advice	Bransholme only

Table 9.3: Key outcomes for the five TPIs

Outcome	Measure	TPI
Reduction in vehicle crime (total and constituent offence categories)	Number of offences	Arrow and Calderdale
Increase in detections for vehicle crime (total and constituent offence categories)	Number of detections	Calderdale
Level of awareness of crime prevention measures	Survey data (incomplete)	Calderdale
Reduction in drug supply/use	Number of relevant offences	DP3
Reduction in level of crime	Number of offences for core crimes (robbery, burglary, motor vehicle crime and shoplifting) and other crimes (pickpocketing, other theft/handling, credit card fraud, violence against the person)	DP3
Reduction in level of disorder	Number of relevant incidents	DP3
Reduction in fear of crime (individual and business)	Responses to survey questions	DP3
Increase in satisfaction within the business community	Responses to survey questions	DP3
Reduction in fear of crime/changes in other community reactions	Questionnaire data – various indices	Tynedale: three surveys Bransholme: in–out surveys but incomplete data
Reduction in disorder	Number of recorded incidents	Tynedale and Bransholme
Reduction in crime	Number of recorded incidents (total notifiable offences and selected categories)	Tyendale and Bransholme

than satisfactorily and the level of output was disappointing. Output failures reflected a range of implementation problems:

- Insufficient problem specification.
- Difficulties in recruiting staff.
- Lack of continuity in project staffing.
- Vulnerability of project activity to competing demands.
- Inadequate timescales.
- Lack of organisational and – in some cases – political support.
- Inadequacies in project management.
- Lack of sensitivities to the dynamics of partnership working and differences in ethos.
- Practical difficulties in developing joint working.
- Deficiencies in contract specification and delivery of outsourced service provision.

Success in output terms was not necessarily reflected in project outcomes, which also present a very mixed picture. The analysis of the project outcomes is illustrated by reference to assessments of all five TPI demonstration projects within our remit.

Tackling vehicle crime: outcomes of the Arrow and Calderdale initiatives

In the case of Arrow, two boroughs – Islington and Southwark – appeared to achieve some success in the initial stages of the project. Decreases in vehicle crime were observed in the first 18 months in the case of Islington and in the first 9 months in the case of Southwark. In the remaining borough, Camden, there was no discernible impact of Arrow on the level of recorded vehicle crime which showed an upward trend throughout the project's lifetime. The downturn in performance in both Islington and Southwark in the latter stages of the project is explicable, to some extent, in terms of competing demands. For example, in Southwark, officers were diverted to a number of murder inquiries, including a particularly high-profile case in late 2000. In Islington, the rise in street crime changed the borough's priorities. All three Arrow boroughs were affected by abstractions following 11 September 2001.

Overall, the data suggest that the implementation of Arrow in Islington and Southwark was associated with a reduction in vehicle crime in the project's first year. In 2000, the performance of these two boroughs was better than or equal to that of their comparator boroughs and of London as a whole. However, this success was not sustained. In 2001, the incidence of vehicle crime was no better – and in most cases worse – than in the comparator boroughs and in the whole of the Metropolitan Police Service (MPS) area.

Calderdale did not achieve its primary objective of reducing vehicle crime over the period of the TPI. However, there was a decrease in theft of a motor vehicle over the project's lifetime. Equally, the number of detections for vehicle crime increased substantially in the project's second year, once the proactive unit became operational, yielding an overall increase over the two-year project period. There is some limited evidence that the TPI did raise the level of awareness of the problem of vehicle crime and encouraged car drivers to take action to avoid becoming a victim. The Calderdale initiative also increased communication between the police and the public and led to co-operation between the police and local organisations, especially the business community, in addressing the problem of vehicle crime.

Tackling drug-related crime: the Dalston Partnership Policing Project (DP3)

In the case of DP3, analysis of the outcome data showed that several of the crimes targeted by project activity decreased over the project period. Changes recorded in the DP3 area were more positive than in the borough as a whole with respect to total crime, street crime, pickpocketing, theft from shops, other theft/handling and disorder. The rise in drug offences observed in the DP3 area is likely to reflect increased attention to these offences arising from the DP3 project.

Comparisons between the DP3 and a similar area again suggest that DP3 activity contributed to the reduction or containment of some of the targeted offences. There is little evidence of displacement from the DP3 area to either the rest of the borough or across the border to Islington. However, the rise in vehicle crime experienced over the course of the project may, at least in part, reflect crime switch.

Survey data from the DP3 project suggest that the proportion of passers-by – the majority of whom lived in Dalston – who felt unsafe and worried about victimisation decreased towards the end of the project period. The increased concern shown in the final survey wave is likely to reflect people's generalised anxiety following the events of 11 September, and specific responses to a reduced police presence. The survey data also suggested that victimisation among the business community had reduced over the project period and that perceptions of the drug problem in the local area were more positive at the end of the project compared with the beginning.

Tackling local problems through mobile offices and CCTV: the Tynedale and Bransholme initiatives

An essential aim of the Tynedale project was to reduce fear of crime and the evaluation involved three postal surveys which examined perceptions of crime, the police and other community safety issues in selected target areas.[1] Although the response rates were relatively low (25, 22 and 18%, respectively), they were satisfactory for postal surveys with no reminders, with each survey generating over 1,000 responses. The surveys provided comparative data about:

- residents' perceptions of their neighbourhood;
- their concerns about community safety and fear of crime; and
- their satisfaction with policing provision.

Only some illustrative examples of the survey findings are highlighted here. The survey data suggested that fear of crime decreased over the project period. The percentage of respondents who felt unsafe walking alone after dark was lower in the third survey than in the second survey (–5%), which in turn was lower than in the first survey (–7%). In the third survey only 16% of respondents felt very or fairly unsafe walking alone after dark (compared with 28% in the first survey). This figure compares favourably with other survey findings. For example, surveys of residents across the Northumbria Police Force area, conducted for Northumberland County Council, report that the percentage of respondents who felt very/fairly unsafe walking alone in their area fell from 45% in 2000 to 21% in 2000. In 2001, the percentage of all respondents to the BCS survey who felt very/a bit unsafe in this situation was 33%. But the percentage of respondents who felt very/a bit unsafe walking alone in their area was significantly higher for non-rural than for rural residents – 37% compared with 23% (Aust and Simmons 2002).

The percentage of respondents in Tynedale who felt the police offered sufficient protection from crime in their area was higher in the third survey than in the second (+5%), which in turn was higher than in the first (+12%).[2] One in every two respondents (47%) felt that the police offered sufficient protection (compared with 30% in the first survey). Although these and other related findings from the survey are encouraging, it is difficult to ascertain whether they are attributable either to the deployment of the mobile office and/or the use of mobile CCTV, or are associated with other interventions or extraneous factors.

Analyses were also conducted of changes in both crime and disorder in southwest Northumberland area command, where the Tynedale TPI was implemented. Assessment of southwest Northumberland against its comparator area suggests that the TPI area's experience of crime was comparable with or better than that of the comparator in 2000 and 2001 but that it was worse than the comparator in 2002. The picture with respect to disorder is more positive. Southwest Northumberland showed year-on-year decreases in the number of disorder incidents in all three years under consideration, while the comparator area experienced increases in both 2001 and 2002.

The Bransholme TPI relied on informal feedback and responses to questionnaires and interviews to assess community reactions to its mobile office known as the 'Cop Shop'. Feedback from local residents indicated that there was some hostility to the Cop Shop when it was initially deployed – the police presence was seen as intrusive and as providing the opportunity for 'spying' on the local community. Since then, public understanding of the Cop Shop has grown and attitudes have changed, such that the benefits of having police based in the local community are more widely recognised. Questionnaire and interview data – although initially limited by the low response rate – have confirmed that the reaction of most sections of the community is now positive and that the office is seen as having contributed to improving life in the neighbourhoods it has visited.

The analyses of crime and disorder on the Bransholme estate over the project period are too complex to detail here as they relate to the deployment of the mobile office for periods of 8–10 weeks at specific locations within the estate. In general, they suggest that the office can contribute to reductions in recorded crime – such as burglary – and incidents of disorder. However, the impact appeared to vary, both across areas and across different offence categories, and the effects were not necessarily sustained after the mobile office moved to a new location.

Overview of outcomes from the five TPIs

Although there were many positive effects of the initiatives, in the majority of cases, targeted crimes were not reduced consistently across the project period. In some instances, they even increased. Table 9.4 provides a summary of the project outcomes.

Even when targeted crime was reduced or contained in the areas addressed by the TPIs, the picture did not always compare well with appropriate comparator areas. Whatever the outcome, it was usually difficult, if not impossible, to determine whether observed changes were due directly to the project interventions. This was particularly true of the projects implemented in London and other urban locations, where there were a multiplicity of concurrent projects associated with areas of high

229

Table 9.4: Summary of outcomes of the five TPIs

Planned outcome	TPI	Summary of observed outcome
Reduction in vehicle crime (total and constituent offence categories)	Arrow and Calderdale	Arrow – some reduction in two out of the three boroughs but not sustained Calderdale – no reduction
Increase in detections for vehicle crime (total and constituent offence categories)	Calderdale	Some increase in detections
Level of awareness of crime prevention measures	Calderdale	Some limited evidence of increased awareness
Reduction in drug supply/ use	DP3	Number of relevant offences increased
Reduction in level of crime	DP3	Reduction in number of offences in some core crime categories
Reduction in level of disorder	DP3	Disorder decreased
Reduction in fear of crime (individual and business)	DP3	Some evidence of reduction in fear of crime
Increase in satisfaction within the business community	DP3	Some evidence of increased satisfaction
Reduction in fear of crime/ changes in other community reactions	Tynedale: three surveys Bransholme: in–out surveys but incomplete data	Tynedale: fear of crime decreased Bransholme: some evidence of decrease in fear of crime
Reduction in disorder	Tynedale and Bransholme	Disorder decreased
Reduction in crime	Tynedale and Bransholme	Initial decrease in crime not sustained

crime and/or deprivation. More generally there were other extrinsic factors relating, for example, to changes in the economic environment.

Cost-effectiveness calculations and comparisons

The final stage of the analysis involved relating outputs/outcomes to costs. This was done by calculating the cost per unit of output for each of the constituent interventions and the cost per unit of outcome for the project as a whole and, where appropriate, by conducting comparative analyses of similar interventions and/or projects.

Costs were related to outputs and outcomes to produce four measures (where appropriate):

1   Average total cost per unit of output/outcome – the output/outcome over the project lifetime compared with the sum of set-up costs, costs in years one and two and the 'shut-down costs' in the exit phase (i.e. excluding the 'sustainability' costs in the exit phase) for the intervention/project.

2   Average variable cost per unit of output/outcome – the output/outcome over the project lifetime compared with the sum of the costs in years one and two (i.e. excluding the set-up and exit costs) for the intervention/project.

3   Average cost per unit of output/outcome in year one – the output/outcome in year one compared with the project costs in year one (i.e. excluding the costs in year two and the set-up and exit costs) for the intervention/project.

4   Average cost per unit of output/outcome in year two – the output/outcome in year two compared with the project costs in year two (i.e. excluding the costs in year one and the set-up and exit costs) for the intervention/project.

Comparing the two years of the project, and perhaps looking at annual patterns, is the closest it is possible to get to assessing marginal costs. However, in many cases this was not possible because of the pattern of activity.

A fundamental element of conducting a cost-effectiveness analysis is the comparison of competing options. Such comparative analyses are only possible, however, when interventions and/or projects are sufficiently similar. In certain instances, initiatives did have some constituent interventions and outputs in common or they addressed similar problems and used the same outcome measures. Where interventions and/or projects were sufficiently similar, it was possible to generate comparative analyses either within or across initiatives.

The process of calculating and comparing cost-effectiveness is illustrated by a case study which focuses on Operation Arrow and the Calderdale initiative, both of which aimed to reduce vehicle crime (theft of, theft from and criminal damage to/interference with motor vehicles).

A cost-effectiveness case study: Operation Arrow and the Calderdale initiative

Applying the cost-effectiveness analysis methodology

Estimates were obtained for the costs of the Arrow and Calderdale initiatives and for each of their constituent interventions. The total cost of Operation Arrow was put at nearly £2.8 million. The implementations of Arrow in Islington and Southwark were estimated to cost between £1.1 and £1.2 million. In Camden, where the operation was terminated early, the cost was estimated to be just under £0.5 million. The percentage of the costs financed directly by the CRP ranged from 16% (Islington) to nearly 25% (Camden and Southwark). The remainder of the costs were covered by levered-in funds, the majority (between 64 and 75%) of which came from the police in terms of provision of staff. The total cost of Calderdale was put at just over £0.4 million. Of this, just over a third (34%) came from CRP funds, with the majority (61%) of the remainder being levered in from police sources.

Having obtained the cost estimates and measures of both output and outcome, cost-effectiveness analyses were then conducted by relating appropriate cost estimates to changes in the relevant measures. Where possible, analyses were conducted for each of the three implementations of Operation Arrow and for the Calderdale initiative in terms of both intervention outputs and project outcomes. The fact that the two initiatives had some constituent interventions and outputs in common and both addressed the problem of vehicle crime meant that, in principle, there was some opportunity for comparative analyses both across interventions and projects. However, the number of comparative assessments that could be conducted in practice was limited by the fact that many of the changes in the outcome measures were in the wrong direction.

Costs per unit of output

Costs per unit of output can give a clear indication of relative efficiency – over time and across projects – and point towards ways in which outputs can lead to better outcomes. They also provide a measure of effectiveness for those working within the project whose responsibilities include ensuring that outputs occur. They may also provide guidance on whether there are economies of scale and, in particular, whether the approach is being used to its optimal extent.

The picture that emerges from analyses of the cost-effectiveness of the projects' constituent interventions differs across interventions. Also, cost-effectiveness in output terms is not always associated with a decrease in vehicle crime. For both focused team/targeted activity and sting operations conducted by the Arrow boroughs, the cost per unit of output is highest in Islington and lowest in Camden. The cost per unit of output for focused team/targeted operations is lower in Calderdale than in any of the three Arrow boroughs. But although cost-effective in output terms neither Camden nor Calderdale recorded a decrease in vehicle crime. Of the two boroughs where there was a decrease – at least in 2000 – Southwark emerges as more cost-effective than Islington in output terms, with respect to both targeted activity and sting operations.

The costs per unit of output for analysts/specialist intelligence unit are higher in Southwark and Calderdale than in Camden where, in turn, they are higher than in Islington. Neither Calderdale nor Camden was effective in reducing vehicle crime. Therefore, of the two boroughs where Arrow appeared to have some impact, Islington's use of analysts was more cost-effective than was Southwark's. The costs per unit of output for publicity are substantially higher in all three Arrow boroughs than in Calderdale, which emerges as the location where the publicity intervention has been implemented most cost-effectively in output terms. But the fact that the costs per output unit are of a different order in Calderdale compared with the Arrow boroughs – pence rather than pounds – suggests that the publicity activity in the two TPIs is of a fundamentally different nature.

Costs per unit of outcome

Vehicle crime went up over the project period in both Camden and Calderdale and so cost-effectiveness comparisons in terms of outcomes were possible only for Islington and Southwark – and then only for the year 2000.

In Islington, the number of vehicle crimes fell by 511 (5.1%) over the two-year project period. However, within the period it fell by 872

(−8.6%) in 2000, but rose in 2001 by 369 (+3.9%). There are various ways of calculating the cost per unit of outcome (i.e. the cost per crime saved), depending on the assumptions made and the baseline against which comparisons are made. The estimates of the cost per unit of outcome in Islington associated with the different scenarios are summarised in Table 9.5. If we assume that the baseline would have been sustained without Operation Arrow and that all the reduction can be associated with that activity, then the overall cost per crime saved was £2,210, while the direct or average variable cost per crime saved was £1,932.

One of the interventions in Islington – the Bullseye communication system – was fundamentally different in nature from the other six interventions and was not aimed directly at vehicle crime reduction in its pilot phase within Arrow. It would therefore not be unreasonable to exclude its associated costs. This would reduce the overall costs to £1,711 per crime saved and direct costs to £1,488.

Were the analysis to focus simply on the year 2000, when there was a large reduction in vehicle crime and when the vast majority of project activity occurred, the cost per unit of crime saved would be far lower – at £586 per crime or £451 (excluding Bullseye costs). However, because a number of costs incurred in 2000 were not accounted for until 2001, this would undoubtedly be an underestimate. (Average cost per unit of outcome were not calculated for 2001 as crime went up in that year.)

Table 9.5: Operation Arrow in Islington: costs per unit of outcome (£)

	Overall cost per crime saved	Direct (average variable) cost per crime saved	Average cost per crime saved in 2000
Time-based comparison within Islington	2,210	1,932	586
Time-based comparison within Islington *excluding Bullseye costs*	1,711	1,488	451
Comparison using Hackney as baseline	847	656	436
Comparison using London as baseline	1,331	1,031	522

Another approach to calculating cost per unit of outcome is to compare the changes in observed crime with those for a comparator borough or indeed for London overall. Over the two-year project period, total vehicle crime went up both in Hackney (+8.1%) – the comparator borough most similar but also adjacent to Islington – and in London as a whole (+3.3%). If it is assumed that Islington – without Arrow – would have experienced the same increases as Hackney or as London, then the costs per unit of outcome are clearly much lower. Applying these figures would imply overall costs per crime of £847 using the Hackney baseline and £1,331 using London as the comparator. Excluding Bullseye costs would reduce these costs to £656 and £1,031, respectively.

It is debatable which of these comparisons is more valid. On the one hand, London includes all the 32 boroughs, encompasses diverse areas and averages over boroughs some of which are very dissimilar to Islington. On the other hand, Hackney's profile is closely comparable to Islington's but there is a real possibility of displacement from Islington to Hackney as a result of Operation Arrow, resulting in an over-optimistic assessment of the cost per crime saved in Islington. (Total vehicle crime fell (–10.2%) over the project period in the other comparator borough – twice as much as it did in Islington – making the interpretation of the comparative analysis problematic.)

The best estimate of the cost per unit of outcome obviously depends upon the scenario adopted. Inspection of the figures in Table 9.5 indicates that the most conservative assumptions lead to an estimate of some £2,000 per crime saved. Using more relaxed assumptions, and focusing only on 2000, produces an estimate of around £500 per crime saved. A best estimate is almost certainly somewhere in between these two figures.

In Southwark, the total number of recorded vehicle crimes fell in 2000 but increased in 2001. In 2000, it fell by 1,235 (–12.1%) but in the following year it rose by 1,494 (+16.7%) bringing the total back above the starting point by 2.5% – an additional 259 crimes. This is undoubtedly in part because of the diversion of general police activity to other problems and priorities in the borough.

As pointed out earlier, there are various ways of calculating the cost per unit of outcome (i.e. cost per crime saved), depending on the assumptions made and the baseline against which comparisons are made. The estimates of the cost per unit of outcome in Southwark associated with the different scenarios are summarised in Table 9.6. The reduction in crime in Southwark in 2000 can be compared with the costs incurred up to the end of 2000 (£612,631) to give some estimate of the

Table 9.6: Operation Arrow in Southwark: costs per unit of outcome (£)

	Overall cost per crime saved in 2000	Direct (average variable) cost per crime saved in 2000	Average cost per crime saved
Time-based comparison within Southwark	496	457	N/A
Comparison using London as baseline	—	—	14,603
Comparison using Newham as baseline	—	—	1,834

costs per crime before the environment changed. This gives a cost per crime saved of £496. Including only 2000 costs (i.e. direct costs) suggests a cost of £457 per crime saved. If it is assumed that crime remained at this level in 2001, the cost per crime saved would have been £969.

Obviously, given the very large increase in 2001, it is not possible to give an estimate of the costs per crime saved using 1999 as a baseline over the whole period. However, comparing with London overall there is some evidence of improvement – even taking account of the problems in 2001. On this basis Southwark did 0.8% better than the average – so the cost per crime saved would be £14,603.

It might be more appropriate to compare with Newham, which suffered from many of the same difficulties associated with inner-city areas. Newham's recorded vehicle crime rose by 8.9% over the two-year period implying that Southwark might have done around 6.4% better. On this basis Operation Arrow would have saved a maximum of 653 crimes – generating a total cost of crime saved of £1,834. On the other hand Southwark did far worse than the other comparator borough Lewisham, which had a pattern of vehicle crime during the period more in line with outer than with inner London boroughs.

It is obviously very difficult to put an accurate figure on the cost per crime saved in Southwark. The estimates vary from £15,000 to around £500. The most appropriate estimates are likely to be the time-based comparisons within Southwark and the comparison using Newham as a baseline. These would yield estimates in the range £500 to £1,800 per crime saved.

Comparative costs per unit of outcome

Depending on the scenario adopted, the cost per unit of outcome (i.e. per crime saved) in Islington in 2000 ranges from around £500 to some £2,000. In Southwark, the lowest estimates of the cost per unit of outcome are £500, £1,000 and nearly £2,000 – the highest estimate is £15,000. These comparative estimates suggest that, in the better case scenarios, Islington and Southwark can be regarded as comparable in terms of their cost-effectiveness. In the worst case scenarios, the cost per unit of outcome in Southwark is some four times that in Islington. Assuming that the appropriate cost per unit of outcome in Islington is likely to be somewhere between the two extremes, the cost-effectiveness of Islington and Southwark would be similar in outcome terms.

Overview of the Arrow and Calderdale initiatives

Despite the Arrow and Calderdale initiatives not achieving many of their intended outcomes during the projects' lifetimes, the two TPIs provided valuable process lessons and implications for good practice. Both projects were based on the assumption that the provision of resources to implement a portfolio of interventions would deter and disrupt criminal activity, thereby reducing vehicle crime over the two-year project period. Although the TPIs had core teams of committed and enthusiastic staff, both projects encountered a range of difficulties, which affected their implementation. Some of these – such as lack of analytic capacity, competition for staff resources and equipment, staff turnover, problems with partnership working and bureaucracy – were related to the project structuring and other internal organisational issues, while others – for example, competing demands and new priorities – derived from extraneous factors.

The evaluation indicates that activity directed at offenders, hot-spots and potential victims can have some success, but only if the project has a problem-oriented focus and coherence, and if project activity – and its necessary resourcing – is endorsed and supported at a senior level. To be effective, a vehicle crime strategy must be based on sound analytic products and must be delivered by a proactive focused team, supported by forensic examination of all vehicles involved in offences, imaginative crime prevention activity and youth initiatives and diversionary activity. It was only in those locations where focused teams were created and where there was enthusiasm and commitment from senior managers that there was any reduction in total vehicle crime. Even then, the decreases were not sustained in the face of competing demands to deal with what were deemed more important priorities.

Cost-effectiveness in output terms differs across interventions and is not always associated with a decrease in vehicle crime. Cost-effectiveness comparisons in terms of outcomes – which were possible only for two of the Arrow boroughs and then only in 2000 – suggest that the costs per unit of outcome are similar in Islington and Southwark. Whether or not these implementations of Arrow are judged to be cost-effective depends upon comparisons with other policing practices.

Overall, both the Arrow and Calderdale initiatives provided officers with the opportunity to test out ideas about how local vehicle crime problems might best be tackled. The officers and partners involved in the projects have a greater appreciation of the need to take a problem-solving approach to vehicle crime and to target their response appropriately. Translating this awareness into action in the wider arena such that it becomes an integral part of action to reduce vehicle crime will not be easy. These projects suggest that an effective vehicle crime strategy will require appropriate resourcing – especially in terms of analytical and response capacity – and organisational commitment and support. Unless the good practice lessons generated by the implementation and evaluation of the Arrow and Calderdale initiatives are recognised and acted upon, there will be minimal return on the substantial investment in these two projects.

Applying the cost-effectiveness methodology: lessons from the TPIs

The relationship between theory and practice

At one level, conducting a cost-effectiveness analysis of a crime reduction project appears to be a simple task – all that is required is the cost of the project and a measure of outcome. But the simplicity of this description hides the complexities of the assumptions underlying the exercise. The guidance provided to evaluators by the Home Office addressed some of the theoretical underpinnings but, in our opinion, a number of ambiguities and points of detail remained.

In particular the methods suggested for data collection, while aiming to simplify the process, were sometimes inconsistent with the fundamental economics of measuring how costs could properly be allocated. Equally, the requirement to focus on a narrow range of outputs and outcomes, while perhaps necessary given the range of projects included, made it impossible fully to assess benefits. The simplifications almost certainly meant that some spillover effects – which are fundamental to the joined-up approach to policing – were missed.

It is true that the projects were very different in nature and therefore the capacity to make direct comparisons was limited – but the fundamental objective of cost-effectiveness and cost-benefit approaches is to enable such comparisons to be made more transparent and consistent. Even at the cost-effectiveness level, comparisons between very different projects can be valuable because they often use similar processes (e.g. targeted action/focused teams; publicity) which can be readily compared. More importantly careful cost-effectiveness analysis is a necessary prerequisite for the more general cost-benefit assessment. At the limit it should be possible to compare, for example, the effective use of mobile offices in reducing anti-social behaviour with the cost of a targeted drugs raid – in terms of the cost per unit of benefit to consumers.

Maintaining the impetus

The approach taken by the Home Office focused more on the practicalities of data collection than on the underlying principles of cost-effectiveness analysis and the assumptions necessary to ensure that the data being recorded would be of some value both in relation to individual projects and – more importantly – in drawing conclusions about different approaches to similar problems and building the baseline for cost-benefit analysis.

At various seminars and meetings, held in 2000 and 2001, it became clear that the infrastructure necessary to facilitate data collection over the course of the various crime reduction programme projects and to permit analysis – especially comparative analyses – after projects had been completed was insufficient.

The baseline for the data collection was changed several times during the evaluation process. For example, requests in the second year of the evaluation that projects be disaggregated in particular ways and categorised under already-defined headings raised a number of concerns. This created problems, not only for the evaluation teams, but also for the project staff, who were disturbed by changes in the demands being made upon them. There were also fundamental issues relating to the value of the results for comparison across projects and for the intended cost-benefit analysis. In particular, the categorisation required by the Home Office reflected different levels of analysis. Some could be described as interventions – the deployment of a mobile police office or the use of mobile CCTV, for instance. Others appeared to represent an ethos or approach – for example, Crime and Disorder Reduction Partnership working – or a process which often underpins all project activity and is not easily separable, such as crime analysis. The project staff would have welcomed more consultation and involvement in saying how their projects were to be defined. Many of them took the view that projects do not fall neatly into separate interventions and that a given intervention often has multiple underlying mechanisms by which it was assumed to affect crime.

What these criticisms make clear is that there needs to be agreement early on with all parties (including practitioners, evaluators and funders) about the terms of the evaluation and in particular what the goals of the evaluation are and how they can be achieved. In the case of the TPIs, this never happened. It must be accepted that there will always be inherent differences in what is wanted at a policy level and what is done and what is useful at the implementation level. These involve trade-offs, but also demand understanding at all levels. Unless these issues are dealt with early in the evaluation process there will be both inconsistency in approach and frustration.

Estimating costs

The production of cost estimates can be a difficult task, not least because economic and financial costs differ significantly. In practice, one is usually forced into a compromise between the ideal of measuring economic costs and what is practicable – measuring resource utilisation and using price to determine monetary costs (cf. Stockdale *et al.* 1999: 18). A practical question is what prices should be used – this will depend on what data are available. Are actual costs (e.g. salaries) available or is one reliant on estimated or average figures? In one sense, it does not matter provided the basis for the costings is made explicit. What is important for the evaluations to be comparable is that the same procedure should be followed by all evaluation teams. In practice, evaluators were advised to use actual costings if they were available; if not, it was suggested they used average local costs – for example, the mid-point of a local salary scale – or, if this was not possible, to use standard costings supplied by the Home Office. As a result, the various evaluations are likely to have used different bases for their costings and – in some cases – the various costings within an evaluation may have been differently generated. Again these problems reflect the importance not only of accurate and consistent data but also data that are fit for purpose. This is a problem for any practical cost-effectiveness analysis – but both far more work and greater agreement are necessary than was possible in this early attempt at large-scale comparison.

Outputs and outcomes

A problem with most outcome evaluations is the temptation to add apples and pears. Many projects have multiple outcomes most of which are not of equal significance or value. One way out is to choose just one outcome measure but this obviously attaches an implicit value to this outcome – it is being designated the only outcome deemed to be of value. Another option is to attempt to value the various project outcomes but this inherently moves us on to cost-benefit analysis and using financial values. Separating the cost-effectiveness and cost-benefit analyses made this approach more difficult.

Giving weights to different outputs or outcomes, or allocating costs across outputs and outcomes, which is the basis for cost-effectiveness analysis, is a difficult task with judgements necessarily reflecting the evaluators' predilections about the benefit of the various project outcomes to the police and to the community in general. This is especially the case when an intervention addresses very different issues such as crime and fear of crime. These raise difficult but interesting questions which are of both theoretical and practical importance. Guidance probably never intended to address these issues but the lack of relevant advice left evaluators unclear about the value of what they were doing. Limited contact between evaluators and the Home Office is likely to have generated inconsistencies in approach and consequently lack of comparability across evaluations.

The opportunity for valid and reliable comparative analysis across projects is always likely to be limited. The problems in this instance were exacerbated by the over-complexity of the approach attempted and the difficulties in obtaining agreement when problems emerged. A clearer baseline, which clarifies the value of different elements, together with an agreed delineation of responsibilities could have very considerable benefits in future evaluations.

Implications

Some of these problems are obviously specific to this set of projects. But the general lesson to be learnt is that, if a complex set of evaluations is to generate broader understanding, more collaboration is necessary early on to ensure that the fundamental template to be followed by all projects is adequate. This involves ensuring both consistency with the principles underlying the specific forms of evaluation and clarity with respect to data collection.

The data collection tool

The data collection tool provided a spreadsheet into which data on different types of cost, their timing, outputs and outcomes were to be entered. The accompanying guidance was intended to clarify definitions and, where appropriate, the values to be used (e.g. for voluntary time or the yearly cost of capital equipment). Such a tool is necessary to ensure consistency. But, it also made transparent many of the problems associated with data collection. As such it was a core element in specifying the form of the overall CRP evaluation and could have offered an opportunity for resolving problems of interpretation. However, a range of difficulties made this impossible and adversely affected the potential for achieving consistency across very different projects.

Most importantly the data collection tool was late and inadequately tested, for reasons mainly associated with the client's procurement process. The data collection tool and its accompanying guidance about its use were not available until mid-way through 2001. A workable version of the tool was not developed until 2002. The associated evaluator guidance (Emmanuel Solutions 2001: 5) stated that the tool: 'was designed as an efficient means to organise and store data as it [*sic*] is collected, during the course of the projects, and facilitates electronic transfer of the data to the Home Office'.

The fact that the tool was not available until most of the round-one TPIs were nearing completion meant that the tool could not be used to store data over the projects' lifetime. Instead there had to be a two-stage process, which meant that some problems did not become apparent until too late to be sure of effective data collection. Even when the tool was available our experience of using it did not confirm its claim to be an efficient means of organising and storing data.

Apart from the overhead costs associated with the tool's use (arising from internal inconsistencies and some incorrect definitions), there was a mismatch between its demands and project content. For example, in some cases the crime categories permitted for entering outcome data did not match those used in the project evaluations. Also, the tool did not sufficiently consider the principles underlying the production of cost estimates, changes in outcome measures and the conduct of cost-effectiveness analyses. For example, evaluators were asked to enter, on a monthly basis, changes in the amount of crime attributable to the project – that is, adjustments were required in terms of what would have been expected to be the case in the absence of the CRP project. Obviously, the evaluators do need to take account of trends over time and/or comparator data, as illustrated in the cost-effectiveness case study above. However, there is little point doing this on a monthly basis. Also, the data collection tool did not permit the collation of the raw changes in recorded crime – only the adjusted figures are entered. These necessarily reflect the evaluators' views about how much any observed changes are attributable to project activity. Such decisions are difficult and do not represent an exact science. Unless the raw data are recorded, there is no way of checking on the assumptions made by the evaluators in reaching their estimates – these must be made explicit.

Essentially, the data collection tool was naïve in its conception and, in our view, encouraged the recording of unreliable data, especially with respect to outcomes. In the end, the data collection tool could not be used to record outcomes or to generate the cost-effectiveness analyses consistent with their underlying principles. It is not surprising that the resources and time involved in setting up the data tool were underestimated. However, it is an important lesson for future evaluations that the tool must be in place before data are collected – and must be internally checked and consistent well before the actual evaluation calculations are required. Equally, the fact that the aims of evaluation are ambitious does not inherently mean that the means should be complex – sorting out priorities for consistency and accuracy could have saved a great deal of effort and tension.

The value of cost-effectiveness analysis

To date there have been relatively few attempts to apply cost-effectiveness analysis to policing activity and POP is no exception. As Leigh *et al.* (1996: 10) pointed out, there has been very little formal evaluation of POP initiatives implemented in England and Wales. The limited evaluation evidence then available focused primarily on the implementation process – especially barriers to adopting a POP perspective – and, in some cases, a basic analysis of one or more outcome measure, such as recorded crime. None of the initiatives considered in their report adopted a framework linking incident identification and analysis with the construction of responses and subsequent assessment of the actions taken. In no case was there any indication that the POP initiative had been costed or that there had been an attempt to assess the value of the initiative in economic terms. The second Brit POP report (Leigh *et al.* 1998), which describes the implementation of POP in various forces in England and Wales, does contain some examples of forces attempting to evaluate the success of POP in the assessment stage of the SARA methodology (scan, analysis, response and assessment). But, as Leigh *et al.* (1998: 43) point out, forces implementing POP do need to recognise the inadequacies in the POP assessment stage.

The authors contended that they were unable to say whether POP works because POP is interpreted and implemented in too many ways to permit any firm conclusion. They might also have added that, typically, there is scant attention paid to project outputs and outcomes – with heavy reliance on a single outcome measure – and no mention of resource inputs or costs, or how these might relate to project activity and impact. Inadequate assessment is not peculiar to POP initiatives. The shortage of good evaluations was also highlighted by Read and Tilley (2000) in their analysis of the more general role of problem-solving in crime reduction.

What, if any, is the value of cost-effectiveness analysis – both to policing activity in general and to POP in particular? Cost-effectiveness analysis is one of a portfolio of economic evaluation techniques, which in turn is one approach to evaluation. All the different approaches have value. Process evaluation tells us about the process of implementation – what were the barriers to effective implementation and what facilitated implementation. Output evaluation can inform us about the level of project activity, while analyses of outcome measures can serve to identify the project's impact.

The particular contribution of cost-effectiveness analysis lies in the linking of resource inputs – and their associated costs – with project activity and outcomes. In the context of scarce or diminishing resources, increased demands for service and heightened emphasis on accountability, cost-effectiveness analysis could – and should – play a role in the evaluation of policing activity and its impact and in informing future decision-making. Although decisions about future action will not necessarily be determined by anticipated costs of resourcing such action, the cost implications need to be made explicit and to be related to both outputs and outcomes to ensure that a rational and appropriate decision is made. Economic evaluation can help provide value for money (VfM) as required by HM Treasury. In particular, as Goldblatt and Lewis (1998: 134) argue: 'to ensure that interventions are only adopted on a large scale when they are shown to be effective, both cost and effectiveness information are required from process and impact evaluations'.

Cost-effectiveness analysis has a range of potential benefits. The application of this technique to well defined, problem-oriented projects can:

- provide an assessment of 'full' costs, as opposed to just the costs associated with overtime or which are directly funded;

- identify cost patterns – over the lifetime of projects – and clarify the relationship of costs to outputs and outcomes;

- permit estimates of set-up, annual running costs, levered-in funds, etc., which would be needed if projects were to replicated elsewhere;

- generate estimates of costs per unit of output and costs per unit of outcome;

- provide comparisons between expected and actual resource demands and associated costs, and between expected and actual outputs/ outcomes; and

- permit a comparative assessment of the return on investment across projects which address similar problems.

However, generating these benefits without incurring a significant resource cost to government, project staff and evaluators alike requires a simple approach to assessing cost-effectiveness. Only if the overheads associated with collecting the relevant data and conducting the analysis are manageable by police personnel will assessments involving cost-effectiveness analysis be used and thereby inform policy and practice. Generally the bulk of any costing is the cost of the personnel associated with a project – the salary bill will involve not just overtime costs but the costs of any officer or other staff member who is diverted to project activity and therefore incurs an opportunity cost. Typically, the costs associated with personnel constitute some 85–90% of the total cost of a project. So, if these costs can be assessed then the other cost categories, such as equipment and premises, can be estimated. (The simplest means of calculating staff costs is to use standard costs – with appropriate guidance about on-costs and overheads.) The TPI showed that the procedures used for cost-effectiveness analyses can be cumbersome, time-consuming and expensive. Therefore, simpler, more efficient heuristics are needed if the technique is to be used more widely.

A basic cost-effectiveness analysis might comprise the following:

- A description of the initiative's set-up phase – specifying the major inputs, the total set-up costs for staff and other inputs and their funding sources.

- Estimation of the percentage allocations of staff and other costs across the project's constituent interventions.

- Collection of yearly costs over the lifetime of the project for staff and other inputs – the costs should be collated in the simplest way possible.

- Calculation of the total yearly costs for each intervention.

- Calculation of the total project costs – subdivided by funding source.

- Specification of the relationship between cost estimates and appropriate output and outcome measures.

Such a template would minimise the demands associated with data collection and analysis, while generating reliable indices of cost-effectiveness.

Cost-effectiveness analysis merits application in the wider arena of policing. The TPI evaluations, which provide the evidence base for this chapter, illustrate how cost-effectiveness analysis might aid the adoption of a problem-solving approach to policing. The analyses of the two initiatives to tackle vehicle crime highlight the differential cost-effectiveness of both the constituent interventions and the projects. The assessments of the two projects which rely heavily on a mobile office not only show how this resource can help the police service to address local problems in both rural and inner-city areas but also permit comparison of the costs and consequences, and of the cost-effectiveness of the two – very different – implementations of the concept.

At a more general level, consideration of the costs per unit of output and per unit of outcome should aid decision-makers' assessments of value for money in relation to the worth of the outputs and outcomes achieved, thereby informing their resource allocation choices and informing decisions about the future roll-out of projects. Moreover, reflection on scale of project funding – in relation both to the size of overall budgets and to the magnitude of resources typically allocated to the problem being addressed – should also serve to highlight the importance of assessing the *real* addition such projects can make to existing inputs and the likely use of such resources in an environment of scarce resources and competing demands.

However, evaluation of initiatives should consider not only project outcomes and effectiveness but also how the findings can be used to build capacity and improve the way in which similar projects work in the future. The suite of evaluations has generated insights into project planning and execution, highlighting both barriers to implementation and good practice lessons, which are worthy of more general consideration and application. Harnessing these insights offers the potential for strengthening and supporting operational policing in the future.

Using cost-benefit analysis – future prospects

Overview of the process

Why should evaluators use cost-effectiveness rather than cost-benefit analysis, which aims to provide a comprehensive and transparent evaluation? Like cost-effectiveness analysis, cost-benefit analysis compares competing options, but on the basis of the input costs relative to the benefits generated across all the outcomes. Where two or more options are being compared, the decision rule is to choose the option with the highest net benefit. But the demands of a full cost-benefit analysis go beyond those of a cost-effectiveness analysis – the technique requires that all outcomes are valued in monetary terms (Table 9.7). The difficulties associated with this task will often mean that, although cost-benefit analysis may be seen as the 'ideal' form of economic evaluation, its use will simply not be practicable.

Valuing benefits

Cost-benefit analysis alone demands the valuing in monetary terms of all benefits deemed relevant to the analysis. The complexities of this process cannot be overestimated. In some cases, it may be possible to

Table 9.7: Key features of cost-effectiveness and cost-benefit analysis

		Cost-effectiveness analysis	Cost-benefit analysis
Inputs	Identify?	Yes	Yes
	Value?	Yes	Yes
Outputs	Identify?	Yes	Yes
	Value?	No	Yes
Outcomes	Identify?	Yes	Yes
	Value?	No	Yes
Definition of success		Lowest cost per unit of primary output/outcome	Highest net value as compared with other use of resources

price the value of a particular benefit (e.g. drugs seized or stolen goods recovered). In others, it may be possible to infer a cost saving. Brand and Price (2000) in their analysis of the economic and social costs of crime provide estimates of the costs of a range of offences. The offence categories considered comprise burglary (dwelling and non-dwelling); vehicle crime (theft of, from and attempted theft); theft from a shop; other theft and handling; criminal damage (against individuals and households and against commercial or public sector property); homicide; violence against the person (serious and other wounding); sexual offences; robbery (of individuals and of commercial or public sector premises); and common assault. Clearly, this list is not exhaustive – several offence categories are not included. However, this work does provide a starting-point for comparing the costs of crimes on society with the costs of preventing them and dealing with their consequences to determine whether the benefits outweigh the costs.

While cost estimates of crime can be useful, they should be treated with considerable caution. As Brand and Price point out, although the estimates they provide are the best estimates of costs given the information available, they are inevitably imprecise and are sensitive to changes in assumptions made or to improvements in the quality of the supporting data. They argue that better estimates are needed of the emotional and physical impact of crime on its victims, the impact of crime on quality of life and fear of crime, the cost of precautionary behaviour, health service costs, costs to offenders and their families and police costs.

Moreover, average cost estimates are, by definition, aggregations of crimes with widely different impacts, such that different crimes within the same offence category will have vastly different costs. These and other potential pitfalls in using average cost of crime estimates identified by Brand and Price highlight the complexities of undertaking cost-benefit analyses of crime reduction initiatives (these are also explored in Dhiri and Brand 1999). Brand and Price conclude that further work needs to be done before average cost of crime estimates can be used with any degree of confidence in the cost-benefit analysis of crime reduction initiatives.

Such considerations mean that, even if one can be convinced that inputs can be comprehensively identified and priced – and even here there may be difficulties – it is very unlikely that it will be possible to generate accurate and realistic estimates of the monetary value of all the benefits associated with a crime reduction initiative. It remains to be seen what success the Home Office has in assessing the cost-benefit of the various TPIs.

Conclusions and recommendations

At this stage the main focus of economic evaluation should be on cost-effectiveness analysis, rather than on cost-benefit analysis, both because it is of more value to those in the field and because some, at least, of the problems can be consistently addressed. As we argued, assessment of outcomes in monetary terms is insufficiently developed and so, at the current time, there is more potential value in using cost-effectiveness rather than cost-benefit analysis (Stockdale *et al.* 1999). Cost-effectiveness has the advantage of building on performance measures while making the cost of an exercise transparent.

Cost-effectiveness analyses have the potential to aid our understanding of our past investment decisions and to inform our future decision-making about the ways problems should be addressed and with what resources. However, our ability to conduct such analyses is constrained by inadequate record-keeping and data collection. Typically management do not routinely collect appropriate data on staff costs; also, levered-in resources, which are especially important in multi-agency partnership working, and sponsorship contributions are rarely considered. There are similar practical problems with the collection of data relating to outputs and outcomes.

Cost-effectiveness analysis can contribute to the assessment element of SARA in POP initiatives. But this will need appropriate problem definition (based on scanning and analysis) and suitable targeted response. We need to consider how measures are assumed to have an impact – i.e. we need to identify the underlying mechanisms and context in which they are implemented (cf. Pawson and Tilley 1997). Also, we need to recognise that there will be no incentive to use evaluation procedures – especially economic assessment – if there is a massive overhead associated with the data collection and interpretation. There is a need to develop simple – but theoretically sound – guidance for assessing costs and outputs/outcomes and for conducting a cost-effectiveness analysis.

POP is seen as good practice (Scott 2000) but there is a clear need to assess the effectiveness of the approach, the associated resource demands and its cost-effectiveness. Economic evaluation should be a routine element of assessing POP – and other policing activity – and associated resource allocation decisions.

However, the use of economic evaluation techniques, such as cost-effectiveness analysis, will not generate significant benefits unless the purpose and value of linking outputs/outcomes to costs are more widely appreciated and the results of such analyses are disseminated.

249

Until then the uncritical transfer of responses will continue to occur, the potential benefits of taking a targeted approach to problems will not be realised and money will continue to be wasted.

In undertaking large-scale, real-time, cost-effectiveness and cost-benefit analyses there are some immediate lessons to draw from our experience. Key issues include the need to:

- agree the project scope and aims/objectives, while recognising that projects evolve;

- establish the rules of the 'game' in advance to encourage mutual understanding of the evaluation requirements;

- recognise what evaluators can and, perhaps more importantly, what they cannot do – not only are they not magicians but they often tread a difficult path between providing an independent assessment of the project and satisfying the expectation that they will provide guidance to project staff;

- ensure that all stakeholders are on board – their commitment and understanding are essential;

- ask those involved on the ground about what they expect to be most important in terms of costs, outputs and outcomes;

- identify the range of potential outputs and outcomes and define appropriate measures;

- make sure as much work is put into improving the quality of output and outcome data as is put into estimating costs;

- implement simple systems for keeping track of inputs, outputs and outcomes;

- try to ensure the availability of relevant baseline and comparator data;

- distinguish carefully what is specific to a particular project and what is more generic;

- ensure all project personnel, partners and other stakeholders and beneficiaries are kept informed – so that the benefits are not all kept until the end; and

- simplify the evaluation process wherever possible – there is no inherent value in complexity.

Taking these suggestions into account increases the chance of economic evaluation being used and of an effective learning cycle for practitioners.

Acknowledgements

The authors would like to thank all those who contributed to the TPI evaluations reported here, especially Jon Jackson whose data management and analytical skills were invaluable.

Notes

1 The Tynedale project and its associated evaluation were extended for an additional year – January to December 2002 – in order to provide a more valid and reliable guide to the implementation and impact of the project.
2 All the differences cited are statistically significant.

References

Aust, R. and Simmons, J. (2002) *Rural Crime England and Wales.* Home Office Statistical Bulletin. London: Home Office.

Brand, S. and Price, R. (2000) *The Economic and Social Costs of Crime.* Home Office Research Study 217. London: Home Office.

Dhiri, S. and Brand, S. (1999) *Analysis of Costs and Benefits: Guidance for Evaluators.* Crime Reduction Programme Guidance Note 1. London: Home Office.

Emmanuel Solutions (2001) *Evaluator Guidance for the Data Collection Tool.* Leatherhead: Emmanuel Solutions.

Goldblatt, P. and Lewis, C. (1998) *Reducing Offending: An Assessment of Research Evidence on Ways of Dealing with Offending Behaviour.* Home Office Research Study 187. London: Home Office.

Legg, D. and Powell, J. (2000) *Measuring Inputs: Guidance of Evaluators.* Crime Reduction Programme Guidance Note 3. London: Home Office.

Leigh, A., Read, T. and Tilley, N. (1996) *Problem-oriented Policing: Brit Pop.* Crime Detection and Prevention Series Paper 75. London: Home Office.

Leigh, A., Read, T. and Tilley, N. (1998) *Brit Pop II: Problem-oriented Policing in Practice.* Police Research Series Paper 93. London: Home Office.

Pawson, R. and Tilley, N. (1997) *Realistic Evaluation.* Newbury Park, CA: Sage.

Read, T. and Tilley, N. (2000) *Not Rocket Science? Problem-solving and Crime Reduction.* Crime Reduction Research Series Paper 6. London: Home Office.

Scott, M.S. (2000) *Problem-oriented Policing: Reflections on the First 20 Years.* Washington, DC: US Department of Justice, Office of Community Oriented Policing Services.

Stockdale, J.E., Whitehead, C.M.E. and Gresham, P.J. (1999) *Applying Economic Evaluation to Policing Activity.* Police Research Series Paper 103. London: Home Office.

Chapter 10

Mainstreaming solutions to major problems: reducing repeat domestic violence

Jalna Hanmer

Introduction

This chapter focuses on the organisation issues involved in the mainstreaming of a successful domestic violence pilot project across a whole police force and its implications for problem-oriented policing. Because wide-ranging and fundamental issues are likely to be present to some degree in any mainstreaming attempt, a thorough evaluation of problems and their interconnections is useful.[1] The model to be mainstreamed, the steps taken to introduce it, the problems encountered and the attempts made to solve them are described first. The mainstreaming process revolved around and interacted with issues of leadership, organisational capacity and culture. The question of why the pilot project was successful, but not its mainstreaming, then follows. The chapter concludes with recommendations for how best to address such a challenging undertaking.

What was to be mainstreamed and where?

The Vulnerable Victims Project (VVP) was based on two initiatives piloted in two divisional areas within West Yorkshire. The first was a successful domestic violence repeat victimisation pilot that involved a graded response in one policing division evaluated by the Home Office (Hanmer *et al.* 1999). The second was a system for responding to repeat victims of racist incidents developed after the publication of the Stephen Lawrence inquiry report (Macpherson 1999) and subsequent reports on progress in implementing the action plan based on the inquiry recommendations (Home Secretary 1999, 2001, 2002). The aim was to mainstream the graded response model developed for domestic violence throughout all the West Yorkshire Police area and also to apply the approach to both homophobic and racially motivated incidents. The desired outcome was to reduce the incidence of repeat victimisation for victims of domestic violence, racist and homophobic incidents through proactive responses to both perpetrators and victims.[2]

The model was to be mainstreamed in a diverse area. West Yorkshire has five local authorities: Bradford, Calderdale, Kirklees, Leeds and Wakefield. There are both urban and rural populations living in villages, small towns and cities. The five districts also differed in population and number of households, ethnic composition, economic and employment profiles. Bradford, Calderdale, Kirklees and Wakefield had higher than average deprivation rankings compared with other districts in England. The exception, Leeds, had the second most diverse economy of any major city in the UK with major financial, legal, professional, retailing and manufacturing sectors. Although Leeds enjoyed the lowest deprivation ranking of the five district councils, they all contained locations of multiple deprivation, particularly in inner-city areas with high proportions of black and Asian residents and areas that were predominantly council estates. Major regeneration programmes were found in all five districts. The crime and disorder strategies for 1999–2002 in the five districts identified domestic violence and hate crime either as a priority or as an aspect of another priority. Through action plans that included tackling repeat victimisation, the Community Safety Partnerships in the five districts were promoting initiatives to reduce the crime and disorder associated with domestic violence and hate crime.

A graded response where interventions increase with each attendance was developed in 1997 to overcome consistent complaints by women about policing responses to domestic violence. These were experienced as erratic and inconsistent and led to the conclusion that the police either could not or would not stop their partners' attacks, while their partners quickly learnt that their violence and abuse were unlikely to be checked by effective police action (Dobash and Dobash 1980; Smith 1989; Mooney 1993). By increasing interventions with each police attendance, the model is designed to convey a message to both parties that the police both can and will assist those who are victimised and both can and will increase their responses to perpetrators, even when arrest and charge are not possible.

Implementing the model requires greater efficiency in the use of resources with limited new resource implications, primarily the allocation of domestic violence officers and clerical support in all divisions. Table 10.1 describes the interventions at each level for the pilot project domestic violence model. Incidents where the perpetrator has either not previously attended, or not within the past year, are to be dealt with at level 1, with one attendance in the previous 12 months at level 2, and with two or more attendances at level 3. However, in assessing the initial level of intervention the full police record of domestic violence is reviewed. Entry at higher levels may be required depending upon the number of prior attendances and previous history, but the entry level cannot be downgraded or remain the same following further attendance. If either downgrading or remaining at the same level were to occur, the implicit message in these actions to both the victim and the perpetrator is that the police either cannot or will not effectively intervene.

Because any officer may initially attend an interpersonal crime, the model interventions begin with their attendance. The model requires continuing input from officers who attend calls and from those who process the outcome of attendances. As multiple attendances increase, the model calls for limited additional tasks to be undertaken by other officers. Partnership working, now part of mainstream policing, is incorporated into the model.

The domestic violence officer (DVO) has overall responsibility for implementing the specific aspects of the model after officers initially attend. The DVO ensures that letters sent out to victims and offenders are tailored to the type of offence and intervention level, and that requests are made for Police Watch and for Cocoon Watch to be undertaken by other officers. The DVO visits women at level 3 and liaises with other agencies that become involved. The reason the assistance of other officers is needed at level 2 and the DVO does not attend until level 3 is because of the large number of domestic incidents. The DVO responds to the most difficult situations, those involving chronic offenders.

Correctly identifying the repeat level of the perpetrator followed by the required interventions was crucial to the success of the piloted model in reducing repeat victimisation. Success was achieved over the year by an increase in the number of single attendances in relation to repeat attendances and also by an increase in the time intervals between attendances. Rigorously applying the model identified systematically chronic offenders and over the year reduced their number. This also encouraged women and their supporters to ask for assistance from the police. Identifying factors associated and not associated with repeat victimisation began to establish who was at risk of repeat attendance and contributed to career profiling of men.

Table 10.1: Domestic violence and repeat victimisation model

Intervention level	Victim	Perpetrator (common law offences)	Perpetrator (criminal offences)
Level 1	• Gather information • Information letter 1 • Police Watch	• Reiterate force policy • First official warning • Information letter 1	• Magistrates – conditional bail/checks • Police Watch • Information letter 1
Level 2	• Information letter 2 • Community constable visit • Cocoon and Police Watches • Target-hardening property	• Reiterate force policy • Second official warning • Police Watch • Information letter 2	• Magistrates – bail opposed/checks • Police Watch increased • Information letter 2 • Crown Prosecution Service (CPS) file jacket and domestic violence (DV) history
Level 3	• Information letter 3 • Police Watch • Domestic violence officer visit • Agency meeting • Panic button/Vodaphone	• Reiterate force policy • Third official warning • Police Watch • Information letter 3	• Magistrates – bail opposed/checks • Police Watch increased • Information letter 3 • CPS file jacket and DV history and contact CPS
Emergency Intervention	Implement – log reasons for selection	Not applicable	Implement and log level of action undertaken

Notes
Common law offences are primarily breach of peace.
Cocoon Watch requests the help and support of neighbours, family and relevant agencies in further protecting the victim by contacting the police immediately if further incidents occur. A Cocoon Watch is only implemented with the informed consent of the victim, and the perpetrator is made aware of the action.

While chronic offenders were systematically identified by the pilot project, there was insufficient time to develop an intervention model aimed specifically at them. The pilot found that the men who were not demotivated by the three model interventions formed a diverse group. Some had no previous criminal records, others had committed other serious criminal offences, while mental health, learning difficulties and addiction problems could also be present. Developing an intervention model for chronic offenders could involve inter-agency assistance as well as proactive investigation and evidence gathering.

The organisational achievements of the pilot included the involvement of all officers in the division. Few additional policing resources were required. Accuracy in recording domestic violence was established and recording categories were developed. These tasks were carried out by the evaluators who set up and maintained the database used both for operational and evaluation purposes. Uneven service delivery both to those victimised and those offending was reduced. The consistent and rigorous approach using appropriate interventions resulted in the demotivation of offenders and the enhancement of victim safety. Agency communication and inter-agency co-operation were improved, particularly with the Crown Prosecution Service (CPS) and the Probation Service.

Types of change and associated problems

In addition to the successful pilot, the West Yorkshire force had one earlier successful example of mainstreamed change in the policing of domestic violence. This previous history of successful change may be part of the explanation why the range of problems that were encountered in the roll-out of the pilot was not anticipated. Each of the two

---

Table 10.1 notes continued

Police Watch provides a visible police presence to both the victim and the offender and involves police patrols within the vicinity of the incident on a twice-weekly basis initially for a period of six weeks immediately following reported incidents.
Level assignment is made on the basis of attendance to the *perpetrator* and not the victim. This is because the perpetrator is responsible for the incident and not the victim. Allocating levels by attendance to the perpetrator means that attendance to previous victims is to be counted in the assignment of the allocation level. The point of the model is to alter the behaviour of the perpetrator, which is only partly accomplished by securing the immediate safety of the victim and possibly providing longer-term support.

prior successful changes was rooted in a different organisational situation and assisted by different factors. Types of change vary from fine-tuning, to incremental adjustment, to modular transformation and, finally, corporate transformation (Dunphy and Stace 1993). Each type of change has different impacts on strategy, structure, people and processes.

Change can be planned or emerge. In the West Yorkshire force the evolution of strategic responses to domestic violence began with continuous external environmental demands primarily from women's groups, punctuated by specific events that increased public pressure for change in the force. Of greatest importance was the length of time it took to identify the serial killer Peter Sutcliffe – some five years after he began killing women, primarily in the West Yorkshire force area. By 1983 the West Yorkshire County Council and the West Yorkshire Police Authority were supporting a proposal for research into the policing of domestic violence, which a newly appointed chief constable agreed could proceed in 1985 and, having accepted the recommendations of the report, introduced fundamental changes in 1988 (Hanmer and Saunders 1987).

These fundamental changes were 'discontinuous' or 'frame breaking' (Tushman *et al.* 1988). They involved radical shifts in strategy, mission, values, structure, operations, technology and management. Changes were introduced through a new policy requiring proactive responses to offenders and the protection of those who were victimised, the setting up of a database to record information gained through police attendance to domestic incidents, training for all officers on the new policy and establishing a headquarters unit led by a detective chief inspector and divisional units that included domestic violence in their remit. Over time, these externally promoted internal changes in the policing of domestic violence gave rise to a small number of committed and knowledgeable officers. The successful introduction of these frame-breaking changes was made easier at that time as the authority and organisational structure of the force were both hierarchical and centralised.

By 1997 the divisions were identifying specific annual objectives and the one division with an objective to reduce domestic violence agreed to participate in a pilot project, which came to be known as the Killingbeck Domestic Violence Project. As is common with pilot projects, those who agree to participate may have been the most committed to trying out new ideas and work practices. In contrast to the changes in 1987, the pilot project change can be characterised as a 'modular transformation' as new processes were introduced in only one division and did not affect the force as a whole (Dunphy and Stace 1993). The mainstreaming project was only possible because of these earlier developments in transforming policing of domestic violence in West Yorkshire and built on their achievements.

The mainstreaming strategy aimed for in the VVP begun in 2000 would require 'corporate transformation'. Corporate transformation involves radical shifts in organisational strategy and calls for changes in core values and mission, the distribution of power and status within the organisation, reorganised structures, procedures, work practices, communication networks, decision-making patterns and new personnel in key managerial positions (Dunphy and Stace 1993). Corporate transformation is qualitatively different from modular change and here it was being attempted in a context very different from the earlier situation. Since the piloting of the model there had been substantial organisational devolution between headquarters and divisions, which was to have a major impact on the process of mainstreaming.

The problems and issues encountered in the mainstreaming of the VVP were identified in earlier studies of domestic violence by Grace (1995) and Plotnikoff and Woolfson (1998). Plotnikoff and Woolfson summed up the issue as the low status of domestic violence within police forces. Problems were located in:

- headquarters management structures;
- divisional management structures;
- links between headquarters and divisions;
- role of domestic violence officers and units;
- co-operation from other officers;
- training issues; and
- views of officers.

Attempts to mainstream the repeat victimisation model also identified problems in relation to the following:

- Organisational location of domestic violence within the force structure.
- Force management information system method of data analysis.
- Most cost-effective use of human and financial resources.
- Centrality of the concept of vulnerable victim.
- Statutory and voluntary partnership arrangements.

While frame-breaking changes were successfully introduced in 1988[3] through the formal subsystem of the police organisation, the informal subsystems of police culture, politics and leadership did not totally relinquish the values and attitudes of the past that underlie the low status of domestic violence. These continued to sustain the view that minimal involvement in domestic incidents and limited roles for women in policing were appropriate. While not uniformly held, such notions influenced work practices and relationships within the force.

While aspects of institutional sexism within the police are raised from time to time, there is yet to be a major public focus that corresponds to that mounted on institutional racism with the resulting changes to operational procedures. Racial and homophobic incidents are primarily same sex, male on male, while domestic violence is cross-gender, primarily male on female. Police forces continue to be dominated by men, numerically and in senior management. The low status of domestic violence is, at root, a gender issue, which intensifies resistance to change.

The relevance of a model developed as a response to domestic violence for racial and homophobic crimes was based on the concept of the vulnerable victim. Victim vulnerability was presumed for inter-personal crimes of violence and abuse and even reflected in the name of the mainstreaming project, the Vulnerable Victims Project. While the characteristics of domestic violence, racial and homophobic incidents and the mode of policing varied considerably, discussion and analysis of differences in crime types and force responses did not occur in advance of the introduction of the VVP. Fundamental differences between domestic and hate crimes and the organisation of policing responses were not conceptualised as impediments to the application of the model. Unlike domestic violence, hate crime was likely to involve both a lack of close relationships and varying numbers of victims and perpetrators, and was routinely policed through crime management. The attempt to apply a systems approach, developed for victims and offenders in a close personal relationship, to racial and homophobic incidents was approached from the view, 'let's see if it works'.

Mainstreaming of the pilot model begins

During the gap between the end of the pilot project in 1997 and the beginning of the roll-out in 2000, different ways of responding to domestic violence developed in the 17 divisions. In the intervening two years, the pilot project interventions and procedures had been 'tweaked' or ignored. No division was implementing the model at the beginning of the roll-out in 2000, although some divisions believed they were, which increased the complexity of introducing mainstreaming. Hate incident responses based on the model were limited to some interventions, par-ticularly the sending of letters and packs to victims of racial incidents.

An advisory committee, the VVP board, consisting of ten members, was set up to oversee the roll-out. The VVP board was headed by the superintendent responsible for community safety and included senior members and co-ordinators of domestic and hate incidents from headquarters community safety, district and divisional crime sections, and also performance review and IT. Senior officers, previously associated with the successful pilot and now members of the board, proposed the extension of the model to hate crime.

After the appointment of the VVP board, the project began with the appointment of headquarters and divisional staff to implement the model. The headquarters domestic violence staff consisted of a co-ordinator and a sergeant. In the 17 divisions, domestic violence officers were already in post or drawn from other areas of work. Hate crime staff consisted of a force co-ordinator for racially motivated and for homophobic incidents; one support member to maintain centralised records; and community safety officers in each division. Additional organisational innovations included establishing hate and homophobic incident panels and community action groups. Each division was allocated a new half-time clerical-support worker post to maintain the database, send out letters and undertake other clerical work.

The plan for rolling out the model required the preparation of a new database for domestic and hate incidents to be designed within the first few months, the appointment and training of staff and obtaining the co-operation of divisional senior managers. All these tasks began to be addressed early on. Although there was time slippage in appointments, training and senior officer co-operation, by the end of the first year it was apparent that a major problem impeding the implementation of the model lay outside the control of the staff directly involved in the roll-out and the VVP board. The failure to complete the partially designed new database gained greater significance as the year progressed.

Inconsistent implementation

Mainstreaming, as with any organisational change, is a dynamic process and not simply a series of events. After a new plan is developed, and as implementation begins, there is likely to be a process involving conflicts, clashes, failures and minor successes. Close monitoring, redoubled efforts and managerial attention to detail are required to continue the implementation process and to achieve the full introduction of the new plan. The change process can be muddled, painful, protracted, tiresome, complicated and energy consuming as it involves emotions, thinking and acting differently (Duck 2001). Successful change is especially difficult to achieve with low-status police work as it affects the organisation at all levels and its processes (Plotnikoff and Woolfson 1998).

Major inconsistencies were present from the beginning. Responsibility for implementing the model was shared between head-quarters and divisional staff. Although there was a direct line of communication with headquarters via the community safety super-intendent and the headquarters domestic violence sergeant, in practice responsibility for implementation of the model across the force area rested with divisional commanders as they controlled the resources necessary for implementation. In relation to divisional commanders, the roles of the headquarters-based community safety superintendent and sergeant were advisory only as was that of the VVP board.

In the divisions, responsibility for domestic violence was usually located in community safety with homophobic and racially motivated incidents in crime management. Prior to the start of the VVP, there was also considerable support for locating domestic violence in crime management, an outcome ultimately rejected by the newly appointed Chief Constable. This meant that, unlike hate crime, located in a consistent and thorough crime management organisational structure, domestic violence did not have a centralised organisational structure. While crime prevention and investigation were relevant to both domestic and hate incidents, their respective histories shaped the approaches adopted.

The Stephen Lawrence inquiry (Macpherson 1999) and subsequent progress reports on the action plan designed to implement its recommendations (Home Secretary 1999, 2001, 2002) reoriented the policing of hate crime in West Yorkshire, while previous inconsistent intervention in domestic incidents continued. The government's detailed action plan on race crime addresses management, inspection and accountability, the handling of racist crime, victims, witnesses and legal proceedings, training and education. Among other aspects, the plan identifies priorities and indicators, the inspection regime, changes in the handling of crimes, complaints and discipline, and the recruit-ment, retention and progression of minority ethnic officers. The results in West Yorkshire were that, unlike domestic violence, all hate incidents were located in crime management with specific procedures for investigation and evidence gathering and close oversight by senior officers.

The roll-out began with variations in divisional staffing levels and distribution of tasks. Although domestic violence officers were, or would be, in post initially their remit varied. All three incident types could be co-ordinated by a domestic violence officer, or racial and/or homophobic incidents could be assigned to one or more officers and domestic violence to another. The way the hours of the newly appointed clerical support workers were shared between domestic and hate crime officers within and between divisions also varied. Officers responsible for domestic and hate incidents changed as the first year progressed. Altogether, divisional organisational structures and approaches lacked consistency.

Training

Training and meetings were major strategies to achieve a specialised group of officers to carry out mainstreaming and to develop a consistent approach in this contextually varied situation. A cascade model was developed. The first training activity was to establish a one-week 'training the trainers' course on domestic and hate incidents. The officer sent by each division was then to cascade train all his or her divisional officers within a specified period of time prior to the mainstreaming start date. The course primarily addressed awareness raising, training facilitation, the law, police practice and procedures and the model to be implemented in relation to domestic incidents.

This plan was not fully carried out and there were divisional variations. Each of the 17 divisions arranged its programme, which varied in content and duration (from three to seven hours). The model could be given little attention as the prioritisation of elements within the course, such as replicating the 'training the trainers' course, domestic violence awareness, legal and police practice and procedures, meant that little time was available to focus on the model itself. Each division organised a series of training sessions as all divisional officers could not be trained on the same date. Even though sessions were repeated, not all staff received the initial training. Lists of attendees were not always kept, reducing effective follow-up. While the force-wide VVP start date assumed the completion of training, there were late starts and not all the training was completed by the launch date of the mainstreaming project.

As the roll-out proceeded, training assumed greater importance. The need for continuous training was identified. Training needs came to be seen as more complex than initially envisaged. For example, a need emerged for specialised training for nominated officers undertaking Cocoon Watch and for area control room (ACR) operators. To follow up the implementation of the roll-out, force co-ordinators arranged regular meetings for domestic violence co-ordinators, hate crime panels and hate crime co-ordinators, but these were unable to resolve major problems in divisions.

Post-implementation drift

After the mainstreaming launch, the roll-out began to lose momentum. With any major organisational change, post-implementation drift should be expected (Duck 2001). Overcoming drift requires an analysis of the specific problems that may differ in intensity and over time. For domestic violence these problems were almost always presented as 'resource issues'. Hate crime did not suffer from the same 'resource issues' problems. Maintaining momentum required engagement with long-standing policing issues that quickly began to be identified at different organisational levels (Plotnikoff and Woolfson 1998).

Revising the model to fit previous police practice in domestic violence units led to deviations from the principle of progressively increasing interventions based on attendance. One example concerned officer assessment of seriousness. The model being mainstreamed, however, only allowed for upward deviation from the normal increase in intensity of response (for instance, emergency interventions). It did not permit downgrading of intensity or remaining on the same level with repeat attendance, a possibility where officer assessment of seriousness shaped the response. Gaining acceptance for the basic principle of stepped response was more complicated than initially envisaged and was never fully achieved. Another example of previous police practices taking precedence over the requirements of the new model related to record-keeping. There continued to be substantial numbers of inaccurate or incomplete final coding of domestic incidents.

Officers found it difficult to implement the model solely on the basis of the number of previous attendances even when emergency increase in levels of intervention was available as required. Police discretion was not totally eliminated by the model, but domestic violence officers continued to apply the model in a discretionary way rather than increasing levels with each repeat attendance. This was partly an issue of a lack of co-operation from other officers in introducing Cocoon Watch and Police Watch with the second attendance, but also an understanding of what being a police officer means. The exercise of discretion is an essential part of this and the previous corporate policing strategy permitted a greater degree of discretion in responding to domestic violence.

In the roll-out, domestic violence officers and clerical support made risk assessment judgements based on initial and later written records rather than following the model. This form of risk assessment was not effective in reducing repeat victimisation. The reasons for this were not that professional staff was incapable of making an assessment of risk, but that they did not have the information to do so. Insufficient detail was provided by patrol officers who had neither the time nor the training to undertake a thorough interview with the victim to determine the history of prior unreported domestic incidents and their meaning for the victimised person, children and other dependants in the household. The recorded account of the incident after a patrol visit did not and could not offer sufficient detail to allow an assessment of these important factors although officers on the scene made immediate risk assessment judgements. With visible injury or aggressive perpetrators these were usually unproblematic, but when it was not obvious what had happened or even who the perpetrator was much more information was needed to assess risk.

Previously unreported incidents by women could be 'none', 'few' or 'numerous' and vary in severity. For example, during the evaluation one interviewed woman had a sword wound in her stomach but did not call the police because she thought her partner would lose his job. She thought this would place her and her children in even greater danger: 'we would be his only focus and he would hurt us more – maybe kill us'. But not all incidents were regarded either as serious or beyond the ability of the interviewed women concerned to sort out. The assumption that all victims were vulnerable either before or after police attendance was not established by the qualitative interviews with women.

There appeared to be incomplete understanding of, or interest in, how the model could reduce repeat offending by divisional command teams. Complacency was reinforced by the location of responsibility for domestic incidents in community safety, rather than crime. Responsibility for domestic incidents was not specifically written in to the job description of divisional senior managers. At headquarters, responsibility for domestic incidents was one activity among others for the superintendent for community safety. The same issues did not arise for hate incidents; located in crime management, the immediate focus was on the suspect. Attention to hate incidents received greater support from senior managers with a location in crime management and a force co-ordinator at inspector rank. The importance of the Stephen Lawrence inquiry (Macpherson 1999) and subsequent action plans (Home Secretary 1999, 2001, 2002) was central to achieving a policing practice where non-crime incidents received the same level of investigation as those that were identified as crime.

Adequate support from divisional senior managers began with resource allocation; that is, the organisation of work within divisions. Organising work in divisions to implement level-2 interventions was never complete in any division, thus reducing the possibility of systematic progression based on reattendance of perpetrators. In the pilot project, an area system based on beats assisted the implementation of level-2 interventions. By the time of the roll-out, allocating officers by geographical area had ended and the divisional patrol system did not provide a close link with specific sublocalities. This may have contributed to level-2 tasks being downgraded in importance, if not ignored altogether.

Resource allocation, expressed through the organisation of work, always conveys a message to staff about the importance given to new working practices. Not introducing, or selectively introducing, pilot model interventions, particularly Cocoon Watch and Police Watch, produced mainstreaming operational problems for domestic violence officers. There were a number of inter-related reasons for this. Senior managers were not always in stable situations as best value reviews over the two mainstreaming years reorganised divisional boundaries and staff positions. This could make the provision of adequate support more difficult. Domestic violence headquarters and divisional officers were at relatively low ranks – constables with the occasional sergeant – which contributed to the low status of domestic violence. Even though approximately one third of reported violent crime was domestically located, a conception persisted of domestic incidents as non-crime.

Headquarters support was also problematic. The creation of a new database for the recording of hate and domestic incidents suffered from a lack of thorough planning from the outset. It began with the recording of domestic incident details on victims and perpetrators, but not actions taken, on a platform meant to be temporary – i.e. Lotus Notes. The database work stagnated in year 1 as IT staff were moved to a district best-value review. In the domestic violence units clerical work spiralled out of control, dominating the progress of the roll-out. This occurred because clerical support and domestic violence officers were required to access two additional databases to obtain information on current and previous incidents, then to create Lotus Notes records of no operational benefit as they did not include the interventions implemented by officers and clerical staff, who were then required to maintain paper files on actions taken.

In the pilot project the research team maintained the standalone database, checked daily all ACR calls for miscoded domestic attendances and, with clerical support, ensured clerical tasks (e.g. sending of letters) were completed for all incidents. The database maintained by the research team for evaluation purposes was also used for operations. The method for the evaluation of repeat rates was based on the perpetrator's history of future repeat attendance. The method was entrant based and prospective and a key element in the operation of the repeat victimisation intervention pilot.

In the roll-out, the database was maintained by the force-wide management information system and the method of evaluating repeat rates was based on incidents and trawling backwards in time for repeat attendance. The method was incident based and retrospective. An incident based retrospective method always produces a progressively lower repetition rate as repetition increases than a prospective entrant-based method.[4] While this may imply that the force is responding effectively to repeat victimisation, this statistical approach artificially reduces the repeat rate by doubling the consideration given to repeat incidents, as these both determine the entry level and are used to register a repeat offence. It is possible to calculate the equivalent management information system (MIS) rate from any prospective entrant-based rate by applying a conversion formula.[5] Even when converted, however, a fundamental problem remains that undermines comparison of repeat rates as perpetrators progress through levels. It is not possible to identify when in the future a repeat attendance will happen with a retrospective method and, for comparative purposes with the pilot findings, this is essential.

The model required that retrospective records should guide the allocation of an entry level only and, thereafter, prospective records-checking should be used to monitor repeat offending. An incident-based retrospective method also departs from a victim/perpetrator-focused analysis where what is important is the continuation of offending. Ultimately it is the entrant or perpetrator that is the focus of police attention, while the incidents signify his behaviour and the required policing interventions.

Getting to grips with problems

As problems were identified new strategies were continually being developed further to co-ordinate and promote the roll-out. The force co-ordinator for domestic incidents arranged meetings with each divisional command team with the aim of gaining greater co-operation and support, particularly for level-2 interventions. In the divisions the force co-ordinator undertook team leaders' briefings on requirements for level-2 interventions, addressed the safety of domestic violence officers on home visits and re-emphasised the importance of officer training, including CID, custody, civilians on the front desk and inspectors. Training was organised separately for ACR staff and guidelines were issued. Clerical support workers received training and, to supplement role profiles, guidance relating to daily tasks. Regular meetings of domestic violence officers continued, with support and assistance to individual officers as required. Towards the end of the second year risk assessment issues were addressed by introducing a proforma for use when officers made Cocoon Watch visits that included a request for consent to refer to another agency.

Because under-recording was established as a major problem during the pilot year, in mainstreaming year 1 the evaluators explored the extent of recording accuracy in information routinely collected and entered by officers and ACR operators. The first of two independent audits checked the 999 call system final coding of domestic incidents for two months, December 2000 and June 2001. At the same time a key-word search system designed to identify incorrectly written-off domestic incidents was created and results sent to domestic violence units for follow-up.[6] The aim was to assist with increasing the accuracy of recording. A way forward on database issues began in the second year with the appoint-ment of an external IT consultant to add operationally useful fields to the Lotus Notes database for domestic incidents. And finally, following intervention by the Home Office Policing and Reducing Crime Unit as a result of the year-1 evaluation report, force headquarters made a re-commitment to develop the VVP database as originally intended. Design plans were underway at the end of the evaluation.

During the second year the evaluation team focused on introducing the model to domestic incidents in two divisions in the hope that recording would improve, a comparative analysis with the pilot project would be possible and systematic allocation of levels as prescribed by the model could be introduced. A second audit of MIS data was undertaken in September 2001 to establish the level of interventions and the allocation of the model responses within each division. Recorded domestic incidents were analysed for correctly identified intervention levels and the allocation of the model responses.

While it was originally intended that hate incidents would also be recorded on the same database, the commitment to their inclusion began to wane during the first year. Although included in the initial plan, data on hate incidents were never systematically collected on the provisional software program for domestic incidents. When the VVP began in April 2000, homophobic and racially motivated incidents were recorded on paper forms and sent to headquarters where limited information was entered on a standalone computer. The force system began to change in June 2000 with a pilot in two divisions recording solely on crime information system (CIS). By December 2001 the extension of CIS recording to the remainder of the force was complete. This securely located hate crime in crime management procedures and processes and no systematic effort was made to apply the Killingbeck model to hate incidents.

Why was the pilot successful and not its mainstreaming?

Major conceptual and value differences were introduced with the mainstreaming project. The pilot was not conceived as a victim-led project, but a systems approach with three participants: the victim, the perpetrator and the police. The focus of the roll-out shifted away from an equal focus on the perpetrator and the victim towards a victim-led approach, thus departing from the values underpinning the pilot. While a focus primarily on the victim may seem to prioritise her right to a life free from violence, diminishing an equal focus on the perpetrator makes this less likely to be achieved. Social values regarding responsibility for violence are also involved in this conceptual shift.

Interviews with women demonstrated the complexity of assessing protection and satisfaction and call into question the rationale for conceptualising domestic violence under the heading vulnerable victims. Why not conceptualise domestic violence as interpersonal crime or violent crime in which some calls for assistance will not involve a criminal offence? This is the approach taken to racist incidents.[7] As with domestic violence, hate incidents both involve criminal and common law offences and, possibly, no offence at all. Naming matters, because the problem and its solution do not lie with those who are victimised but with their abusers. While a qualitative conclusion, the lack of progress in implementing the VVP seems in part to be expressed through a concept that, however unintended, minimises the importance of the perpetrator to repeat victimisation and, therefore, to domestic violence as potential crime. Overemphasis on the victim foregrounds a social-welfare policing approach; an inevitable outcome as those who are victimised are not the subject of criminal investigation.

On reflection, the basic problem with the roll-out can be expressed as the adoption of a 'hard systems model' of change in an organisationally 'messy' situation. A 'hard systems model' is described as an appropriate choice where organisation systems are simple and those involved in the change situation share common interests, have values and beliefs which are highly compatible, largely agree upon ends and means, share decision-making and act in accordance with agreed objectives (Flood and Jackson 1991; Senior 2002). A hard systems model of change provides a rigorous and systematic way of determining quantifiable objectives for change which are tested against a set of explicit criteria. These approaches are described as useful in situations where change is sought to the means whereby things are done and where a problem can be solved (Ackoff 1993; Senior 2002). A hard systems model was successful for the pilot project, but not for the roll-out. There are a number of reasons for the different outcomes.

The recommended stages of development were followed for the pilot (Paton and McCalman 2000; Senior 2002), but not with the roll-out. At the beginning description phase, agreement was reached between senior officers in the division selected for the pilot, the headquarters domestic violence and child protection unit, and researchers on what was involved, and objectives set. In the options phase the same group selected the most appropriate interventions. The implementation phase that followed consisted of putting feasible plans into practice and evaluating the results primarily by quantitative methods.

Problems with both correct coding and with implementing Cocoon Watch and Police Watch arose in the pilot and were successfully resolved, but not in the roll-out. With the pilot, the support of the divisional superintendent, crime manager and other senior officers made it possible to raise the standard of domestic violence coding through a system of requests for clarifications. Constables and their supervising sergeants and inspectors came to accept a higher standard as part of their work. Considerable improvements were made in the number of Cocoon Watch visits and successful take-up of the Cocoon Watch system by a training event introduced by the divisional commander who remained in the room until the session was over. Inputs were made by other senior officers in the division and from headquarters, from the divisional domestic violence officer in the division and the evaluators (Hanmer *et al*. 1999: Table 2, pp. 16–17). Police Watch follow-through received equally systematic monitoring and management. This unambiguous expression of commitment by senior officers provided the leadership needed to achieve changes to work practices by other officers.

With the roll-out, given the success of the pilot, the project moved immediately into the implementation phase. This missed out stages that enabled senior officers to learn about the model, the different roles of officers in the division, the resources that would be required to implement it, how it fitted in with other policing demands and activities and potential problems. As with the pilot, the roll-out provided training sessions for all officers in each division and senior officers rarely attended. But attendance was not necessary with the pilot as senior officers were informed through their participation in the stages of development. Participation in the stages led to acceptance of the pilot by senior officers who gained consent from other officers through the operation of the authority structure.

Pilot studies are particularly relevant for a hard systems model of change as implementation is rarely a problem (Senior 2002). Pilot studies help sort out any problems before more extensive change is instituted. The hard systems model of change is particularly relevant for bureaucratic organisations. In the pilot, the authority structure support enabled another basic difficulty, that of negative gendered social relations and values, to be suppressed.

By the time mainstreaming began, the policing structure was less hierarchically organised and more managerial authority and responsibilities were devolved to policing divisions. The force system was veering towards the 'messy'. Messes, in contrast to difficulties, are unbounded by being spread throughout the organisation where they constitute an inter-related complex of problems which cannot be separated from their context. Messes involve many people of different persuasions and attitudes. They have a long history within organisations where there is little agreement on what constitutes the problem and its solution, and there is an absence of knowledge and uncertainly about what needs to be known. Messes have serious and worrying implications for all concerned and are qualitatively different from difficulties (Senior 2002).

Complex systems characterised as 'messy' require a different problem-solving approach. While the men and women who make up the system have basic shared interests, their values and beliefs diverge to some extent along with agreement upon ends and means, although compromise is possible (Flood and Jackson 1991; Senior 2002). Messy situations call for dissolving problems, through organisational development, an approach difficult to implement in bureaucratic organisations. Organisational development implies organisational learning as a means of improving an organisation's capacity to change. It is characterised by change over the medium to long term, involves the organisation as a whole, is participative, has top management support and involvement and a facilitator who takes on the role of change agent, concentrates on planned change but can adapt to a changing situation (Senior 2002).

The VVP roll-out illustrates the factors requiring mess management. The decision to mainstream was made at headquarters command team level, but implementation and resources were at divisional level. Also, later during the first year, the headquarters command team gave priority to strategic decisions that had a detrimental impact on the introduction of the VVP. The withdrawal of IT staff from the VVP database planning process to work on a district-level best value review was followed by force reorganisation through amalgamation of divisions.

At headquarters the VVP was located within community safety – a structure that in relation to divisions could advise only. Although headed by a superintendent, the same rank as divisional heads, the day-to-day liaison was carried out by a sergeant, which further reduced the impact of headquarters on divisional implementation. Further, as authority and resources to implement were devolved to divisional level, although headquarters decreed domestic incidents were to be located within community safety, divisions could decide not to do so. Some chose instead to locate domestic incidents within crime. This difference of opinion between the chief constable and his senior team, and divisional superintendents and their senior teams, remained un-resolved, raising the issue of corporate strategy.

The power division between headquarters and divisions was also demonstrated by the responses to attempts to improve the rate of correct coding of domestic incidents. Presentations were made to meetings of divisional crime managers and chief inspectors operations by senior headquarters staff detailing the individual responses of officers sent on domestic calls, but this did not result in improved correct coding. There seemed to be no drivers to ensure compliance. The use of information on the roll-out as a management strategy – to appraise and improve the progress of individual officers – did not happen with sufficient rigour to facilitate the implementation of the model. Only in the force-wide service (the call centres) was information supplied to management on individual operators acted upon, and then only after the second evaluation showed no improvement in correct coding by call centre staff.

The headquarters-based management information system provided statistics on the number of attendances and their outcomes, which at divisional level were not always regarded as reliable, thus reducing the impact of headquarters influence over divisions. Unlike the pilot, there was weak supervision of staff, and weak monitoring and use of data. Domestic violence officers complained of a lack of contact, support and supervision by divisional officers.

Officers within divisions were no longer organised in a way that made it obvious who should carry out Cocoon Watch. Various attempts were made to substitute for the lack of a system where an individual officer was associated with a specific area (for example, community constables). Several divisions experimented with establishing new organisational forms – in particular, volunteers were requested and found from each patrol shift. Patrol sergeants did not give officers sufficient time to conduct the visits, as either they or more senior officers decided something else was more important.

The most commonly introduced alternative was a rationing or gate-keeping system introduced by domestic violence officers where only the incidents judged most pressing were sent out for a Cocoon Watch visit. The pressure on domestic violence officers to maintain good relations with fellow officers at the same rank was considerable. As most domestic violence officers were women and patrol officers were men, issues of gender also contributed to the devaluation by male officers of the work of domestic violence officers. The devaluation, or low status, of their contribution to policing was a consistent feature of the work culture that required negotiation on a day-to-day basis.

Very similar outcomes occurred with Police Watch. Although Police Watch did not require direct contact with the men and women involved in the domestic incident, there was resistance to implementing Police Watch by officers in patrol cars. Police watch in the pilot was carried out by officers in patrol cars on their way to other non-emergency jobs. By the time of the roll-out this was no longer promoted by senior managers as contributing to divisional efficiency by maximising the use of time spent driving from one place to another. Given the resistance from fellow officers, once again a rationing or gate-keeping system became the major mode of response by domestic violence officers. However, on occasion when relationships between individual officers in patrol groups and in domestic violence units were particularly strong for personal or shared value reasons, extra effort could be forthcoming for both Cocoon Watch visits and Police Watch drive-bys.

Dissolving problems

Elements of both hard and soft complexity emerged in the roll-out. The organisational culture, entrenched power bases and established leadership styles, as well as simultaneous reorganisation of the force, combined to make the process of change more complex, diffuse and confused. The VVP board and headquarters staff faced more of a mess than a difficulty. Problems can be resolved, solved or dissolved (Ackoff 1993). With mainstreaming, not one but a complex of problems needed to be dissolved. To dissolve problems, it is necessary to redesign the characteristics of the larger system containing the problem; that is, to change the organisational culture, structures, systems and/or processes.

During the roll-out one division attempted to adopt a problem-dissolving approach that involved structure, problem ownership, communication and the participation and commitment of the people involved in the change process itself. Domestic violence officers reported directly to the crime manager and specific officers were identified to undertake Cocoon Watch. Ways to increase the number of Patrol Watch drive-bys were introduced. Monthly meetings on domestic violence unit work were chaired by the crime manager and included officers undertaking Cocoon and Police Watch and other relevant divisional officers.

During the second year of the mainstreaming project this division added a structured approach to perpetrators who were not demotivated by the three model interventions (see Figure 10.1). In this, level-3 interventions were repeated for the fourth attendance and, on the fifth, perpetrators were referred either to the community-based team or the crime manager for allocation to CID. The domestic violence officers assisted with gathering evidence, inter-agency liaison and continuing contact with those who were victimised. All requests to drop charges by those who were victimised went to domestic violence officers who interviewed and on occasion refused to allow it.

Allocation to the community team or CID depended upon the severity of the attack. Where there was no apparent danger, but perpetrators were recidivists, the referral was to the community-based team. As deadly attacks may occur even when risks of serious harm appear to be slight and police resources continue to be called upon with repetition, the aim was to target all recidivists and not just those repeat perpetrators where the victim was clearly in danger. This aim, however, could not be fully implemented particularly in relation to criminal investigations. Officers were withdrawn from normal work duties to emergencies and their aftermath in other divisions, and domestic violence competed with other crime types for investigation and evidence-gathering attention. While some progress was made in changing work practices, the sustained withdrawal of officers for duties in other divisions made it almost impossible fully to implement this problem-solving approach.

A feature of organisational messes is a lack of agreement on what constitutes the problem and what changes are required. This lack of agreement by officers also applied in the pilot, but the commitment of

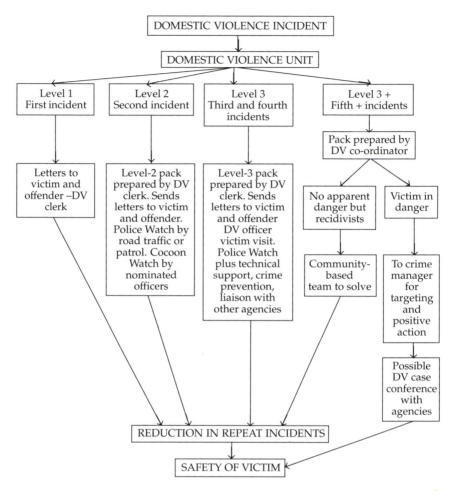

Figure 10.1. Police implementation and extension of the model.

senior officers meant it largely remained unexpressed. The assumption of the evaluators that the change in responding to domestic violence would 'bed in', as the pilot year had demonstrated major successes, proved not to be justified as senior officers were replaced by others who had not participated in the development of the pilot. By the time the roll-out began, the pilot division had returned to its previous practice and could not be distinguished from the other divisions. Another division, however, as a result of the experience gained by senior officers through participation in the pilot, invested more resources into their domestic violence unit than other divisions, with the sergeant in charge reporting directly to the crime manager. When work practice problems arose, the crime manager conveyed to other officers within the division his expectation that domestic violence crime would be investigated and evidence gathered.

Mainstreaming recommendations

The lack of an integrated corporate response affected the policing of domestic violence negatively across the force. The evaluation included interviews with senior and other officers on mainstreaming problems and their potential solution. This led to recommendations on management and the organisation of domestic violence.

Headquarters

Implementing a corporate domestic violence response requires a headquarters command structure headed by a senior officer, such as a chief superintendent, located in crime management with the sole task of overseeing the implementation of effective and efficient policing of domestic and other family violence.

Headquarters–divisional links

Implementing a corporate policy on domestic violence requires greater standardisation across divisions. To achieve this, domestic violence units should come under a headquarters organisational structure.

Divisions

Attaining a corporate response at divisional level has several elements. The first is a unified and consistent approach from officers tasked with delivering specific interventions, such as Cocoon Watch and Police Watch. The second is the management, monitoring and assessment of the work of individual officers to ensure and maintain standards. The corporate response fails if co-operation from other officers, including senior officers, is not forthcoming and the policing experience of domestic violence officers is underutilised.

Organisational location

Locating hate incidents in crime management ensured investigation and evidence gathering. Domestic incidents require the same crime focus and location.

Views of officers

The evaluation established that the policing system is resistant to recognising the importance and relevance of violent domestic crime. Occupational inertia is difficult to shift, but dedicated officers are allowed to carry on and to shoulder the enormous emotional and work burdens that result from being given inadequate assistance. Sufficient human resources are required to respond to all incidents.

Co-operation from all officers

Attaining more co-operation from other officers is first and foremost a management issue. Officers need to be allocated time to undertake tasks involved in implementing the model and given sufficient training to enable the task to be carried out effectively.

Training issues

Training on the domestic violence operational model should be continuous as, over a relatively short period of time, efforts to train all staff inevitably fall short of that goal and also staff change posts and new officers and clerical staff enter the force. There should be refresher and additional training for those who remain in post for longer periods or who are appointed to new posts. Training curricula should be standardised.[8]

Role of domestic violence officers

Implementing the model requires domestic violence units with sufficient officers and clerical support workers to ensure that all incidents receive all interventions in good time.

Domestic violence officers are in a unique position to develop and utilise skills appropriate for a specialist service within policing and the community. Specialist skills are required to confront a wide range of violent behaviours, sexual as well as physical, and the less obvious psychological, emotional and financial abuses. Specialist skills are also required for multi-agency liaison (e.g. with mental health, substance abuse, social and child welfare, women's refuges).

Under-valuing domestic violence officers results in an erosion of policing skills, and a non-integrated approach to incidents that make up a high volume of police work. This not only squanders financial and human resources, it also results in a reduction in the quality of life of those who are victimised and deterioration in the standing of the police within the community.

While a focus on victims is needed, perpetrators cannot be marginalised as they are the primary cause of calls for assistance. In order to support victims, domestic violence officers should share responsibility for investigations and evidence gathering in conjunction with other officers. These policing activities distinguish domestic violence officers from welfare workers and represent an efficient use of experienced officers.

Because domestic violence officers respond to all incidents, they are best placed to identify and to develop strategies to target chronic offenders for whom the model is not effective. If the response to chronic offenders is to be passed on to other officers (e.g. CID or problem-oriented policing teams), a full briefing from domestic violence officers with a continuing exchange of information is necessary in order effectively to support those who are victimised.

Role of clerical support

Clerical work underpins the implementation of interventions on a day-to-day basis. In domestic violence units the clerical support staff require-ments are similar to those in child protection units. The model calls for an in-depth understanding of domestic violence, its impact on victims and a number of police computer systems and procedures. In smaller units particularly, clerical support staff will answer telephones and speak to victims and agencies when domestic violence officers are not in the office. Maximising the effectiveness of clerical support requires initial and ongoing training. Mainstreaming experience suggests that the knowledge, motivation and skills required to maintain an accurate and complete database are not easily transmitted to operational personnel. Inadequately prepared clerical staff waste resources in several ways, through personal inefficiency and the negative impact on the work of domestic violence officers. If computer entry of incidents and sending letters and other communications are not completed, domestic violence officers must assist with this work as it is a pre-condition for the fulfilment of their policing role. Sufficient and appropriately trained clerical support is therefore essential.

Information management system

The recognition that severity and frequency of domestic attack often increases with repetition intensifies the need for reliable data, which is vital to assess resource needs and to obtain additional resources. In order to be able to provide reliable data for nationally monitored performance indicators, under-recording due to incorrect coding must be eliminated which, it must be accepted, will lead inevitably to an increase in the reporting rate. Greater reliability requires correcting under-recording through incorrect coding of incidents, while success in achieving greater reliability requires an increase in the reporting rate and therefore more work for domestic violence and their clerical support.

The major question, however, is 'reliability for what purpose?' More is required for effective policing than statistical overviews, however useful these may be for other purposes. To further corporate responses and to increase officer efficiency, management information systems should provide managers with information on attendance by individual officers at domestic violence incidents. The information that could be useful to managers for the review of officer performance and for crime management begins with the coding of these attendances and includes actions taken by officers. In addition, to further crime management by obtaining the maximum amount of information on offenders, the method of recording should be entrant based and prospective.

Increasing the cost-effective use of human and financial resources

The pilot project demonstrated that cost-effective actions follow from consistent implementation of the model. While there are a number of reasons why this was difficult to achieve, inconsistent implementation increased the theoretical cost of the programme to the force. If the good practice mainstreaming checklist points had been implemented in the right order at the right time, considerable savings in time and more effective implementation of the model would have occurred. Disorganisation has major implications for repeat victimisation and costs. Based on pilot project data, potential cost savings of a fully mainstreamed model were estimated as between £2.66 million and £2.88 million for the two-year period April 2000 to March 2002.

Partnership

Agency views were influenced by the different organisational ways the police respond to domestic violence and racially motivated and homophobic incidents, and by the different contexts and meanings these three incident types had for agency respondents. Multi-agency organisation for responses to hate crime was more highly structured than for domestic incidents. There was a corporate strategy for racial and homophobic incidents that involved active collaboration with community agencies. Partnership activities with domestic violence agencies in the voluntary sector were less systematic and structured. In the statutory sector, structured relationships were developed within the criminal justice system and with social services, but not health. Partnership activities with domestic violence and other agencies were being developed in a somewhat haphazard way, unlike hate crime partnerships, which benefited from a focused corporate strategy.

Good practice mainstreaming checklist

Mainstreaming the VVP identifies the type of issues likely to be associated with the roll-out of any pilot or new plan of action. Training, information and problem sharing, introduction of new procedures and processes to move beyond sticking points and to achieve managerial recommitment to change are standard requirements. Successfully evaluated pilots cannot be assumed to work automatically when transferred to other departments or geographical areas. Managers need to step back to examine operational procedures and issues prior to importing new working practices if similar outcomes are to be achieved across an organisation.

Hindsight suggests a series of steps that could usefully have been taken before the roll-out began. These extend beyond this project and offer a starting-point for developing good practice checklists in any mainstreaming projects:

1   Before mainstreaming begins ensure that systems for recording and monitoring required information are in place. The VVP roll-out would have been greatly assisted by prior preparation of the new database that included the capacity to relate to other relevant databases and the area control room.

2   Ensure that a detailed handbook for staff on how to implement the programme is in place before mainstreaming begins. Initial detailed instructions for officers and clerical support on implementing the VVP model and the supporting database would have aided and complemented training.

3   Ensure training is delivered to a standard format, quality and timescale across the force. Considerable pre-planning is required to achieve this outcome in a large and complex organisation where different staff groups require different inputs. For the VVP roll-out, focused training on the concepts that underlie the model to be mainstreamed and the roles of different officers required greater emphasis. Achieving training consistency and applying the same start date for mainstreaming demonstrate a coherent strategy agreed by senior managers.

4   Build divisional senior management support with a core team to manage and implement the project prior to mainstreaming. This will be time and effort intensive, but essential. The VVP roll-out would have benefited greatly from consistent senior management support across divisions.

5   Acknowledge and address problems previously identified by pilots before mainstreaming begins. The VVP roll-out would have been less problematic if strategies for improving the recognised problem of initial incorrect or incomplete recording of incidents had preceded the roll-out.

6   Think of worst case scenarios and how these can be tackled before starting the roll-out. Not all one's worst fears will become reality, but something unexpected is likely to happen. Agreed systems for trouble-shooting, coupled with a willingness to reconfirm commitment in difficult moments, are required to mainstream innovation successfully. The VVP built in trouble-shooting through force co-ordinators and the VVP board, but this small group could be somewhat isolated on occasions.

7   Recognise that mainstreaming change takes time and everyone involved is on a learning curve.

Post-implementation drift is probably inevitable, even with thorough and successful pre-planning. Not everyone will be committed or understand what is required and why. Some may even wish to oppose changed ways of working. It may not be possible to avoid other unanticipated issues and demands for staff time and financial resources.
   Overcoming drift requires:

• knowing what is really going on among those tasked with implementation;

• using information, data and evaluation to assess progress;

• constant engagement with problems, their analysis and possible solutions;

• endless striving for greater ownership for the changes to be mainstreamed;

• redoubled efforts just at the moment when problems seem overwhelming;

- constant demonstration of commitment to those tasked with implementation by their senior manager;

- reaffirmation by the headquarters command team that the changes to be mainstreamed have their continued support; and

- always avoiding complacency.

Conclusion

To introduce the new policing model required appropriate structures, committed and effective management, staff co-operation and co-ordination, and relevant information management data. Achieving only partial success in these aspects led to system malfunction during the first two mainstreaming years. Attempts to compensate for system failure by those most committed introduced further distortions in the delivery of the new work process. Some of the problems encountered were previously identified in research on policing crime in general and on policing domestic violence, in particular. Additional issues were identified through a detailed evaluation of the VVP.

Developments continued after the end of the two-year Home Office funding for the VVP. The post of force co-ordinator for domestic violence was extended for a third year. Divisional clerical posts were added to mainstream funding and domestic violence officer posts in divisions continued. Included in mainstreaming messages are the recommendations from three proposals for organisational change initiated by those in the VVP and circulated within the force. Independently of the mainstreaming project, hate crime developments continued to expand with increases in community-based reporting centres and planning for more hate crime panels. Getting to grips with problems became a continuing process. In the view of the VVP board, to introduce the pilot model to domestic incidents always required a minimum of three years.

Notes

1 The evaluation of the Vulnerable Victims Project was carried out by Jalna Hanmer, Sue Griffiths, Debra Wigglesworth, Denise Hutchinson, Dave Jerwood and Samuel Cameron.

2 The primary objectives of the VVP were to:
   - develop a more accurate recording rate for domestic violence, racist and homophobic incidents;

- reduce incidence of repeat victimisation for domestic violence, and for racist and homophobic attacks;
- introduce measures to support the victim at the earliest opportunity;
- generate multi-agency problem-solving approaches for lasting solutions; and
- improve satisfaction levels for victims in domestic violence, racist and homophobic crimes.

The secondary objectives of the VVP were to:

- reduce levels of assaults across the force in the long run;
- reduce multiple attendances and thereby officer time spent on incidents; and
- develop a more sophisticated form of risk assessment for victim and offender.

VVP targets and performance indicators were to:

- reduce repeat attendance for domestic violence to 30%;
- reduce repeat attendance rate for racist and homophobic incidents to 10%;
- reduce to 10% domestic violence, racist and homophobic incidents reattended within 5 weeks;
- develop strong links with other agencies able to assist with the repeat victimisation issues;
- maintain or improve the satisfaction rate of 92.7% for victims of domestic violence, racist and homophobic crime; and
- to set a violent crime reduction target.

3 The research of Sandra Jones (1986) describes the formal and informal policing culture of this decade with its emphasis on women as suitable for a social-welfare service role while men face risk and danger. These understandings of gendered social relations were observed in the 1985 research. The police members of the project committee refused to accept the report if the authors left in the recommendation that officers who abuse their wives should be disciplined, reasoning that male police officers did not behave like that. They also argued strenuously against substantially increasing the percentage of women in the force. The recommendation on disciplinary procedures was withdrawn and, after negotiation, a 50% increase in women officers was agreed, raising the proportion of women officers in the force from 9 to 13%. The major argument against the increase was rhetorically to ask 'Do you want to see women beaten up outside pubs?', thereby identifying the macho culture of 'real policing' and women's unsuitability for police officer work. These views are yet to be fully eradicated and were structurally expressed in the VVP through the appointment of civilians to undertaken the work of domestic violence officers in several divisions and the location of domestic violence, unlike hate incidents, in community safety not crime.

4 The hypothetical repeat rate for these two methods of calculating repetition is given below (Dave Jerwood, University of Bradford). As the percentage of repeat incidents increases, the divergence between an incident retrospective and an entrant-based prospective method also increases. The table shows that a 5% repeat rate using a prospective entrant method becomes 4.76% using a retrospective incident method. A 50% repeat rate using a prospective entrant method becomes 33% using an retrospective incident method. A 75% repeat rate using a prospective entrant method becomes 43% using a retrospective incident method.

Hypothetical repetition rate (%)

Incident-based retrospective	Entrant-based prosective
4.76	5
9.09	10
13.04	15
16.67	20
20.00	25
23.08	30
25.93	35
28.57	40
31.03	45
33.33	50
35.48	55
37.50	60
39.39	65
41.18	70
42.86	75

5 For details of the conversion formula, contact Dr. Dave Jerwood, University of Bradford.

6 Although officers thought there was under-recording of hate incidents, a key-word approach to examining recording accuracy could not be established given the lack of key-word consistency in reports of incidents.

7 Recommendation 13: 'That the term "racist incident" must be understood to include crimes and non-crimes in policing terms. Both must be reported, recorded and investigated with equal commitment' (Home Secretary 2002).

8 This issue was highlighted in the report by Kelly (1999).

References

Ackoff, R.L. (1993) 'The art and science of mess management', in C. Mabey and B. Mayon-White (eds) *Managing Change*. London, Paul Chapman Publishing.

Dobash, R.E. and Dobash, R. (1980) *Violence against Wives: A Case against the Patriarchy*. Shepton Mallet: Open Books.

Duck, J.D. (2001) *The Change Monster: The Human Forces that Fuel or Foil Corporate Transformation and Change*. New York, NY: Crown Business.

Dunphy, D. and Stace, D. (1993) 'The strategic management of corporate change', *Human Relations*, 45(8), 917–18.

Flood, R.L. and Jackson M.C. (1991) *Creative Problem Solving: Total Systems Intervention*. Chichester: Wiley.

Grace, S. (1995) *Policing Domestic Violence in the 1990s*. Home Office Research Study 139. Policing and Reducing Crime Unit.

Hanmer, J., Griffiths, S. and Jerwood, D. (1999) *Arresting Evidence: Domestic Violence and Repeat Victimisation*. Paper 104. London: Home Office Policing and Reducing Crime Unit.

Hanmer, J. and Saunders, S. (1987) *Women, Violence and Crime Prevention*. West Yorkshire Police Authority (published by Gower, Aldershot, 1993).

Home Secretary (1999) *Stephen Lawrence Inquiry: Home Secretary's Action Plan*. London: Home Office.

Home Secretary (2001) *Stephen Lawrence Inquiry: Home Secretary's Action Plan, Second Annual Report on Progress*. London: Home Office.

Home Secretary (2002) *Stephen Lawrence Inquiry: Home Secretary's Action Plan, Third Annual Report on Progress*. London: Home Office.

Jones, S. (1986) *Policewomen and Equality: Formal v. Informal Practice*. Basingstoke: Macmillan.

Kelly, L. (1999) *Domestic Violence Matters: An Evaluation of a Development Project*. Home Office Research Study 193. London: HMSO.

Macpherson, Sir William (1999) *Stephen Lawrence Inquiry of an Inquiry by Sir William Macpherson of Cluny. Advised by Tom Cook. The Right Reverend Dr John Sentamu and Dr Richard Stone*. Cm 4262–1*Report*. London: HMSO.

Mooney, J. (1993) *The Hidden Figure: Domestic Violence in North London*. London: Islington Council Police and Crime Prevention Unit.

Paton, R.A. and McCalman, J. (2000) *Change Management: A guide to effective implementation*, London: Sage.

Plotnikoff, J. and Woolfson, R. (1998) *Policing Domestic Violence: Effective Organisational Structures*. Police Research Series Paper 100. London: Home Office Policing and Reducing Crime Unit.

Senior, B. (2002) *Organisational Change* (2nd edn). Harlow: Pearson Education.

Smith, L. (1989) *Domestic Violence*. London: HMSO.

Tushman, M.L., Newman, W.H. and Romanelli, E. (1988) 'Convergence and upheaval: managing the unsteady pace of organisational evolution', in M.L. Tushman, and W.L. Moore (eds) *Readings in the Management of Innovation*. New York, NY: Ballinger.

Chapter 11

The role of the centre

Gloria Laycock and Barry Webb

We were both involved to varying extent in the planning, execution and delivery of the Home Office Crime Reduction Programme (CRP).[1] This chapter comprises our personal reflections on what we see as avoidable weaknesses in the central management of the programme. These weaknesses account to some extent for the shortcomings in the work ultimately delivered, as revealed in several of the chapters of this collection. This is an opportunity to explain what we think might have been, and what still could be, an opportunity to learn from some mistakes.

It is important to note that the discussion is focused upon the role of the centre (generally the Home Office), and primarily the first round of the Targeted Policing Initiative (TPI). It considers the way in which the early planning developed and some of the tensions that existed between senior Treasury and Home Office officials and researchers, both within and outside central government and the police. These issues are important in that they set the early framework for the initiative and formed the basis of later work. Our purpose in recording them is twofold. First, some of the issues raised are significant in that they help to explain what might be interpreted as the limited outcome of many of the first-round projects and some of the later proposals. Secondly, although the operations have moved on and evolved, some of the issues remain and need to be addressed to improve future programmes. For both of us working on this programme was a frustrating experience, and the reader may sense this in the tone of the chapter. We make only limited apology for this, and in defence refer to Christie's (1997) insightful paper on the oversocialisation of criminologists.

In the remainder of this chapter we outline the background to the initiative from our perspective and set out, with the benefit of hindsight, what seem to have been the assumptions of those who were required to deliver the scheme. In effect this means senior civil servants in the Home Office and Treasury. We then address the extent to which we think these assumptions were justified, drawing on other research and some of the key points from the earlier chapters of this book. A 'lessons learnt' section follows, again focusing on the central management process and its associated assumptions. This has implications for the future prospects both of problem-solving within the policing environment and for the delivery of crime reduction.

The background

The new UK Labour government of the late 1990s was a breath of fresh air on the crime reduction scene. First the Crime and Disorder Act 1998 created a framework within which locally targeted and data-based strategies could be devised and agreed with communities, and then the CRP (Home Office 1999) followed on its heels, with what was seen as a vast investment in evidence-based crime reduction. The sums allocated to the programme, as set out in Chapter 1, are by British standards spectacular. The funding for targeted policing, within the CRP, was £30 million over three years. The Home Office permanent secretary at the time, whose background was in defence, described it as half an aircraft wing, but for those of us in the research community investment on this scale was unprecedented, and there was a commitment to evaluating all that was good and new.

The Home Office was not used to outcome-focused project management on this scale, in which 'delivery' was primarily by agencies outside their direct control and there was a strict spending timetable as required by the Treasury. There are two senses in which 'time' was short. First the whole CRP, of which the TPI was a part, was to be delivered within a short period – three years. This included all the business of organising the programme and making funding decisions as well as delivering actual projects across a range of initiatives. Secondly, and consequently, the time provided for police forces to prepare and submit bids for funding under the TPI was very tight indeed. Despite initial Treasury promises (later partially withdrawn) that the money could be 'rolled over' to later financial years, which should have served to take the pressure off, there remained a sense of increasing panic to get projects off the ground and money spent as fast as possible.

The influx of funds coincided with a growing interest in problem-oriented policing (POP) and the opportunity was taken to devote some of the money to supporting it directly. In essence the TPI expected the police to use a problem-oriented approach – to collect data, analyse them, develop a response, implement and monitor. Invitations to the police to bid for the money were issued in two rounds, as described in Chapter 1. In round one potential bidders were told that of the order of £400,000 was available per project.

In hindsight, there were a number of assumptions made in inviting bids in this way, most of which were implicit and none of which was subject to adequate critical scrutiny by the Treasury officials and senior civil servants in the Home Office policy groups who orchestrated the CRP. It was assumed that:

1. the principles of POP were sufficiently well understood in police forces that they could do what they were being asked to do – that is, to carry out an analysis of local data and make a reasoned case for financial support to address an identified problem;
2. the necessary local data were readily available to support bids, and agencies shared, or would be easily persuaded to share, their data;
3. forces could reasonably respond to the invitation to bid within the one month or so they were allowed;
4. forces would bid for the money that was needed to do the job, rather than bend the job to fit the amount of money available;
5. sound implementation and project management skills were widely available locally;
6. expenditure of money, once allocated, would be straightforward;
7. all the projects would be sufficiently well articulated and challenging to merit formal independent evaluation;
8. the importance and value of independent academic evaluation would be understood and facilitated;
9. it would take few people with conventional civil service skills and experience at the centre to manage the programme effectively;
10. policy groups would embrace the CRP as an opportunity to develop more evidence-based policy initiatives; and
11. the criminology or evaluation community had the capacity to carry out the evaluation work required on the TPI and that they would do so in a uniform way with sufficient expertise.

To varying extents most of these assumptions proved questionable. That this was the case was either known or suspected by the research community from the start. Suggestions, however, that a slower, more circumspect approach might provide for a more securely based programme were ignored, in part because of an impatience to act quickly, and in part because of the government's financial spending regime. Government funding generally requires expenditure in the financial year to which it applies, which accounts for the rush to spend as the end of the financial year approaches. This did not seem, to us, a sensible way to manage money. The difficulties with many of the assumptions became clearer as the projects emerged and implementation began. These are discussed in the next section.

Were the assumptions right?

In this section we make some rather sweeping statements for the sake of simplicity. The evidence for them comes largely from the research literature that predates the CRP, from the chapters of this volume and from our experience in attempting to manage at least part of the process. As Bullock and Tilley note in Chapter 1, the projects discussed here are not an exhaustive set of the TPIs, never mind the whole CRP, but they do represent a significant subset and formed part of a £30 million investment just on project costs (i.e. excluding the evaluation costs). They are, in our view, an acceptable set of projects from which to draw some conclusions and we know of no evidence that the other parts of the CRP were so much better as to negate what is said here.

A fuller account of the CRP, including the TPI, is set out by Bullock and Tilley (2003). It describes limited achievement at almost all stages of the process but does not go into detail as to why the achievement was so limited. Part of our purpose in articulating and discussing these assumptions is to begin that process. It may be painful, but we feel it is necessary if real progress is to be made in delivering crime reduction – an outcome which we all want, from senior politicians to the citizens on the streets.

The assumptions set out above are discussed in turn below, in the light of what we now know.

1. That the principles of POP were sufficiently well understood in police forces

We knew from a number of the Home Office's own research studies that POP, while a good idea in principle, was proving difficult to deliver in practice. A few police forces had dabbled with POP in the early 1980s but it had not taken off. Towards the end of the 1990s there were more serious attempts across whole force areas to develop a problem-oriented approach, and these were documented by the Home Office (Leigh *et al.*

1996, 1998). On the whole they were not successful although the reports were of the 'snapshot' variety, with implementation ongoing.

The state of problem-solving in the police service nationally had been examined by Her Majesty's Inspectorate of Constabulary in 1997 (HMIC 1998). HMIC found it 'unacceptable' that so few forces adopted problem-solving as the approach to crime reduction. Of 234 crime reduction initiatives submitted by forces to the inspection as successes, only 17 (7%) could be judged to have followed a problem-solving process and be able to evidence their claim to have reduced crime. Analysis of problems was found generally to be poor, resulting in too much 'unfocused' effort. Monitoring and evaluation in particular were 'not valued processes', being seen generally as too difficult and a waste of effort that could be spent on the next initiative.

That report was followed up by a subsequent inspection to monitor progress. This was conducted almost in parallel to the CRP, and produced another somewhat critical report (HMIC 2000). While some improvements in problem-solving were found, it was clear that many forces still had a good way to go, and there remained some key obstacles, particularly good analysis of crime problems.

The research report that accompanied the inspection was later published by Read and Tilley (2000). The title, *Not Rocket Science*, goes some way towards explaining the difficulty that both the Treasury and Home Office policy units have in accepting that what seems like such an obvious approach to crime control is actually a radical shift in behaviour for the police. Analyse the problem with relevant data, develop a solution, implement it and evaluate – the essence of the problem-solving approach – is simply not rocket science. What else would you do? But the fact is that the police in the UK, and in just about every other jurisdiction that has been investigated, seem to have the most enormous difficulty in doing it (Knutsson 2003). They are demand led – responding to calls for service is rightly a first requirement of the public – and creating the time for a more thoughtful approach which might enable a longer-term reduction in the scale of the presenting problems is a luxury few forces seem able to afford. Nor do they have the trained analytic capacity to do so.

In a recent publication, Herman Goldstein (2003), father of the approach, lists five reasons for this:

1. The absence of long-term commitment from police leaders to strengthen policing and the police as an institution.
2. The lack of analytic skills within a police agency needed to analyse problems and evaluate strategies for dealing with the problems.

3. The lack of a clear academic connection.
4. The absence of informed outside pressure.
5. The lack of financial support.

The CRP provided the necessary financial support, and some projects were fairly clearly tied to academic institutions, but in the absence of the other 'essential ingredients' this may not have been enough. As Bullock and Tilley (2003) put it: 'the Crime Reduction Programme may have provided inadequate and inappropriate support for problem-oriented policing, and thus comprises a flawed test of police analytic potential (p. 147)'.

The poverty of knowledge about POP within forces and lack of training in effective problem analysis and how to generate appropriate responses were particularly important missing 'ingredients' that were not addressed by the TPI. The scale of this particular problem, and its importance, became more and more evident as bids began to roll in to the Home Office, and it remains an issue which needs urgent attention in forces.

There was no evidence, then, from previous recent research that the police could adopt a problem-oriented approach, and the optimism that the CRP, by providing funds for projects, would somehow of itself make a difference, proved unfounded. For example, Bullock *et al.* (2002) assessed the quality of problem analysis as good in only 3% of bids. Some emergency repair work was instigated. Experienced academic researchers were dispatched to the project areas, prior to funding being agreed, to sharpen the proposals and link them better to the local area data and some rudimentary ideas about what might work, so that projects had at least a fighting chance of making a difference to crime and disorder. The researchers' interventions, however, were interpreted by some as academics trying to ensure that the projects were capable of being evaluated, and unnecessarily delaying the start of projects. As initially conceived, most of the proposals were so poor that they should not have been funded without considerable further work. Indeed it is doubtful that the project proposals could ever have been drafted well given the limited analytic skills available locally and the punishing time-frame.

2. That the necessary data were readily available to support bids, and agencies shared, or would be easily persuaded to share, their data

Quite simply the data were not readily available and such data as there were were often incomplete and inaccurate. Furthermore, despite the fact that the Crime and Disorder Act was intended to facilitate data sharing across agencies, this has often not happened. Two thirds of bids had no data from other agencies when clearly in many cases this would have been extremely useful (Bullock *et al*. 2002). Problems included data protection as well as practical difficulties arising from different agencies using different computer systems or organising their data in different ways. We find that in some areas significant amounts of project time are lost while access is discussed. Harris *et al*. (Chapter 7) describe an extreme case where in the North Town project partners failed to agree a data- sharing protocol by the end of the funded period. Not surprisingly this caused considerable unease among agency personnel. Similar experiences were found in other parts of the CRP, for example in the domestic violence projects, where it created all sorts of problems for the reduction of repeat victimisation. This is an area where it is obviously important to have information at individual level.

3. That forces could reasonably respond to the invitation to bid within the one month or so they were allowed

We have noted the lack of skills at local level to produce the kind of analysis that was required to sustain a credible TPI. The reality is, however, that *within the time frame allowed* it would have been extremely difficult in any case to provide what was being asked. To quote Harris *et al*. (Chapter 7): 'the two projects did not have a full picture of the stolen goods market when they put their bids into the Home Office – indeed with the nature of the activity it is unlikely that they ever would have'.

The POP process is just that – a process – which involves a number of iterations and data searches as planners move from first ideas to a properly thought-through plan which includes some thoughts on implementation and assessment (Clarke and Goldstein 2002). The TPI, as initially conceived, was predicated on the assumption that a single analysis would lead to a set of proposals (as set out in the initial bids) which could then be funded and delivered. No allowance was made for the iterative nature of the process, and the possibility that the response might evolve. Bullock and Tilley (2003) describe the impact of this thus: 'In so far as the funding regime of the Targeted Policing Initiative itself provoked premature closure over problem-definitions and measures to address them, ironically it may, of course, have undermined that problem-orientation it was intended to promote (p. 173)'.

In some of the later projects a more iterative approach was, in the event, taken. This was usually the case where the project researchers felt strongly that an action research model would be the more appropriate.

This more flexible approach was possible in round two of the TPI but was less likely in round one.

To make matters worse the police and many of their partner agencies were simultaneously being invited to bid, in competition with each other, for money in other parts of the programme. For example, the burglary reduction work, which involved planned expenditure of some £50 million, resulted in funding being allocated to over 60 development projects and around 190 'mainstream' projects over the same time-frame as the TPI.

4. That forces would bid for the money that was needed to do the job, rather than bend the job to fit the amount of money available

Not unreasonably some potential bidders were keen to know just how much money might be available to support the projects. In round one they were told that it was of the order of £400,000. It should have come as no surprise, therefore, that all but one of the subsequent bids were for about that amount. Clearly this is not necessarily a criticism, although it does raise the possibility that the work was being tailored to the funds available rather than the other way around. Within the Reducing Burglary Initiative, which focused on one particular kind of problem, it became possible to devise a formula which ensured that the amount of funding was linked to the scale of the problem. In the TPI, however, which covered many different kinds of problem, it was difficult to see how a similar kind of guidance could have been devised.

5. That sound implementation and project management skills were widely available locally

Implementation failure has been shown to be a persistent problem in crime prevention work for decades (Hope and Murphy 1983; Laycock and Tilley 1995). Somehow the announcement that a project has been funded or an award made, and the articulation of a strategy or action plan, is assumed automatically to result in its delivery. The least that seems to be required for successful implementation is establishing dedicated posts, recruiting staff, training them (often ignored in this context) and ensuring that they have the necessary leverage to deliver change in other agencies and organisations.

While some areas were fine, the necessary skills were not widely available. As a consequence, in some projects there was implementation failure (e.g. in attempting to mainstream the reduction of repeat domestic violence and hate crime); in others implementation was partial (e.g. gun crime in Manchester); and in yet others there was significant drift (e.g. the South Town market reduction work where there was a significant change of emphasis).

Dedicated posts were provided to support some of the projects, but few staff were in post in time to assist with the initial development work. Recruiting dedicated staff often took much longer than expected or in some cases failed. This process was hindered, at one stage, by uncertainty about whether the TPI would fund dedicated project managers if they were also serving police officers. The result was staff (often not those initially involved in the development of the project) having to manage the TPI project in the margins of their day job. This is problematic when we know that an important success factor for crime reduction projects, particularly those that involve inter-agency work, is the presence of dedicated project managers (Hedderman and Williams 2001).

6. That expenditure of money, once allocated, would be straightforward

It was expected that grants, once allocated, would be spent by forces on the agreed initiatives to the planned timetables. The extent to which this did not happen proved something of a shock to funders. Original spending profiles produced by projects turned out to be wildly unrealistic, with the allocated funds not spent as expected for a number of reasons.

Slow implementation was a major problem. Practical difficulties such as staff recruitment, getting people to do things and unanticipated lengthy procedures all conspired to slow down expenditure considerably and many initiatives simply did not happen. As projects progressed, some wanted to change the initiatives originally agreed with funders, because these no longer seemed appropriate in the light of new experience. Also, relaxed invoicing procedures could slow down expenditure, a particular problem for the centre as it struggled to work out how much money was actually likely to be spent within each financial year.

A fairly relaxed view of these problems was taken in the early days of the CRP, because it was expected that unspent funds could be rolled over into the next financial year. The withdrawal of this facility by the Treasury marked a turning point in the urgency with which project and financial monitoring was dealt with, since slow expenditure now threatened to produce serious shortfalls in future Home Office budgets. A formal CRP Programme Board was established and regional teams were put under considerable pressure to produce regular and accurate spending predictions for projects, a demand which proved difficult in the absence of good local auditing of projects and expenditure profiling skills.

The academics employed to evaluate the projects provided the closest thing that the centre had to local auditors, and were often the only people who really knew what was going on. Once the problem of implementation failure and its impact on future Home Office budgets became recognised, there was some pressure from Home Office programme managers, particularly in regional offices, for the evaluators to provide regular updates to them on how individual projects were progressing, and in particular to flag projects that were in difficulty.

While this may not appear to be an unreasonable request, in practice it put the evaluators in a difficult position. The Treasury, in the early days of the CRP, insisted on a 'Chinese Wall' between the evaluators and the projects they were evaluating, and that evaluators should try to avoid as much as possible any action that would taint their role as independent and objective observers of the projects as funded. Evaluators, for their part, were very concerned to avoid being seen as Home Office 'spies', to ensure that projects would give them full and frank access to data without fear of being 'grassed up'. Such a request from Home Office programme managers, therefore, contradicted the model of evaluation which had been agreed with the Treasury and presented evaluators with real ethical difficulties and potentially jeopardised their evaluation work. Mario Matassa and Tim Newburn have described these problems in some detail in Chapter 8.

Various devices were created to enable any problems in projects spotted by evaluators to be dealt with while protecting their independence. For example, it was agreed that any serious implementation failure and certainly misuse of funds would be reported to regional teams immediately. These arrangements were, however, unsatisfactory as substitutes for adequate programme management from the centre.

7. That all the projects would be sufficiently well articulated and challenging to merit formal independent evaluation

It was envisaged originally by central government that all CRP projects would meet funding criteria that would justify their independent evaluation, and in this way the knowledge base about effective crime reduction would be very significantly enhanced. In round one of the TPI there was therefore a commitment to evaluate all the successful bids. However, even after the academics and others worked with the local projects to clarify their round-one proposals, a number of difficulties remained.

As a result of this experience, and increasing pressure on budgets arising from slow expenditure, the Home Office decided to be much more selective in what was evaluated formally. A more strategic approach was taken whereby only projects which promised to fill 'knowledge gaps' about effective crime reduction would be evaluated. Among other things, poor-quality proposals, or proposals that included little that was new or innovative, would not merit a formal independent evaluation on the grounds that not much would be learnt and money therefore wasted. Consequently evaluations were commissioned for less than half of the funded round-two projects, revealing how far the TPI had drifted from the original expectation and how mistaken this particular assumption had been.

8. That the importance and value of independent academic evaluation would be understood and facilitated

The technical complexity of the evaluations required is well described by Janet Stockdale and Christine Whitehead (Chapter 9). Measuring cost-effectiveness is rare in crime reduction research, and it is clear that for many projects the challenges and demands of providing the data for such evaluations were a shock for which they were quite unprepared. In addition, there were concerns and uncertainties about the actual role of the evaluator. Projects often sought to involve evaluators more in their development than was strictly allowed (see Chapter 9).

Most projects, to their credit, appear to have co-operated as far as they were able in meeting evaluators' needs. Many of the problems evaluators encountered arose more from the difficulty of undertaking complex evaluation work in projects which often had poor baseline data, were poorly thought through and were having implementation problems (Bullock and Tilley 2003). In this context, the model of evaluation being applied across the CRP seems inappropriate, and makes understandable the desire in some projects to involve the evaluators more in the development of the project as well as its evaluation.

POP is essentially a scientific endeavour. It is characterised by analysis, study and evaluation. SARA, as Townsley *et al.* (2003) note, is essentially a stripped-down version of the scientific process of hypothesis development and testing. To separate the evaluation process from the rest for special and separate funding, commissioning and conduct begs the question 'why?', especially when we know the other processes will be poorly done. To insist that the evaluation does not influence the development of the project itself runs completely counter to the process that the TPI was designed to encourage. This was made worse by the fact that many projects did not see the need to assess their work because the evaluators were doing that, and that the evaluation was where learning was taking place. A more compatible model of evaluation would be what some would call action research, where specialist researchers and evaluators work with projects to help and support them in conducting the whole of the SARA process. In addition to producing a better product and body of knowledge, other benefits would include building capacity within police forces for problem-oriented work and developing more productive relationships between academics and police practitioners that would hopefully survive beyond the life of the particular project. In effect, such a model of evaluation is helping to mainstream the approach.

9. That it would take few people with conventional civil service skills and experience at the centre to manage the programme effectively

The CRP as a whole was managed by a small central administrative team within the Home Office, with various policy groups taking responsibility for various parts of the programme. There was an understandable concern that the CRP should not spawn a huge bureaucracy at the centre, which would both reduce the amount of money available for projects and slow down local expenditure and action on the ground. It was also hoped that by getting different policy divisions across the Home Office to take responsibility for various parts of the programme, these would be more effectively incorporated into the policy development process.

Both aspirations proved optimistic within a tight timetable. It is now quite clear that there were insufficient staff at the centre to manage the volume of bids as well as the process of maximising the quality of funded projects. There were around 170 bids for funding under round two of the TPI alone. The creation of crime reduction teams in the regional government offices helped, but quality control remained a problem. In relation to the TPI, it proved difficult to locate within a policing policy division, and was initially managed by the central team that also had responsibility for the Reducing Burglary Initiative. This small team consequently had the task of managing the two largest of the original CRP initiatives, accounting for over a third of the original £250 million CRP programme (not counting CCTV).

10. That policy groups would embrace the CRP as an opportunity to develop more evidence-based policy initiatives

Policy groups varied in the extent to which they made use of the CRP as a means of developing more evidence-based policy initiatives – from those that simply went through the motions to those that developed new initiatives on the back of emerging findings. The recent campaign to reduce student victimisation is an example of the latter, emerging from the Reducing Burglary Initiative.

In relation to the TPI, various policy divisions took an interest in those projects targeting particular problems for which they had responsibility, for example one policy group would follow the progress of vehicle crime projects while another would follow the anti-social behaviour projects. While understandable in an organisation focused on the reduction of particular crime problems, the disadvantage here of 'picking off' individual TPI projects is that the 'bigger picture' is lost. This is a particular risk when, as here, the central team responsible for the TPI was not located in a policing policy group. It thus became difficult for the TPI to influence the development of more co-ordinated Home Office policy on POP, including a strategic approach to how the Home Office could support and promote POP more generally as a style of policing.

11. That the criminological or evaluation community had the capacity to carry out the evaluation work required on the TPI

The criminological and evaluation communities were being stretched by the demands for evaluation and assessment associated with the CRP in general and the TPI in particular. At one point we felt that virtually every senior criminologist in the country was working on various parts of this programme. One academic was asked to review a TPI proposal and was only prepared to do so provided that he was allowed to bid in competition later to carry out the work. We had to agree to this – there simply was nobody else that could be found, in the time-frame, that could have helped to develop the TPI bid in the way that was needed. As noted in the *Guardian Education* (17 July 2001), there was so much money (£25 million for research and evaluation) that there was a shortage of grant applications. Indeed, some later parts of the CRP were unable to attract evaluators with relevant skills at all because they were all too busy. Inevitably, then, some of the evaluations were carried out by less experienced staff and they all brought their own style to the process.

297

Further lessons for the centre

In this short section we pick up on some of the lessons for the central management of innovative work which go beyond the challenge to assumptions discussed above. We also summarise the lessons from the TPI as a whole.

We should first note that the way in which round two of the TPI was rolled out, and indeed some of the developments associated with round one, took account of emerging results. So, for example, a more flexible approach was taken to the funding; the Treasury turned its attention elsewhere and the senior researchers and policy advisers within the Home Office worked more closely together (at more junior levels it is probably fair to say that this was always the case).

Although what was delivered under the TPI fell far short of what was expected and hoped for, the chapters in this volume point to implementation failures rather than theory failure. In other words the notion of evidence-based problem-solving still seems the right one. There is certainly a case to be made, however, that the difficulty in introducing what at first sight looks like an obvious and straightforward process into the policing environment has been underestimated. Some of the reasons for this are described in a recently published book edited by Knutsson (2003).

Out of this review, in our opinion, ten lessons emerge for the centre in developing and managing outcome-focused programmes such as the TPI:

1. For large programmes, designate one senior individual as responsible for delivery. Clearly they need a direct line to ministers.
2. Take account of what you know to be true even if it is inconvenient.
3. Don't mistake a lack of knowledge or expertise for delivery failure.
4. Accept that it takes time to plan, recruit staff, train them, establish monitoring procedures etc.
5. Be aware that funding short term projects is not the way to change mainstream budget expenditure.
6. Expect implementation failure. If it is to be avoided it needs specific care and attention.
7. Agree roles and responsibilities at all levels, and at an early stage.
8. Discuss and agree the role of the researcher – specifically, is action research needed?
9. Don't keep asking for progress reports. It distracts local staff from delivery.

10. Aim to secure agreement across key stakeholder groups on the aims and objectives of the programme before the launch.

If these lessons are to be acted upon, some key issues need to be addressed.

Leadership

Within the Home Office itself there was no clear leadership of the whole CRP, including the TPI. There were two equally senior civil servants notionally in charge. It was not a full-time post for either of them and they, or their staff, disagreed in some important respects about the way in which the programme should have been conceptualised and delivered. If there had been more time to discuss these differences and less pressure to spend the money, then the final product would have been the better for it. We feel then, that for new and major projects, involving significant public expenditure, there needs to be sufficient time for discussion and planning at all levels, but particularly at the centre, if programmes are to be developed on the basis of evidence and stay on track.

Funding regimes

More flexibility in the way in which government funding operates is also clearly needed. The fact that funding streams are not approved until the start of any given financial year, or even later, together with the imperative to spend money before the end of that same year, distorts the whole process. Even where funding is spread over more than one year, there is insufficient flexibility and rarely is account taken of the time required to recruit suitable staff, train them and ensure that management systems are in place.

At the end of the day we should be moving towards financing new and effective ways of working by the redirection of mainstream budgets, not through short-term project funding. Methods need to be developed to facilitate this process. The opportunity cost of bidding for money is considerable and this, together with the demands placed on statutory agencies by the performance management regime, leaves little time for professional staff to maintain their expertise or develop new skills.

Training

Much more attention needs to be paid to training. We feel that this is the case at all levels, including central government, and in the police and partner agencies. It applies particularly to the crime analysts and the police staff who 'task' them. If POP is to develop as is hoped then there are huge training challenges to be met. Furthermore the better integration of what might be called academic experience is also a necessity. At present to call something 'academic' in this field is to insult it. Indeed, in one version of the *Oxford Dictionary* it is defined as 'scholarly; abstract, unpractical'. This is not the sense in which we mean it! Rather we feel that academics have ready access to bodies of knowledge about behaviour modification in general and crime reduction in particular. The police and their partners need access to that knowledge and it is incumbent upon the 'academics' to render it accessible to practitioners working in real-world situations with day-to-day challenges that need to be addressed. That way we can all live in a better world.

Note

1 Gloria Laycock was Head of the Policing and Reducing Crime Unit (PRCU) in the Home Office Research, Development and Statistics Directorate when the first round of targeted policing initiatives was launched. She then left to take up a fellowship at the National Institute of Justice in Washington, DC. Barry Webb remained in PRCU throughout the period and was responsible for organising and co-ordinating the evaluation of all the initiatives funded under the CRP.

References

Bullock, K., Farrell, G. and Tilley, N. (2002) *Funding and Implementing Crime Reduction Initiatives*. On-line Publication. London: Home Office.

Bullock, K. and Tilley, N. (2003) 'The role of research and analysis: lessons from the Crime Reduction Programme', in J. Knutsson (ed.) *Problem-oriented Policing: From Innovation to Mainstream*. Cullompton: Willan.

Christie, N. (1997) 'Four blocks against insight: notes on the oversocialization of criminologists', *Theoretical Criminology*, 1(1): 13–23.

Clarke, R. and Goldstein, H. (2002) 'Reducing theft at construction sites: lessons from a problem-oriented project', in N. Tilley (ed.) *Analysis for Crime Prevention*. Crime Prevention Studies. Vol 13. Cullompton: Willan.

Goldstein, H. (2003) 'On further developing problem-oriented policing: the most critical need, the major impediments, and a proposal', in J. Knutsson (ed.) *Problem-oriented Policing: From Innovation to Mainstream*. Cullompton: Willan.

Hedderman, C. and Williams, C. (2001) *Making Partnerships Work: Emerging Findings from the Reducing Burglary Initiative.* Briefing Note 1/01. London: Home Office.

Her Majesty's Inspectorate of Constabulary (1998) *Beating Crime. HMIC Thematic Inspection Report.* London: Home Office.

Her Majesty's Inspectorate of Constabulary (2000) *Calling Time on Crime. A Thematic Inspection on Crime and Disorder.* London: Home Office.

Home Office (1999) *Reducing Crime and Tackling its Causes: A Briefing Note on the Crime Reduction Programme.* London: Home Office.

Hope, T. and Murphy, D. (1983) 'Problems of implementing crime prevention: the experience of a demonstration project', *The Howard Journal,* 22: 38-50.

Knutsson, J. (ed.) (2003) *Problem-oriented Policing: From Innovation to Mainstream.* Cullompton: Willan.

Laycock, G.K. and Tilley, N. (1995) 'Implementing crime prevention programs' in M. Tonry and D. Farrington (eds) *Building a Safer Society: Crime and Justice. A Review of Research.* Vol.19. Chicago, IL: University of Chicago Press.

Leigh, A., Read, T. and Tilley, N. (1996) *Problem-oriented Policing: Brit Pop.* Crime Prevention and Detection Series Paper 90. London: Home Office.

Leigh, A., Read, T. and Tilley, N. (1998) *Brit Pop II: Problem-oriented Policing in Practice.* Crime Prevention and Detection Series Paper 75. London: Home Office.

Pawson, R. and Tilley, N. (1997) *Realistic Evaluation.* London and Thousand Oaks, CA: Sage.

Read, T. and Tilley, N. (2000) *Not Rocket Science? Problem-solving and Crime Reduction.* Crime Reduction Research Series Paper 6. London: Home Office.

Townsley, M., Johnson, S. and Pease, K. (2003) 'Problem orientation, problem solving and organisational change', in J. Knutsson (ed.) *Problem-oriented Policing: From Innovation to Mainstream.* Cullompton: Willan

Index